# Security
# Automation
# Essentials

## About the Authors

**Greg Witte** has been building and securing computer systems since 1985 and leads G2's support for U.S. federal civilian customers. His experience with both configuration management and information security naturally led to his role in establishing SCAP and related standards. He lives in southern Maryland with his wife, Stacey, and his daughter, Melissa.

**Melanie Cook** is an information systems engineer at G2 in Annapolis Junction, Maryland. She previously worked at the National Security Agency, where she contributed to security guides and evaluated the security of fielded systems throughout the Department of Defense. She has also been responsible for implementing security on Department of Defense systems. Most recently she contributed to SCAP efforts at NIST, focusing on the United States Government Configuration Baseline (USGCB) and SCAP product validation programs.

**Matt Kerr** is G2's Director of Research & Development and has been a system administrator and software developer since 1999, with a focus on security for most of those years. He helped develop the DISA Gold Disk application, the primary compliance assessment utility for Defense Department systems.

**Shane Shaffer** is the Technical Director of Security Automation for G2. He served as the lead architect of the Department of Defense's Vulnerability Management System and has been a key contributor to the development of SCAP from the inception of its individual component standards. He continues to support enterprise security management by encouraging adoption and improvement of the current standards and through identification of new, emerging models.

## About the Technical Editor

**Stephen Quinn** is a senior computer scientist at the National Institute of Standards and Technology (NIST). He is the co-originator of the Security Content Automation Protocol (SCAP) and was instrumental in implementing the U.S. government's secure desktop configuration initiative known as the Federal Desktop Core Configuration (FDCC), now the U.S. Government Configuration Baseline (USGCB) program.

Prior to joining NIST, Steve worked as a consultant to the Department of Defense and large commercial endeavors with Wall Street banking firms and insurance companies. His research experience includes computer viruses, intrusion detection systems, vulnerability/misconfiguration identification, categorization, and remediation.

# Security Automation Essentials

## Streamlined Enterprise Security Management & Monitoring with SCAP

Greg Witte
Melanie Cook
Matt Kerr
Shane Shaffer

New York   Chicago   San Francisco   Lisbon
London   Madrid   Mexico City   Milan   New Delhi
San Juan   Seoul   Singapore   Sydney   Toronto

The *McGraw·Hill* Companies

**Cataloging-in-Publication Data is on file with the Library of Congress**

McGraw-Hill books are available at special quantity discounts to use as premiums and sales promotions, or for use in corporate training programs. To contact a representative, please e-mail us at bulksales@mcgraw-hill.com.

**Security Automation Essentials:**
**Streamlined Enterprise Security Management & Monitoring with SCAP**

1234567890   DOC DOC   1098765432

ISBN    978-0-07-177251-8
MHID       0-07-177251-0

| | | |
|---|---|---|
| **Sponsoring Editor**<br>Amy Jollymore | **Technical Editor**<br>Stephen Quinn | **Composition**<br>Cenveo Publisher Services |
| **Editorial Supervisor**<br>Patty Mon | **Copy Editor**<br>Lisa Theobald | **Illustration**<br>Cenveo Publisher Services |
| **Project Manager**<br>Anupriya Tyagi,<br>Cenveo Publisher Services | **Proofreader**<br>Claire Splan | **Art Director, Cover**<br>Jeff Weeks |
| **Acquisitions Coordinator**<br>Ryan Willard | **Indexer**<br>Jack Lewis | **Cover Designer**<br>Pehrsson Design |
| | **Production Supervisor**<br>George Anderson | |

This book is dedicated to the memory of Paul F. Bartock, Jr., who taught us that we can achieve better security through teamwork than any of us could achieve alone. His dedication to building more secure systems and networks was an inspiration to all who knew him, and his legacy lives on through the automation he pioneered.

# Contents at a Glance

# Contents

# Foreword

It's no secret that individuals, companies, and whole nations are struggling with the challenge of cyber security. In cyberspace, the Bad Guys have the upper hand: low cost of entry, speed, anonymity, high leverage, global information sharing, and rapid adoption of new technology. Meanwhile, cyber defenders are, in effect, pinned down by relatively mundane problems like missing patches, poor configuration choices, and unenforced policies. And they are saddled with a bewildering array of tools that must be managed independently and that rarely can communicate with each other. It's not that the defenders don't care, or that they lack good solutions; it's that cyber defense is operationally very difficult, especially at large scale.

I believe that the essential first step to major progress in cyber security is to take a classic "80/20 Rule" approach. In the security context, the 80 percent solution is that pile of mundane tasks—this "network hygiene" as some call it—things that we know we should do every time, automatically, but that are easy to neglect. These are known problems with known solutions, theoretically simple but real-world difficult. And our conceptual goal should be to accomplish this with 20 percent of our resources. All of this speaks to the need for much more automation and standardization to simplify the problem, to operate our defenses at machine-speed, and to free humans for work worthy of their talents.

But security automation and standards are not just about the management of mundane tasks. They are the essential "plumbing" we need to standardize the flow of defensive information throughout the environment. We must be able to monitor and assess the state of risk continuously in our networks. When new flaws are discovered in our basic technology, we must be able to assess our vulnerability and remediate any flaws rapidly. When we learn about new threats in one part of our environment, we must be able to use that information everywhere. We must be able to share new threat information rapidly among trusted partners. And we need to do all of this at machine-speed, using a variety of tools from multiple vendors, at manageable cost, and manage them coherently at large scale, without asking overworked humans to be the primary data integration engine.

This is the promise of SCAP (Security Content Automation Protocol) and the many related partnerships that have sprung up across government agencies and the private sector, and with other standards organizations such as the Trusted Computing Group. There's a lot of talk about information sharing in the name of cyber security, but efforts like these are about the use of information, and this will be the key to empowering defense.

*—Tony Sager*

# Acknowledgments

The authors wish to thank their colleagues, Paul Green, Matt Barrett, Roger Chapple, Steven Bennett, and Joe Wulf, who reviewed drafts of this document and contributed to its technical content. The authors also thank our automation colleagues at NIST, Homeland Security (including US-CERT), and Department of Defense (including NSA and DISA) for their leadership and vision. Special thanks to Steven Hanna of Juniper Networks, Ed Bellis of HoneyApps, Karen Scarfone of Scarfone Cybersecurity, Joe Wolfkiel, Shon Harris of Logical Security, and Mike Schiffman of CISCO for their keen and insightful assistance throughout the development of the document.

Thank you to our families that have supported us and to our great friends at McGraw-Hill for their patience and guidance: Amy Jollymore, Ryan Willard, and Patty Mon.

# Introduction

## WHY THIS BOOK?

Although the practice of using automated tools to help perform effective risk management is not new, it is an exciting and dynamic field of study. The data exchange protocols we describe in this book grew out of the work of many engineers who foresaw a "better way" of learning and sharing information about security risks, collaborating about the best way to mitigate those risks, and reporting on the residual risk that comes with operating an information system in the real world.

This book collects much of the information about those standards that is currently scattered. It provides a convenient description of the benefits and practical use of security automation protocols.

## WHO SHOULD READ THIS BOOK

This book is written for the security practitioner who wants to learn more about the broad array of security automation methods available for security practitioners today. It is useful for information system managers and system security officers who want to learn about the use and practical application of these standards.

*Security Automation Essentials* is intended for those who have seen automation methods (such as SCAP) beginning to appear in common use and who would like help navigating the various acronyms and specifications.

## WHAT THIS BOOK COVERS

*Security Automation Essentials* guides the reader through many of the information security automation models that have been built by security practitioners worldwide. The book helps you make sense of the broad array of data exchange standards that government, commercial, and nonprofit organizations have created to combat the ever-growing threats to our information security. Leveraging the standards described in this book will help any organization to implement an effective continuous security and monitoring solution as part of an effective risk management framework. Attacks are increasing and security budgets are strained; through the methods described herein, we share the progress made in a decade of making security measurable and manageable and invite the reader to get involved and continue that progress.

# HOW TO USE THIS BOOK

Readers will be able to use this book as both an introduction to the concepts and also as a reference guide. In concert with checklists and utilities available at the companion website, the tables and reference materials will help users create and adapt automation content for use with their own systems.

# HOW IS THIS BOOK ORGANIZED?

Part I, "Security Automation Essentials," introduces the basics of security automation, describing the reason for automation, some of the underlying challenges, and improvements that have been developed during the past decade. Chapter 1 explains why automation is necessary and considers some parallels in other types of technology. Chapter 2 describes the Security Content Automation Protocol (SCAP), providing a high-level overview of its components and purpose.

Part II, "Using SCAP," provides a more detailed look into SCAP's underlying data exchange models. Chapters 3 through 6 explore the purpose and uses of specific SCAP components that enable organizations to establish and monitor information security controls on business systems.

Part III, "Putting It All Together," describes the practical use of the specifications, including how to create the digital automation files and how to use those for practical application within the enterprise. Chapter 7 outlines the specific instructions for creating SCAP-compliant content for use in common security products, and Chapter 8 outlines some real-world examples.

Chapter 9 wraps up by exploring the current application of security automation and how that automation is being used to create healthy and resilient cyber security solutions.

# Part I

## Security Automation Essentials

# Chapter 1

## The Security Management Problem

As long as there has been information, there has been the need to protect its confidentiality, integrity, and availability. Although the methods to protect that information have evolved over the years, the complexity needed to ensure that protection hasn't changed much.

At its core, *security management*, the process of securing a system and maintaining security throughout its life cycle, requires a broad array of technical, management, and operational steps. To achieve effective security, these steps need to be well-planned, shared with anyone required to help implement them, and tracked along the way to ensure that they are achieving the desired outcomes. Depending on the value of the information being protected and the known threats to the system itself, the requisite steps can be tailored to the measured risk to the system.

Among the challenges to this model is the simple fact that security management often depends on humans to do their part correctly to secure the information system. Humans are important, but they do introduce limitations and inconsistency, and history is filled with occasions where human security failures led to catastrophic results. A significant part of that challenge comes from the sheer number of actions needed to achieve effective security management in today's information systems—system administrators, auditors, and other personnel with security responsibilities cannot keep up with security management demands through solely manual means.

## SECURITY MANAGEMENT CHALLENGES

Even with all the security knowledge, tools, and other resources available to organizations today, it is a constant struggle to secure computers and keep them secure. Information security can be an incredibly frustrating endeavor, because organizations spend so much time and money on it, yet many attacks against computers still succeed and cause staggering amounts of damage. The underlying problem is that managing security has become so complicated and dynamic that most organizations simply can't keep up with it with their current resources. We need a way to bridge this gap, ensuring that we can determine what security changes are needed on each computer; implement those changes quickly, correctly, and consistently; and verify the security configuration of each computer on demand.

| Challenge | Security Management Issues |
|---|---|
| The need to address the complexity of modern security management | New vulnerabilities and security updates on thousands of applications on hundreds of new platforms and operating systems make it difficult to keep current, patched, and properly configured. |
| The need for security management to be a continuous process | Adversaries don't work according to your schedule. Malicious software is already lurking, ready to create havoc in your information systems. |
| The need to have a comprehensive picture of enterprise security | Information Technology is pervasive, especially with the proliferation of mobile devices. Security managers need to understand the state of security across a wide range of devices, locations, and business areas. |
| The need for standardization in security management | Disparate security products, many with proprietary reporting formats, can't communicate. Incompatibility hinders correlation and the aggregation of security data. Conflicting terminology among security practitioners and security products further hampers monitoring and security response. |
| The need for compliance with multiple security requirements from regulations and other sources | Security managers must dedicate significant time and effort achieving and monitoring compliance with numerous laws, regulations, international standards, and other frameworks. |

**TABLE 1-1** Security Management Needs

Table 1-1 highlights several of the major needs that confront today's security manager. Each of these challenges are defined and explored in the following sections.

## The Number and Variety of Systems and Software to Secure

Most software manufacturers provide their own methods of maintaining security updates, each with unique notification, patching, and verification processes. These disparate approaches make it complicated for organizations that have many devices to secure such as user devices (desktops, laptops, and smart phones) and IT infrastructure components (servers, network devices). Each system has at least one operating system to be secured, and the advent of virtualization software can increase the complexity by enabling multiple operating systems on a single host computer. There are numerous applications to be secured on each system, including some (such as web servers and database applications) with complex configuration requirements.

Across an enterprise, dozens of operating system versions and hundreds or thousands of applications may be in use, each with unique security characteristics and mechanisms for configuration management. For example, the mechanisms for changing a configuration setting are completely different on Windows, Mac OS X, and Linux systems. Many applications, such as the Mozilla Firefox web browser, run on top of each individual operating system and have a vast array of different potential configuration settings.

In addition, instances of a single type of software may need to be secured differently on different systems. For example, a web server that contains sensitive data and is directly accessible via the Internet might need a more stringent security configuration than a similar server without sensitive data deployed to an internal network and accessible from only a few computers. And a desktop computer on an internal network, protected by layers of network-based security controls, might have less stringent security configuration requirements than a laptop computer that is intended for use on unknown external networks. A single piece of software could have several security configurations across an enterprise, each tailored to mitigate risk while permitting necessary functionality.

With so many different security configurations possible for each system, it is a daunting task to determine which configurations are relevant in each case, implement those configurations, and verify them upon demand, all manually. What's needed is a way to understand the relevant configurations for each system and ensure that those configurations are implemented and maintained properly.

## The Need for Continuous Security Management

Historically, security management has largely been performed according to rigid schedules. For example, new security patches might be deployed to computers once a quarter, except in emergency situations. And computers in many organizations undergo security audits infrequently, perhaps just once every few years. These timeframes aren't frequent enough to keep up with today's security needs, however. New, exploitable software flaws are being discovered every day—several thousand of these vulnerabilities are publicly disclosed each year. Most of these are corrected through patches; given the number of patches that need to be installed in an enterprise, organizations often have to prioritize patching to ensure that the most important vulnerabilities are patched more quickly than other vulnerabilities. Less important vulnerabilities often remain unpatched for weeks or months, or they are never patched at all. We need a means to identify when new patches are available, help prioritize their installation, and ensure that they are installed in a timely fashion and any supporting actions taken (for example, rebooting systems off hours to complete patch installation).

Attacks can target software security misconfigurations or can take advantage of weaknesses in security controls. Mitigating attacks that target these types of security issues often requires the ability to reconfigure security controls or software security settings rapidly throughout an enterprise. In worst-case scenarios, an organization may need to perform drastic actions immediately, such as temporarily disabling a service to prevent its compromise.

In addition to being able to change the security state of a system on demand, you also need to be able to verify quickly that the system is properly secured. These go hand in hand—how do you know that you need to change a system's security unless you already know its security state? It takes a lot of work for a person to verify all of the security configuration elements of a system—that all patches are present and installed, that all software has its security settings configured correctly, and so on. A single system can have thousands of security configuration settings for its operating system and applications. There are also many more requirements to audit security than there used to be—meeting various mandates, for example.

Security researchers such as those at Carnegie Mellon University's CERT Coordination Center (CERT/CC) have demonstrated that the majority of security intrusions could be prevented by effective patch-management techniques. It is clear that timely software updates to and proper security configuration of information systems is the best defense against the rising tide of computer attacks. But the speed and complexity of those attacks is too fast to continue relying upon humans to detect and respond manually. Evasive maneuvers will be possible only when the computer systems can recognize an attack and implement defenses automatically.

## The Need for a Comprehensive Picture of Enterprise Security

Continuous security management is invaluable, but it is most valuable if it extends throughout the enterprise. Today that is rarely the case. For example, most organizations audit only a representative sampling of their systems because of the immense resources needed to perform audits. If an organization has 50,000 laptop computers that should be configured similarly, for example, it is common practice to audit just a few of them, or even to audit the baseline security configuration that they are all supposed to have. These approaches are understandable, given the resources needed to audit large numbers of computers, particularly when deployed to a variety of locations, but these approaches are very risky. They are based on an assumption that is generally wrong—that security controls, once implemented, will not be changed or removed.

Security controls can be altered in many ways. Software patches, upgrades, and other updates can add security features, change existing features, and reset security configuration settings to default values. Installing a new application can alter configuration settings used by another application, particularly if they share components. Users who have administrator-level privileges can alter, disable, or remove security controls, particularly if a user thinks that the security controls are preventing him or her from doing what needs to be done or are otherwise irritating the user. Another frequent problem is malware or other attacks that compromise a system by disabling or otherwise changing its security controls.

By auditing only a sampling of systems, all the security weaknesses of the unsampled systems will go undetected and uncorrected, with obvious adverse consequences. Also, without full auditing, you cannot get a true picture of security throughout the enterprise. Often, one of the challenges to monitoring the security posture of the whole network is the problem of identifying the person(s) responsible for the relevant assets. Security managers need a way to organize groups of assets into assessable business units that can be reviewed and reported upon. This would enable products such as security dashboards to provide integrated views of the organization's security posture by owner or system.

## The Need for Standardization in Security

Many security tools, such as vulnerability scanners, patch management software, and intrusion detection systems, use proprietary formats, nomenclatures, measurements, and terminology for their security content. Without standardization, simple tasks take more time and are more difficult. For example, when security products do not use consistent names for known vulnerabilities, it might not be clear to security staff whether multiple products are referencing the same vulnerabilities in their reports. This can cause delays and inconsistencies in security assessment, decision making, and remediation. Having proprietary formats for security reports creates disjointed information that requires manual intervention, customized application development, or specialized third-party software to facilitate data exchange. Using proprietary formats for checklists and their components means that a single checklist has to be re-created for each security tool that needs to use it.

Standardization is particularly helpful when multiple products within a single organization perform the same function, such as vulnerability identification. This happens often—it may be desirable, for example, to have multiple products performing the same function so that you can compare their results to validate their accuracy. Also, different groups within a single organization (centralized IT, local IT, auditors, and so on) may use different tools. External parties, such as external auditors or penetration testers evaluating an organization's system security, are likely to use different tools as well.

One of the greatest benefits of standardization comes from the increased ability to correlate, aggregate, and summarize the results of security checks and monitoring. The underlying requirements and controls to be assessed may be shared with multiple organizations, each with disparate products and processes, but a standardized language for what to check and how to report the results avoids subjective interpretation and inconsistent reporting.

## Security Requirements from Regulations and Other Sources

Some organizations must periodically demonstrate that their computers meet security requirements mandated by national or regional laws, industry regulations, international standards, and other sources.

In the United States, many organizations are subject to security requirements from Sarbanes-Oxley (SOX), the Health Information Portability and Accountability Act (HIPAA), and other laws. States such as California and Massachusetts have begun to impose their own privacy protection requirements, requiring specific management and technical security controls to protect privacy-related information from unauthorized use. Internationally, the Payment Card Industry (PCI) Data Security Standard (DSS) applies to millions of businesses and other organizations that process credit card transactions.

The security requirements in these laws, regulations, and so on are often written at a very high level, far removed from the individual security configuration settings, patches, and other security elements that are necessary to meet the requirements. For example, the PCI DSS version 2.0 requirements include statements such as "the personal firewall software is configured by the organization to specific standards" and "access control systems are configured to enforce privileges assigned to individuals based on job classification and function." When organizations must present proof that they comply with a set of high-level security requirements, they need to know how to link those requirements to all of the low-level details that collectively provide the necessary evidence, which is where automated security checklists come into play. The use of shared security content also enables the results of the assessments and monitoring components to report findings in a consistent way and using common references that enable reviewers to monitor security trends and report compliance findings.

# THE SECURITY AUTOMATION SOLUTION

"Security automation" refers to the use of standardized specifications and protocols to perform specific, common security functions such as those described in the following sections. Security automation technologies are an integral part of IT operations within most organizations today. Much of the work we describe in this book refers to a collaborative effort among commercial security product vendors, U.S. government agencies (especially the Department of Defense [DoD], the Department of Homeland Security [DHS], and the Department of Commerce, National Institute of Standards and Technology [NIST]). The federal government maintains millions of individual computer systems and deals with significant information security challenges every day. The scale and complexity of achieving effective risk management on those systems led the government to help sponsor much of the research and development we discuss in upcoming chapters.

To understand the value of using automation in the first place, consider the analogy of the development of the mechanical assembly line, such as that exemplified by Ford Motor Company in the early 20th century. The assembly line did not replace previous manufacturing steps, but instead took advantage of standardization, consistent processes, and automation. Using specifications for interchangeable parts and automated delivery mechanisms, efficiency increased and quality improved. Similarly, through the use of specific interchangeable assessment and reporting specifications, achieving security requirements becomes more effective, more accurate, and less costly.

A common example is patch management software. This software performs several patching-related tasks that used to be performed manually, such as identifying when new patches are available, downloading the patches from vendors and verifying their integrity, determining which systems within an enterprise need each patch, and distributing the patches to the appropriate systems and installing them. Consider this scenario on a network with thousands of computer systems and hundreds of applications, and you quickly realize the challenge of scalability.

Another common form of security automation technology is vulnerability assessment software. This software operates on an information system to perform a series of checks for vulnerabilities, such as missing patches or incorrect security configuration settings, instead of having someone manually perform each check.

Automation supports many areas of security management, beginning with the very need to understand what it is that's being managed. Well-known areas of IT service delivery such as asset management and configuration management may overlap with security management activities to help form a well-rounded system management approach. These automation components work together as interlocking gears to enable effective management and monitoring of business systems, as illustrated in Figure 1-1.

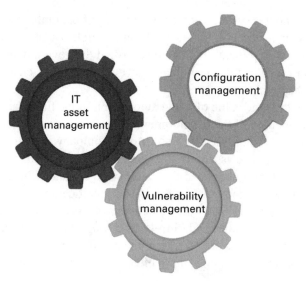

**FIGURE 1-1** Automation component examples

Here are some of the ways that security automation and common business processes complement each other:

- **IT asset management (ITAM)**  Automated processes collect information about the various components of an information system (and related data, such as the asset's location, purpose, owning organization, and so on) and support the overall understanding of what should be secured. The automated tools can, for example, provide near-real-time information about licenses being used or notification of a new host on a network. In turn, the ITAM processes provide important information back to security management and monitoring tools, for example, by informing assessment or monitoring tools of which hosts to check for compliance.

- **Configuration management**  Many organizations rely upon automated configuration systems (such as IBM's Tivoli or Microsoft's System Center Configuration Manager) to keep software versions updated and to track system characteristics (for example, how many machines use a particular type of processor). Such products are a natural choice to use for validating that specific security settings are properly in place, and they will have a role in the eventual methods for standardized, automated remediation of misconfiguration.

■ **Vulnerability assessment**   Specific approaches and tools look for known or potential vulnerabilities inherent to the information system. Integrating the products that identify vulnerability with other IT processes helps ensure that the whole security life cycle is operating effectively. For example, the IT asset management process can supply a list of registered network devices to inform the vulnerability scanner of what to check, and the vulnerability product can report discovered devices back to an inventory service to support inventory processes. This process often includes verification of software updates ("patch management") to correct the identified vulnerabilities.

These examples are simply ways that security and IT service delivery work together to support the organization. Service processes such as asset management and configuration management encompass more than we have described here, but these examples show how many automated processes work hand-in-hand to provide both better information security and effective information resource management. Each of these current processes, such as vulnerability, configuration, compliance, and asset management are important essentials and represent the first wave of capabilities that security automation supports. Security automation practitioners are working on an exciting set of challenges for future automation capabilities, including event management integration, automated incident reporting, standardized and automated remediation, structured threat modeling and identification, improved supply chain tracking, and many more new possibilities waiting to be discovered. These processes, and the products that support their automation, leverage external information to achieve their purpose: *security management content*, or *security content*. The *content* informs the automation product regarding how to complete its task: for example, informing patch management software which patches apply to specific versions of an application, or notifying a policy compliance checker which registry settings to review to ensure compliance with a particular configuration requirement. Leveraging common security content within an organization or among a group of security practitioners begins to enable consistent and repeatable security management practices, supporting a common understanding of the true security posture of the information systems being maintained and facilitating effective reporting of that security management status.

There are thousands of examples of security content within global repositories such as the U.S. National Checklist Program. Software manufacturers, security researchers, and government agencies continually share their expertise through electronic mailing lists and Internet sites. Major forms of security content include the following:

- Knowledge about individual security elements
- Security checklists
- Security requirements from regulatory mandates and other sources

These security content forms are described in more detail in the following sections. NIST's Special Publication 800-70, "National Checklist Program for IT Products—Guidelines for Checklist Users and Developers" describes how to create and maintain those checklists and how they might be used by those implementing security automation components.

Table 1-2 highlight some ways that security automation helps address the needs described earlier.

# SECURITY AUTOMATION BASICS

Each of the security automation technology components is valuable when used individually, but you can achieve great benefits by using multiple standards together. Numerous organizations and vendors have defined ways to combine these standards and enable the components to work together; these group definitions are often referred to as *security automation protocols*. A single standard is often used by multiple protocols, each building upon its component standards by defining how the pieces should be used together for a particular purpose.

The best known security automation protocol, and the focus of this book, is the *Security Content Automation Protocol (SCAP)*.

| Challenge | Security Automation Solution |
|---|---|
| The need to address the complexity of modern security management | Automated security management systems are predeveloped for the vast array of platforms and system types, with a global community helping create updated definitions together. Interoperable and machine-readable data exchange helps security managers review many devices much more quickly than manual capabilities. |
| The need for security management to be a continuous process | Automated systems can quickly adapt to system changes and/or new threats. Digitally expressed security alerts enable rapid detection (and in some cases remediation) of security risk. Continual review of security posture helps the manager quickly detect new risks such as rogue devices on the network, unauthorized software, and misconfiguration. |
| The need to have a comprehensive picture of enterprise security | The use of automation enables a rapid review of the security posture of a wide range of devices, locations, and business areas. |
| The need for standardization in security management | Adoption of consistent data exchange standards promotes interoperability, common reporting format, and effective security information sharing. |
| The need for compliance with multiple security requirements from regulations and other sources | Automation of security assessment (and, in some cases, implementation of security settings) supports rapid and frequent audits. Continually ensuring compliance helps avoid costly infractions. Automated checking supports reuse of compliance review results, simplifying audit responsibilities and reducing burden on security officers and administrators. |

**TABLE 1-2** Security Automation Solutions to Management Challenges

SCAP uses standards from all three of the automation families (enumeration, language, and risk measurement) to provide a consistent way to perform checks and to interpret results. Chapter 2 goes into greater detail about these standards and how they work together within SCAP.

Organizations can use SCAP to help with security configuration, patching, vulnerability checking, technical security control compliance verification, and security risk measurement. Dozens of software products and security services have already adopted SCAP and its component standards. NIST maintains a broad array of information about SCAP, including a list of officially validated SCAP-compatible products at http://scap.nist.gov.

## Knowledge About Individual Security Elements

The phrase "individual security elements" is a catch-all term for vulnerabilities, attacks, patches, security log entries, and all of the other little pieces of security knowledge that cumulatively contribute to the understanding of information systems' security posture. A wide variety of information is continually monitored and managed to maintain knowledge of overall information security, including the following:

- Platform/architecture
- Configuration (including relevant software patches or version updates)
- Vulnerability
- Threats
- Audit/log information
- Operational status and availability

Various security processes and tools are used to determine and report discrete information related to these security elements, the results of which enable a security manager to maintain appropriate security. Although each process and tool collects unique information, we can generalize the individual security elements into several common types, as described next.

One of the security manager's most fundamental data requirements is the ability to determine what hardware platform/architecture a system uses and which operating system and application versions are installed thereon. This foundational knowledge forms the basis for determining which vulnerabilities, patches, attacks, and so on, are applicable to the system in question. For example, consider a single piece of software: the operating system Windows 7. It comes in several editions, including Starter, Home Basic, Home Premium, Professional, Enterprise, and Ultimate. Most of these editions support a unique subset of the possible Windows 7 features. Most of these editions also distinguish 32-bit and 64-bit processor architectures, and the Windows 7 installation is significantly different depending on which architecture is present. Because of these differences in features and installations, many patches and security configuration settings will apply to some, but not all, of the Windows 7 editions and architectures. This is why it's so important to know exactly what software is installed on a system before trying to secure it.

Built on top of the knowledge of hardware and installed software is an understanding of how to read and modify all security configuration settings for installed operating systems and applications, including what the options are for each setting. It's also often necessary to know how these settings relate to each other: one setting is often dependent on others, such as setting A being ignored unless setting B is set to "enable." For example, a setting for which algorithm to use for disk encryption is ignored if disk encryption is set to be disabled.

Additional types of security elements include knowledge about vulnerabilities, patches, and known attacks, such as the following:

- Which vulnerabilities/patches/attacks affect a particular piece of software

- How to identify the presence or absence of a vulnerability/ patch/attack on an installed piece of software

- What name or ID number to use when referring to the vulnerability/patch/attack

- How the vulnerability/patch/attack could alter the security of affected computers

Yet another type of security element is security log entries. Each entry has information on one or more security events observed by the system. Basic knowledge about these log entries include the relative significance of each event (for example, informational, error, policy violation, and so on), which pieces of information are captured for each event, and how each type of event might map to particular vulnerabilities, patches, attacks, or other security elements.

Security automation is an ideal solution for performing audits, because it can perform them so much more quickly than a person could, and it saves people from the generally boring job of performing all of the verification checks, allowing them to focus on the much more interesting job of analyzing the check results. Security automation also allows audits to be performed much more often, which has distinct benefits. The primary benefit is that it allows problems to be identified and fixed much more quickly, thus reducing the attackers' window of opportunity. A secondary benefit is that it deters system administrators and others from altering security configuration settings simply for the duration of an audit and then rolling them back to the previous, less secure settings.

All of these types of individual security elements are building blocks with which you can form an understanding of the state of security for information systems. With the knowledge of the state of an information system provided within the individual security elements, the security manager can then compare that state with defined requirements (per policy or standards of good practice), perhaps using a checklist to determine any differences between required state and actual conditions. The individual security elements are the raw materials of security, and the security requirements and checklists act as recipes for combining those materials to achieve the desired level of security. Security automation technologies bring together these raw materials and recipes, providing faster security management capabilities and giving security professionals a single point of access to a much wider range of security knowledge than they would otherwise have. This allows system security to be dealt with more holistically and completely than could be accomplished without security automation.

## Using Checklists to Achieve Compliance

A *checklist* provides instructions and/or procedures for configuring and implementing a given set of security requirements, such as those that might be mandated in a particular security policy. Such a checklist may also be used to verify compliance with that security policy. For example, an organization might have a checklist that specifies all of the security configuration settings and security patches that the organization requires for a particular version of Microsoft Internet Explorer.

A checklist often addresses a particular role or environment, such as "all mainframes" or "all systems in the Human Resources division," because different levels of security might be appropriate for each. A laptop used in external locations might need a more stringent security configuration than a desktop running the same software but used only on the organization's internal, protected networks. For this reason, it might make sense to have two checklists: one for each scenario, sharing much in common, but each tailored to support unique security needs. Checklists help implement and review many types of information, as you'll see in the following paragraphs, but we're focusing primarily on the role of security checklists and the benefits of automating those.

Early versions of information security checklists were lists of items for a person to implement or verify manually, often with step-by-step instructions that described the actions to be performed, such as navigating an operating system or application's menus to view a particular configuration setting's value. These narrative checklists are often referred to as *prose checklists*. Sometimes a prose checklist is accompanied by a configuration file or a script for implementing or checking settings. With a prose checklist, the expectation is that an administrator will use the checklist (along with supporting configuration files or scripts, if available) to implement or verify settings and will manually document any conflicts or other problems that occur.

The simplest prose checklists are very high level and are not product-specific. An example of an item from such a checklist is, "Verify that the system enforces a password history of at least 24 passwords." A checklist at this level of abstraction places a large burden on the people who must follow it, to know or learn how to perform each of dozens or hundreds of checks properly, each of which is likely to have significantly different procedures among disparate products, and to be relied on to be consistent and accurate when performing the checks.

The next step in the evolution of checklists was product-specific prose checklists. Figure 1-2 shows a Windows object that you might check in response to a sample prose checklist for securing Windows: "Verify that the computer enforces password history." To do so, open the Local Security Policy. Double-click Account Policies, and then click Password Policy. Double-click the item for Enforce Password History. Look at its value and confirm that it is set to 24 or higher.

Having product-specific checklists makes it easier for people to use the checklists, but it takes considerable resources to develop such checklists for every piece of software that needs to be secured.

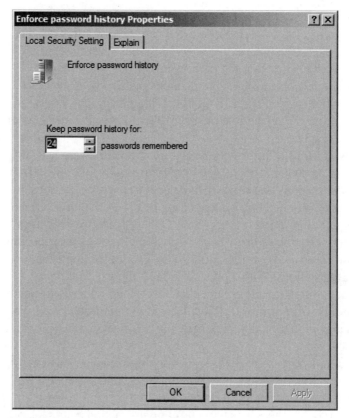

**FIGURE 1-2** Example password history policy

Product-specific checklists can reduce the amount of effort for people performing the checks, but they can introduce a new problem. As the checklists become more detailed and complex, it is easier for the people using them to make mistakes with the checklists themselves—to skip a step, to transpose steps, or to make other mistakes.

The concept of a checklist has expanded from prose checklists to include automated means of checking and implementing security configuration settings, patches, and other security control components as you will see later in this chapter. Just to give you an idea of what an automated checklist looks like, here's an excerpt that is roughly the equivalent of the prose checklist example for Windows presented earlier in the chapter:

```
<Value id="password_enforce_history_var" type="number" operator="greater than
or equal">
  <title>Enforce Password History</title>
  <description>The number of passwords remembered</description>
  <value>24</value>
  <value selector="5_passwords">5</value>
  <value selector="24_passwords">24</value>
</Value>
[...]
<Rule id="enforce_password_history" weight="10.0">
  <title>Enforce Password History</title>
  <description>This setting determines how many old passwords the system will
remember for each account.</description>
  <reference>
    <dc:type>GPO</dc:type>
    <dc:source>Computer Configuration\Windows Settings\Security Settings\
Account Policies\Password Policy</dc:source>
  </reference>
  <ident system="http://cce.mitre.org">CCE-8912-8</ident>
  <check system="http://oval.mitre.org/XMLSchema/oval-definitions-5">
    <check-export export-name="oval:gov.nist.usgcb.windowsseven:var:17"
     value-id="password_enforce_history_var" />
    <check-content-ref href="USGCB-Windows-7-oval.xml"
     name="oval:gov.nist.usgcb.windowsseven:def:4" />
  </check>
</Rule>
```

This checklist example is obviously more complex than the prose examples, but that's not a problem, because it's intended to be read by machines, not people. However, it's written in an open XML-based format, so you can look at it and understand parts of it immediately, without knowing anything else about the standards involved in this checklist. (In Chapter 3, we will talk in much more detail about checklists such as this one.) The benefit of using such a checklist in an automated tool is that it can check numerous devices consistently in seconds, compared to a much longer delay for manual verification. The rapid execution, combined with greater accuracy and consistency, makes automated checking valuable.

Checklists don't have to be long; many include only a few lines of code and include checks that look for evidence of a particular malware infection or to identify a particular vulnerability. Checklists can deliver questionnaires to designated people in various compliance roles, collecting information regarding management or operational security requirements, such as collecting training results or reviewing physical facility security controls.

From a technical standpoint, there's really no difference between using a checklist to verify one set of characteristics versus another. For example, on a Windows laptop, the checklist can just as easily contain nonsecurity checks such as configuring network communication settings. The same is true for patches; the mechanisms for installing a security patch are the same as those for installing the latest version of a PDF reader.

# THE EVOLUTION OF SECURITY AUTOMATION TECHNOLOGIES AND STANDARDS

Security automation technologies are nothing new; they have been in widespread use for many years. They have been based almost exclusively on proprietary mechanisms and concepts, which, as explained in the previous section, cause a variety of problems. However, that doesn't mean that there haven't been efforts to standardize the format and nomenclature by which software communicates security information. Efforts to develop standards for security automation have been underway nearly as long as security automation technologies have been around. Standards development is a slow, complex process, but when done well it can ultimately result in major improvements to products and the industry as a whole. The past few years have experienced a sharp increase in the adoption of security automation standards, and this trend is expected to continue, helping to unify security tools and security content even more.

There have been many security automation standards efforts—too many to attempt to present a comprehensive list of them in this book. Instead, we highlight several recent and current efforts that are particularly noteworthy, grouped into families: enumeration, language, and risk-measurement standards. The rest of this book will dig deeply into a subset of these efforts that has been most widely deployed in commercial products and services to date.

Many organizations and individuals have contributed to security automation standards, most of which have been true community efforts. That being said, certain organizations have played significant roles:

- The U.S. federal government has put forth considerable funding and research effort in security automation standards development, particularly NIST, DoD including the Defense Information Systems Agency (DISA), and DHS.

- In support of the federal programs, the MITRE Corporation was an early pioneer in the field of security automation standards and continues to lead and manage many of the standards.

- International organizations such as the Forum of Incident Response and Security Teams (FIRST), whose members come from industry, government agencies, and educational institutions, have also led standards development efforts.

- Many software vendors, particularly in the security software industry, have also been major contributors to these standards.

## Enumeration Standards

A *security enumeration standard* defines a naming format (or nomenclature) for a security automation element. It often provides for a dictionary of items expressed using that nomenclature, as well. The most widely used security enumeration standard is Common Vulnerabilities and Exposures (CVE), which provides unique identifiers for publicly announced software flaw vulnerabilities.

CVE was originally released for public use in 1999. Since then, more than 40,000 CVE identifiers have been issued. Products ranging from vulnerability scanners to intrusion detection systems use CVE identifiers when referring to software flaw vulnerabilities. Software vendors routinely include CVE identifiers when they issue advisories on new vulnerabilities in their products. Figure 1-3 shows an example of a CVE identifier, CVE-2011-1308. The identifier has an associated description and a list of references, which provide the supporting details for the vulnerability.

Several other similar enumeration standards exist as well. Common Configuration Enumeration (CCE) provides unique identifiers for software security configuration issues, such as

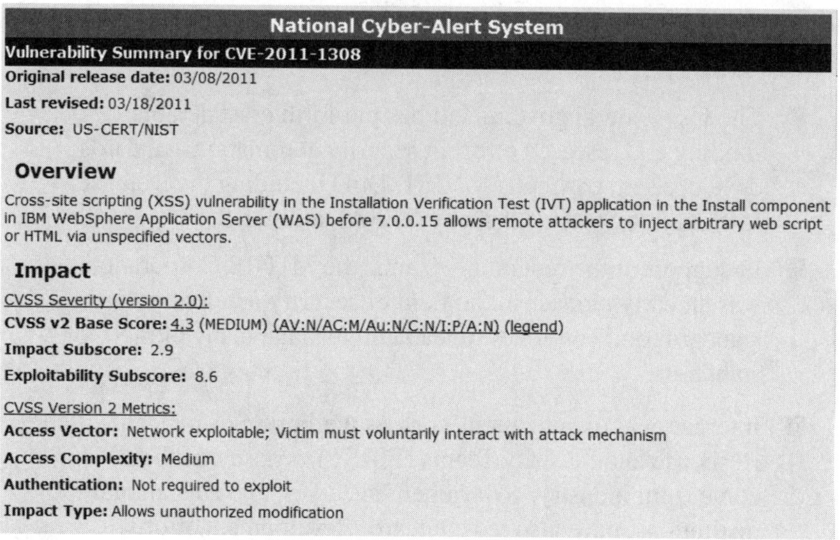

**National Cyber-Alert System**

**Vulnerability Summary for CVE-2011-1308**

**Original release date:** 03/08/2011

**Last revised:** 03/18/2011

**Source:** US-CERT/NIST

### Overview

Cross-site scripting (XSS) vulnerability in the Installation Verification Test (IVT) application in the Install component in IBM WebSphere Application Server (WAS) before 7.0.0.15 allows remote attackers to inject arbitrary web script or HTML via unspecified vectors.

### Impact

CVSS Severity (version 2.0):

**CVSS v2 Base Score:** 4.3 (MEDIUM) (AV:N/AC:M/Au:N/C:N/I:P/A:N) (legend)

**Impact Subscore:** 2.9

**Exploitability Subscore:** 8.6

CVSS Version 2 Metrics:

**Access Vector:** Network exploitable; Victim must voluntarily interact with attack mechanism

**Access Complexity:** Medium

**Authentication:** Not required to exploit

**Impact Type:** Allows unauthorized modification

**FIGURE 1-3** Example of a CVE identifier

individual configuration settings for a particular operating system. Common Platform Enumeration (CPE) provides unique names for versions of hardware, operating systems, and applications.

We use enumerations every day to help specify details that we need to describe, such as automobile makes and models, or the 'Red Delicious' and 'Granny Smith' apple cultivars. Automated products leverage the same technique, using enumeration to specify what to check, and determining how to do so with languages, as described next.

## Language Standards

A *security language standard* provides a standardized vocabulary and conventions for expressing security information, such as security policies, security checklists, or mechanisms for performing individual technical checks. Where the enumerations help specify what to check, the languages detail how to do so, either by presenting a series of checks in a profile or by instructing the product about the technical mechanism used to perform that check.

## Checklist Language Standards

The primary uses of a checklist language standard are authoring checklists and executing checklists (evaluating a system based on the criteria defined in a checklist). The Extensible Configuration Checklist Description Format (XCCDF) is a checklist language most often used for security checklists, but it is flexible enough to be used for nonsecurity purposes as well (such as to validate that power conservation settings are properly applied on a set of devices). XCCDF also defines basic capabilities for reporting the results of a given set of checks, so that reporting tools can automatically consume the results of an automated checklist and provide the relevant data to products that understand the language, such as a situational awareness dashboard.

## Check Language Standards

Some language standards are specifically designed for performing security checks, such as verifying security settings, looking for known vulnerabilities, confirming the presence of patches, and collecting other information from computers. The most widely known check language standard is the Open Vulnerability and Assessment Language (OVAL), which is used for performing individual security checks and reporting the results of each check performed. You can evaluate individual OVAL checks directly, or you can use an XCCDF checklist to evaluate lists of OVAL checks and generate a single consolidated report for the results of all of those checks. A common operating system compliance review includes several hundred tests; although you could launch hundreds of individual checks, it is definitely easier to compile that list of target checks into a single XCCDF checklist and let XCCDF do the work of calling the required OVAL tests.

Recently, an additional security language standard was created to complement OVAL. The Open Checklist Interactive Language (OCIL) is a language for representing checks that collect information from people or from existing data stores made by other data collection efforts. For example, OCIL could be used to present a questionnaire to users, asking them questions regarding their security responsibilities. Like OVAL, OCIL questionnaires can be called individually, or they can be called by an XCCDF checklist. A single XCCDF checklist can

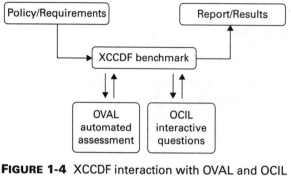

**FIGURE 1-4**  XCCDF interaction with OVAL and OCIL

call both OCIL questionnaires and OVAL checks, and any other check language standards, and produce a single report that encompasses the results of all the checks. As shown in Figure 1-4, XCCDF works with both OVAL and OCIL to perform the checks required and return the results in a manner in which the assessment product can understand what the checking languages reported.

## Event Language Standards

Event language standards are used to document the characteristics of computer events, including security events, so that they can be expressed in a standardized format, particularly in log files. One example is from the Open Group, a global consortium that develops information technology standards to support business needs. Their XDAS Distributed Audit Services audit specification defines sets of generic events, such as end-user system sign-on and the initiation and termination of communication sessions between components.

A related event language standard is Common Event Expression (CEE), which includes a dictionary of event fields. By providing a common language for reporting that "something noteworthy happened," defining how to share that with those who need to know, and describing how the receiving systems should interpret the event, CEE helps the security automation community share information more effectively.

## Asset Language Standards

Asset language standards provide a framework for documenting information related to a variety of assets, including computers, networks, software, and hardware. The Asset Identification (AI) standard allows unique identification of assets and standardized expression of the information that is used to identify them. A complementary standard, the Asset Reporting Format (ARF), defines how to express information about assets in a way that can be transported from one computer to another, including standardized reporting formats. This allows information about assets, including security information, to be reported and correlated throughout and among organizations.

### Remediation Language Standards

Remediation language standards allow software vendors and others to define how vulnerabilities, such as software flaws and security misconfigurations, can or should be remediated. Examples of remediation actions are installing patches, disabling a service, and changing a configuration setting. These standards are in much earlier phases of development than the other categories of standards described here.

## Risk Measurement Standards

A *security risk measurement standard* is a set of measures that correspond to elements of risk, along with formulas to calculate a relative risk score. Current risk measurement standards focus heavily on measuring vulnerability characteristics and assigning a severity score to each vulnerability. The most widely used risk measurement standard is the Common Vulnerability Scoring System (CVSS), which applies to software flaw vulnerabilities. CVSS complements the CVE standard for software flaw vulnerability enumeration, and the two standards are frequently used together.

CVSS has been the basis for several other risk measurement standards such as the Common Misuse Scoring System (CMSS), which measures risk for software misuse issues, and the Common Weakness Scoring System (CWSS), which measures risk for weaknesses in software design and coding. A significant addition is the Common Configuration Scoring System (CCSS) that has been included in Version 1.2 of SCAP, which we will cover in the next chapter.

# Chapter 2

## What Is SCAP?

In Chapter 1, we mentioned the Security Content Automation Protocol (SCAP), a well-known security automation protocol that is used throughout the world. In this chapter, we will provide more detail about SCAP's history, its composition, and how the individual pieces fit together. This chapter is intended to show you the big picture and whet your appetite for what's to come in later chapters that examine SCAP in much greater technical detail.

## THE HISTORY OF SCAP

The original motivation behind developing SCAP was the need to automate execution of security checklists (as discussed in Chapter 1). Although many organizations have been involved in SCAP's development, the leader has been the National Institute of Standards and Technology (NIST). In 2002, NIST was tasked by the U.S. Congress with the responsibility of creating and maintaining a publicly available repository of security checklists. At that time, most of the checklists were prose checklists, readable only by people, and they lacked standardization and interoperability. Although a repository of such checklists was valuable, NIST staff and others realized that the checklists would be much more valuable if they were in a standardized format that allowed for automation. This need for standardization, and the need for consistent technical methods for assessment and reporting, led to the creation of SCAP.

Early efforts toward developing SCAP focused on what SCAP's intended goals should be, what specifications would be needed to achieve those goals, and what work needed to be done to get the necessary specifications in place. Most of the specifications already existed or were in development, but nearly all of the individual specifications needed modifications to be able to support the broader vision. For years, a partnership of government agencies, companies, academic institutions, and individuals worked diligently to modify the specifications in a way that would allow them to be used together. Each individual specification accomplishes its own goal, and using them all together properly enables a new level of effectiveness and efficiency in security management.

As the individual specifications matured, NIST and its partners began to concentrate on developing SCAP itself. This work was expedited in 2008, when NIST was directed to lead the creation of standardized, automated checklists to be used in securing Microsoft Windows XP and Vista computers throughout the federal government—in millions of desktops and laptops. NIST used drafts of the original SCAP specification as the basis for constructing these checklists, and in turn the checklist work helped to mature SCAP quickly. The official SCAP specification was finalized in late 2009.

In just a few years' time, SCAP has achieved widespread adoption. Dozens of major security software products and services support it and 39 products have been validated as having successfully implemented the SCAP specification. It has been widely deployed at U.S. government agencies, but it has also been adopted by large companies, foreign governments, and many other organizations. A common misconception is that SCAP is intended for the U.S. federal government only, when, in fact, it was developed with extensive participation and input from many viewpoints, including government, commercial, and academic institutions from around the world. There's nothing in the SCAP specifications that is specifically tailored for U.S. government use. All of the details of SCAP are publicly available, free for anyone to use, and many have.

Another misconception is that SCAP is useful only for checklists. Although that use was a driving force behind the creation of SCAP, its developers were mindful that SCAP and its components could be used for other purposes as well. SCAP is designed to be flexible and extensible. Since SCAP decomposes configuration items of interest into base components, those details may be used in a host of applications such as intrusion detection, incident response, and malicious code detection. SCAP is already being used for several purposes besides checklists, as we'll discuss later in this chapter.

The development of SCAP is still ongoing. The protocol is expected to continue to evolve and expand in support of the growing needs to define effective security controls and measure their effectiveness, assess and monitor ongoing aspects of information security, and successfully manage systems in accordance with mandates and other externally imposed requirements.

# THE PARTS OF SCAP

At its core, SCAP is a protocol specification; it defines how other specifications can be used together to achieve something greater than would be achieved by using the same specifications independently. For example, suppose that you have a checklist for verifying the security configuration of a particular piece of software. The checklist itself, which is written using one of the SCAP component specifications, references system test procedures that are written using a different SCAP component specification. The SCAP protocol specification defines how the checklist must reference the system test procedures, how it must interpret the results of executing those test procedures, how it must handle errors that occur, and so on. This allows the same checklist to be used with different products, freeing you from being tied to a certain assessment tool just because you want to use a particular checklist.

The SCAP specification, and several of the individual specifications that it references, have been used for years to record certain types of security information, such as security checklists and vulnerability information, in standardized, open formats. This information, recorded in SCAP formats, is known as *SCAP content*. The specific types of SCAP content and how they are used within SCAP will be explored later in this chapter.

In the first part of the chapter, we'll talk briefly about the individual SCAP component specifications and the composition of the SCAP protocol specification itself. Then we'll look at the major types of SCAP content.

## Component Specifications

SCAP comprises component specifications from all three security automation families described in Chapter 1: enumerations, languages, and risk measurement. Figure 2-1 shows the SCAP components included in Version 1.2; Table 2-1 provides a brief description of their primary functions.

Each SCAP component specification offers unique functionality and is useful independent of SCAP; however, most of those specifications have been adjusted or expanded over time to support interoperability with the other SCAP component specifications, to provide additional functionality for SCAP, and to otherwise provide greater support for SCAP use.

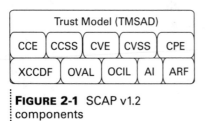

**FIGURE 2-1** SCAP v1.2 components

| Specification | Description |
|---|---|
| Asset Identification (AI) | Language for representing asset identification information (information used to identify assets uniquely) |
| Asset Reporting Format (ARF) | Language for expressing information about assets, including reports of asset results |
| Common Configuration Enumeration (CCE) | Enumeration for software security configuration issues |
| Common Configuration Scoring System (CCSS) | Risk measurement specification for the relative severity of software security configuration issues |
| Common Platform Enumeration (CPE) | Enumeration for IT product names and versions (for example, operating systems, applications, and hardware) |
| Common Vulnerabilities and Exposures (CVE) | Enumeration for software flaw vulnerabilities |
| Common Vulnerability Scoring System (CVSS) | Risk measurement specification for the relative severity of software flaw vulnerabilities |
| Trust Model for Security Automation Data (TMSAD) | Integrity specification for digitally signing SCAP content and the results of SCAP operations |
| Open Checklist Interactive Language (OCIL) | Language for representing checks that collect information from people (through questionnaires) or from existing data stores made by other data collection efforts |
| Open Vulnerability and Assessment Language (OVAL) | Language for specifying low-level system testing procedures and for reporting the results of those tests |
| Extensible Configuration Checklist Description Format (XCCDF) | Language for authoring security checklists and for specifying how the checking product(s) should format results |

**TABLE 2-1** SCAP 1.2 Component Specifications

It is noteworthy that SCAP makes extensive use of the Extensible Markup Language (XML), a well-known language itself that is used to store and transport data in machine-readable form. It is well defined in the XML Specification and there are already some excellent books on the subject, so we won't go into detail here about the language, but anyone interested in working directly with SCAP content will need to get to know XML and how to use XML tools.

## How the SCAP Component Specifications Fit Together

So far in this chapter we've looked at the individual pieces that are part of SCAP. Now it's time to look at how these pieces fit together. Because the pieces of SCAP are open and extensible, they can be used together in many ways. One of the most common ways in which the SCAP pieces are combined is in a security checklist. Let's use a typical SCAP checklist as an example to illustrate how the pieces work together.

The core of a checklist is XCCDF, the language used to define the checklist itself, and is constructed as an XML document. In turn, the XCCDF references enumerations from the other component specifications:

- CPE descriptions express for which products and product versions the checklist is valid.

- CCE descriptions link checks with standardized identifiers for security-related settings.

- CVE descriptions specify which software flaws/ vulnerabilities to look for.

These enumerations simply indicate what needs to be checked; they don't directly include any instructions for performing the checks. Technical instructions are documented in OVAL checks, also known as *OVAL definitions*. Each OVAL definition defines a single system check, such as which security configuration settings or files need to be examined to verify something. Suppose, for example, that you wanted to ensure that the screen saver on a personal computer started after 15 minutes of inactivity and required a password upon the user returning to work. The checklist would specify a review of particular CCEs (CCE-10051-1 to confirm that the screen saver is enabled, CCE-9730-3 to ensure that password protection for screen saver was enabled, and CCE-10148-5 for the number of seconds [900] before it launches).

OVAL definitions often go hand-in-hand with the CPE, CCE, and CVE enumerators. The enumerator says, at a high level, what needs to be checked, and the OVAL definitions provide the low-level details of how those checks should be performed. This distinction is important, because often multiple OVAL definitions are options for a single enumerator. For example, a single web browser product might work on several operating systems, but the details of how to check the browser's security settings might be different for each of those operating systems. So the single enumerator (a CCE enumerator for checking an encryption setting, for example) might have several associated OVAL definitions, each providing the details of how to check that setting for a single operating system (designated by a CPE enumerator).

Additional checks that cannot be performed through fully automated means can be documented in OCIL questionnaires. These questionnaires can be presented to users, system administrators, and other individuals who know or have access to the requested information. Each questionnaire contains one or more questions, along with restrictions on which types of answers are valid, such as a list of multiple-choice answers or a true/false designation. Questionnaires can also be used to collect evidence (or artifacts) from people, such as copies of security configuration files or security documentation that was written specifically for a particular system or person. These OCIL questionnaires support the same layer of the SCAP model as the OVAL definitions; each supplies an assessment product with the details of how to gather certain pieces of security information for the checklist.

Checklists often leverage another layer—risk measurement. The CVSS specification provides measurements of the relative severity of vulnerabilities, such as those defined by CVE enumerators. The most common source for CVE and CVSS information is NIST's National Vulnerability Database (NVD), which provides a searchable list of CVEs and associated CVSS measurements. For example, Figure 2-2 shows a portion of the CVEs related to Internet Explorer 8.

Figure 2-3 shows the SCAP components within each layer of the example SCAP 1.2 checklist. Each layer is labeled by the types of component standards it contains: checklist language, check instruction languages, enumerations, and risk measurement. Each arrow indicates content from one component referencing content from another component. For example, the arrow pointing from XCCDF to OCIL indicates that an XCCDF checklist may reference an OCIL questionnaire. Note that the enumeration components may be referenced by both XCCDF and OVAL.

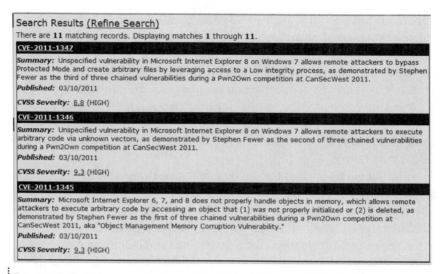

Search Results (Refine Search)
There are 11 matching records. Displaying matches 1 through 11.

**CVE-2011-1347**

*Summary:* Unspecified vulnerability in Microsoft Internet Explorer 8 on Windows 7 allows remote attackers to bypass Protected Mode and create arbitrary files by leveraging access to a Low integrity process, as demonstrated by Stephen Fewer as the third of three chained vulnerabilities during a Pwn2Own competition at CanSecWest 2011.
*Published:* 03/10/2011

*CVSS Severity:* 8.8 (HIGH)

**CVE-2011-1346**

*Summary:* Unspecified vulnerability in Microsoft Internet Explorer 8 on Windows 7 allows remote attackers to execute arbitrary code via unknown vectors, as demonstrated by Stephen Fewer as the second of three chained vulnerabilities during a Pwn2Own competition at CanSecWest 2011.
*Published:* 03/10/2011

*CVSS Severity:* 9.3 (HIGH)

**CVE-2011-1345**

*Summary:* Microsoft Internet Explorer 6, 7, and 8 does not properly handle objects in memory, which allows remote attackers to execute arbitrary code by accessing an object that (1) was not properly initialized or (2) is deleted, as demonstrated by Stephen Fewer as the first of three chained vulnerabilities during a Pwn2Own competition at CanSecWest 2011, aka "Object Management Memory Corruption Vulnerability."
*Published:* 03/10/2011

*CVSS Severity:* 9.3 (HIGH)

**FIGURE 2-2** CVE examples from the National Vulnerability Database

Figure 2-3 also illustrates how the component specifications relate to each other. SCAP products and content follow this basic architecture, omitting the pieces that are not relevant for the particular security automation need being addressed. For example, a checklist might be written only to validate software configuration settings, so the CVE specification would not need to be used for that particular checklist.

SCAP version 1.2 was released in 2011 and builds upon original SCAP architecture by updating several component versions and adding several new component specifications: ARF and AI specifications have been added to XCCDF's layer because they supplement XCCDF's reporting capabilities. The CCSS specification joins CVSS as a companion specification. The final piece of the SCAP 1.2 architecture is the Trust Model for Security Automation Data (TMSAD),

**FIGURE 2-3** SCAP component interaction

also known as "Digital Trust"—this specification is used by several components to ensure the integrity and authentication of content.

## SCAP Data Streams

When one or more SCAP language component specifications (XCCDF, OVAL, OCIL, ARF, AI) are being used, their collective XML content and output is called an *SCAP data stream*. An *SCAP source data stream* holds the inputs (such as the XCCDF checklist, OVAL check definitions, and OCIL questionnaires) and an *SCAP result data stream* stores the outputs, the results from running the specified checks. Both the source and result data streams point to SCAP reference data, such as enumerations or scores, as needed. Each major element of a data stream, such as the XCCDF or OVAL portion, is referred to as a *stream component*. The SCAP protocol specifications define which stream components are required for certain SCAP uses.

# THE SCAP PROTOCOL

The SCAP protocol specification is formally defined in publications from NIST. The first such publication is NIST Special Publication (SP) 800-126, "The Technical Specification for the Security Content Automation Protocol (SCAP)." SCAP Version 1.0 was released in November 2009, and each new version of SCAP is documented in a separate revision to NIST SP 800-126. Each of the NIST specification revisions is freely available from NIST's Computer Security web site.

Each revision of NIST SP 800-126 provides similar information for its particular version of SCAP. The protocol specification lists which versions of each SCAP component specification are used by that SCAP version. The protocol specification starts with the requirements of the designated component specifications and adds requirements for how those specifications must be used with each other as part of SCAP. An example is defining the filename conventions to use for SCAP XML documents. The individual specifications don't place requirements on filenames, but SCAP needs them so that tools can automatically identify and differentiate

| SCAP Component Specification | SCAP 1.0 | SCAP 1.1 | SCAP 1.2 |
|---|---|---|---|
| Asset Identification (AI) | N/A | N/A | 1.1 |
| Asset Reporting Format (ARF) | N/A | N/A | 1.1 |
| Common Configuration Enumeration (CCE) | 5 | 5 | 5 |
| Common Configuration Scoring System (CCSS) | N/A | N/A | 1.0 |
| Common Platform Enumeration (CPE) | 2.2 | 2.2 | 2.3 |
| Common Vulnerabilities and Exposures (CVE) | Included | Included | Included |
| Common Vulnerability Scoring System (CVSS) | 2.0 | 2.0 | 2.0 |
| Trust Model for Security Automation Data (TMSAD) | N/A | N/A | 1.0 |
| Open Checklist Interactive Language (OCIL) | | 2.0 | 2.0 |
| Open Vulnerability and Assessment Language (OVAL) | 5.3 and 5.4 | 5.8 | 5.10 |
| Extensible Configuration Checklist Description Format (XCCDF) | 1.1.4 | 1.1.4 | 1.2 |

**TABLE 2-2**   SCAP Component Versions Included in Each SCAP Version

all the SCAP XML documents that are bundled together, such as the components of a checklist.

Table 2-2 lists the SCAP components included in each of the versions of SCAP: 1.0, 1.1, and 1.2. The appropriate version or versions of each SCAP component specification are listed in the table except for the CVE specification, which does not have versions. "N/A" indicates that the SCAP component specification was not included in that SCAP version. See the current revision of NIST SP 800-126 for the latest information on the versions and components included in SCAP.

For most implementations, we strongly encourage the reader to adopt version 1.2 or later. Among the improvements that SCAP 1.2 brings are the following:

- **Asset Identification and Reporting**   As described, asset management and inventory references provide security knowledge that is crucial to providing effective risk management and continuous risk monitoring. The AI and ARF components bring significant improvement to SCAP's capabilities, helping to ensure comprehensive coverage, enabling trends and risk mitigation tracking, and helping to correlate and aggregate security reporting.

■ **Conditional applicability** SCAP versions 1.0 and 1.1 did not support the ability to determine what software or services were installed and should be assessed during scanner runtime. As a result, the static list of configuration settings were all assessed, and in some cases inaccurate results were reported. This happens when configurations (that is, the IPv6 settings) are assessed when the service is not enabled. In SCAP 1.2, the state of the service will be assessed at runtime and the applicable settings will be assessed (or not) according to the detected state. Rather than having to predict the system state in advance, newer versions of XCCDF (supported by improved OVAL 5.10 tests) are better able to determine the appropriate checks to perform and report.

■ **PowerShell support** Microsoft's corporate decision to embrace PowerShell as its normative API across its product line required SCAP to expand to assess configuration settings for new platforms. The ability to assess the next version of Windows and fully assess current versions of MS SQL Server, Office 2010, and MS Exchange Server require the use of PowerShell as incorporated SCAP 1.2's OVAL 5.10 language.

As these examples show, each version improves upon the version before it by adding new capabilities and by correcting previous errors and/or ambiguities in the SCAP specification. Each new version involves years of planning, coordination, review, and testing by the security automation community. Participation in this process is open to all, but the parties most frequently involved include the organizations developing the SCAP component specifications and the vendors that use SCAP in their security products and services. For more information on the SCAP release cycles, see http://scap.nist.gov/timeline.html.

After a new version of the SCAP protocol specification has been finalized, vendors and developers are provided time to integrate new features and capability into products. Those that want their products to be formally evaluated and independently certified to abide by the SCAP specification (referred to as "SCAP Compliant") have a limited time from the announcement of the final release to demonstrate compliance with the SCAP Validation Program Test Requirements. Initial validation procedures did not exercise a broad spectrum of the XCCDF and OVAL capabilities, so keep in mind that not all SCAP-validated products will be able to execute all checklists. The validation program for SCAP 1.2 provides a more exhaustive test suite that is intended to improve interoperability among validated products.

## SCAP Content

There are two types of SCAP content. The first type is known as *SCAP reference data*. This is information that is universally used by SCAP implementations. Each enumeration specification references its own global dictionary, which defines the master list of identifiers that everyone must adopt when using that component. For example, the CPE dictionary includes a reference to cpe:/o:redhat:enterprise _linux:5. While the CPE specification describes how that entry will be constructed and how that CPE may be used by companion protocols, that particular entry always relates to Redhat Enterprise Linux version 5. The dictionary information can be thought of as reference material that's used by all implementations of SCAP and its specifications. Another example is the central OVAL Repository that contains thousands of standard OVAL checks, such as those for assessing the value of a particular product's security configuration setting or confirming that a given patch has been installed. Each of these checks has a unique identifier.

SCAP reference data is available from several authoritative public sources. MITRE Corporation hosts the official OVAL database. The NVD, maintained by NIST, hosts all of the official SCAP enumeration dictionaries. This public reference data can be used by products in multiple ways—for example, the NVD offers XML and RSS feeds for fully automated retrieval of the dictionaries, plus web interfaces for people manually searching for information on particular enumeration entries.

There are also private sources of SCAP reference data; these are often security products that start with the authoritative public data and add supporting information, although this information is technically not part of the SCAP specification. An example of this is a security product vendor that employs its own team of vulnerability researchers. These researchers may analyze certain vulnerabilities, discover additional details about their characteristics, and make these details available to their customers as supporting information alongside the SCAP reference data for the vulnerabilities.

The second type of SCAP content is *general* SCAP content other than the SCAP reference data. An example of general SCAP content is a security checklist for a particular software product version. Some general SCAP content is available publicly; for example, the National Checklist Program (NCP) hosts a free repository of security checklists, including SCAP checklists. Other general SCAP content is created and distributed by software vendors and service providers to help their customers secure their systems or is developed by organizations for their own internal use (for example, to secure internally developed applications throughout the enterprise).

## Alternate Reference Data

When using SCAP, you can't currently use your own enumerations or other reference data in place of SCAP's, but you can complement the official reference data by adding data that is specific for your products, environment, and/or requirements. One enterprise, for example, directs vulnerability scanners to point to internal sources for patch information rather than referencing the official Internet sites (for example, Microsoft or Adobe.) Complementing the reference data enables the scanners to use common platform (CPE) and vulnerability (CVE) data from the official sources while permitting the results to recommend corrective action from an internal patch site.

## SCAP Content Validation

The SCAP specification describes which individual SCAP components must be included together, and in what manner, to create a valid data stream. An SCAP data stream that is simply performing an inventory process may not need to leverage components such as CVE or CCE—it would include a checklist (XCCDF file) that, in turn, calls the OVAL inventory definitions and returns the appropriately formatted results. The combinations can be tricky, though, especially as the number of component specifications grows and as each component gains new features.

To help the content author ensure that a data stream is written in accordance with the specification, NIST provides a content validation tool (known as SCAPVAL) on the SCAP web site. A user executes the SCAPVAL utility and specifies the location of the data stream to be reviewed, after which the utility provides a report on the review findings including any warnings about the construction of the file and any errors that must be corrected. It is important to note that SCAPVAL is not a replacement for testing content files to ensure their suitability. As NIST describes it, "SCAP Content Validation Tool is designed to validate the correctness of a SCAP data stream for a particular use case according to what is defined in SP 800-126." Keep in mind that SCAPVAL isn't intended to confirm that the content correctly performs the assessment for which it is written; it simply verifies that the various pieces are constructed the right way—it will not warn a user if he is searching for the wrong setting in the right way.

# THE VALUE OF SCAP

SCAP was designed with several common uses in mind, all of which are valuable for security operations and management. Because SCAP is based on open specifications, it is highly flexible, and organizations can extend it to be used for many other security-related and nonsecurity-related purposes (such as collecting license information or checking power-conservation controls). It's not possible to list every conceivable use of SCAP, so instead we've surveyed today's common uses and grouped them into five categories:

- Determining what software is installed on a system
- Identifying security issues for a system
- Monitoring the security state of a system
- Quantifying risk
- Having common terminology for platforms, vulnerabilities, security checks, and so on

Let's look at each of these in turn, concentrating on the benefits of these uses, the SCAP tools and content available today to implement them, and the possibilities for expanding these uses in the future.

## Inventorying Installed Software

One of the simplest and most common uses of SCAP is to determine what software is installed on a particular system. This might sound like a rather trivial function, but it's fundamental to many other uses of SCAP. As mentioned in the checklist example, when someone attempts to use a checklist to verify a particular system's security, the checklist can specify for which software versions it's valid. This prevents someone from applying a checklist to a system that does not have the corresponding software installed. Possible negative outcomes of using the checklist on the wrong system include misleading results, such as a report saying no vulnerabilities were found when the product actually checked for the wrong vulnerabilities. And if the product executing the checklist has been extended (through non-SCAP means) to change incorrect security configuration settings, install missing patches, and so on, then applying the checklist to the wrong system could cause serious security and operational problems.

There are significant limits to identifying which software and software versions are installed on a system. Each relevant version of each piece of software must have its own OVAL definition. The global OVAL repository contains many definitions for widely used products, but many other pieces of software aren't yet in the repository. Also, significant lags can occur between the availability of a new piece of software or software version and the inclusion of an OVAL definition in the repository. And, of course, custom software, such as an application written by an organization for its own internal use, would not be in the repository. However, organizations may write their own OVAL definitions for identifying software, and if these definitions would be useful to others, the organizations are encouraged to submit them to the global repository maintained by the MITRE Corporation. More details on how to do so are available at http://oval.mitre.org.

Because the ability to determine which software versions are installed on a system is foundational to checking for patches, managing configurations, and assessing vulnerability, this function is used by all SCAP tools and content in those categories. It's also useful for general IT technologies such as asset management tools.

## Identifying Security Issues

SCAP has been heavily used to identify security issues on systems. Originally, SCAP version 1.0 enabled checking for a given vulnerability by examining the versions of a product installed or executing an OVAL test against a known flaw or configuration setting. Although that use case is still very important, it has evolved to include not only that original vulnerability identification capability but also the ability to identify potentially compromised computer systems through automated detection of suspicious files and settings.

### Vulnerability Identification

SCAP offers multiple ways to identify particular types of vulnerabilities on systems: software security flaws, misconfigured security settings, and missing patches. One identification method is to use an XCCDF checklist with associated SCAP reference data (CVE and CCE enumerations for vulnerabilities of interest).

As an example, a checklist might be used to look for systems susceptible to CVE 2003-0109, a buffer overflow problem in some older versions of Microsoft Windows. The assessment product would follow checklist instructions to determine whether a given target system had one or more of the vulnerable CPEs, and, if so, the tool might execute OVAL definitions to query the version of a file that's associated with a known attack (such as ntdll.dll). The presence of a known vulnerable version or the confirmation of vulnerability would be returned with the data results as specified in the original checklist.

SCAP versions 1.0 and 1.1 were limited to identifying system vulnerabilities that can be verified through automated technical mechanisms (OVAL definitions). SCAP version 1.2 expands upon this with the addition of the OCIL specification. OCIL allows questionnaires to be posed to users, system administrators, and others who have knowledge of security practices that cannot be verified through technical checks. An example is a questionnaire that asks users about their recent security awareness training or their physical security practices, such as keeping their offices locked or enabling password-protected screen savers whenever they step away from their desks. Another example is asking a system administrator to verify security settings that cannot currently be accessed through fully automated means, such as a setting only available through a proprietary GUI. Information collected from people can reveal important vulnerabilities that cannot be identified through direct system examination. So SCAP version 1.2 is capable of producing a more complete picture of system security than earlier SCAP versions were.

A few important limitations of current SCAP vulnerability identification functionality must be noted. First, it works only for identifying post-compilation vulnerabilities—that is, vulnerabilities in fully compiled software. It is not designed to be used to look for vulnerabilities in source code or other precompilation states. Second, as of this writing, SCAP is capable of vulnerability identification only, not vulnerability mitigation. However, many security product vendors have proprietary (non-SCAP) extensions that can mitigate the vulnerabilities identified by using SCAP. Meanwhile, the security automation community is working on developing a companion remediation protocol specification and a corresponding suite of lower level remediation specifications that will provide a standardized means of vulnerability remediation in the future.

## System Compromise Identification

As described earlier, SCAP can be used to examine a system's technical characteristics, such as Windows registry values, configuration files, or other elements, for vulnerabilities. In much the same way, SCAP is used to identify potential compromises on systems by checking those systems for technical characteristics left behind by a compromise. Many successful attacks leave detectable traces on the systems they have exploited. If the method for finding evidence of a particular attack can be determined—such as the checksum of a malicious file or the existence of a malicious service—then the check can be expressed in an SCAP format. This can be done by creating new OVAL definitions or by creating a mini-checklist with XCCDF and OVAL. This SCAP content could look for a single sign of compromise or various combinations; it could also check to see if the system is vulnerable to the attack, allowing vulnerable systems to be identified and fixed before they are attacked. Some sophisticated attacks will be able to fool a suspect computer into providing false information back to SCAP, but many threats aren't that advanced and SCAP checks (that is, OVAL tests) are getting better at spotting hosts that return fraudulent information.

When a new attack, such as a new form of malware, is affecting organizations, the software vendors, incident response teams, and other organizations can rapidly write new SCAP content to detect that malware's presence on a system and then make that SCAP content available through appropriate means (post on web site, push to security products through automatic updates, and so on). As soon as this information is publicly available, any organization can use it with all of its SCAP-validated tools, instead of having to wait for each tool vendor to perform the necessary research and develop, test, and distribute the check information. The ability to use the same SCAP check information with many tools permits an organization to conduct the checks and identify problems much more quickly, thus reducing the window of opportunity for successful attacks.

## Monitoring the Security State

Monitoring the security state of systems has traditionally involved performing periodic audits. As discussed in Chapter 1, without security automation, an audit can be incredibly time consuming, requiring auditors to check hundreds or thousands of security configuration settings, patches, and other elements of security manually on each system. Because of the level of effort, it's been common for audits to occur only on a sampling of actual systems and only occasionally, such as once every few years. This severely reduces the value of auditing, because so many security problems go undetected and unresolved for so long.

With the help of security automation technologies, organizations are shifting from conducting periodic security audits to performing continuous monitoring of their systems' security state. You can think of continuous monitoring as performing audits all the time through automated means. The goal is to identify problems as soon as they occur and fix them right away so that the window of opportunity for attackers to take advantage of those problems is as small as possible.

Although identifying vulnerabilities is critically important, monitoring the security state of systems is much broader than that.

It typically includes providing evidence of compliance with sets of security requirements and gathering enterprise security metrics. SCAP offers capabilities that help with both of these functions.

All SCAP versions support security checklists that contain mappings between the low-level checks and the high-level requirements that those checks support. For example, suppose that a business is required to comply with a law that includes requirements for how personally identifiable information (PII) must be protected. One requirement of that law is that the business must properly manage its authenticators, such as passwords, to prevent unauthorized access to the PII. An XCCDF checklist can map that high-level requirement to the low-level checks that support it, such as verifying that passwords are required, that the minimum password length is acceptable, and that passwords must be changed regularly. Many organizations must provide evidence that their systems comply with several high-level sets of requirements for security, ranging from laws and regulations to standards and guidelines from industry, government, and others. SCAP not only offers an excellent way to gather this information, but it also makes all the details of its checks available, so that others can understand the basis of each piece of evidence. As an example, the NVD provides a data feed that correlates CCE dictionary entries with the related security controls as described in NIST Special Publication 800-53, "Recommended Security Controls for Federal Information Systems and Organizations."

## Security Measures and Metrics

The standardized nature of SCAP enables an organization to collect enterprise security metrics consistently and with clarity. Security managers can create questionnaires that enable clear and accurate collection of security actions or remediation steps, enabling the creation of specific performance measures to track security trends, confirm the success of a training program, calculate the value of a security change, and so on. Specific measures can also leverage automated collection capability: mean time to remediate a vulnerability, average number of vulnerabilities per site, and the number of authorized users that have passed a given mandatory security training course are all examples of this. Additionally, the reporting capabilities provided by components such as XCCDF, ARF, and AI can be used to report security metrics data in consistent XML-based formats that are processed and analyzed by other security tools. Ultimately, organizations use the SCAP-collected security metrics data in support of security-related risk decisions.

As the security automation data exchange models mature, we expect the use of this technology to request and receive such metrics to increase dramatically. The evolution of the U.S. government's Federal Information System Management Act (FISMA) requirements is a good example of this progress. Originally, security mandates were transmitted in a written memorandum, requiring written responses that had to be manually integrated. Today, web-based data feeds ingest dynamic data sets, providing near real-time information on the security posture of dozens of agencies. Results of activities and improvements are rapidly observed as a change is implemented and scan results collect the objective data; armed with these measurement data points, today's security managers can prioritize action and continually monitor the results through automation.

## Quantifying Risk

Historically most efforts to measure computer security risk have been qualitative in nature, based on a person's opinion. Such measurements lack consistency; they can vary greatly from person to person. For example, one auditor might believe that a particular security issue is of grave concern, while another auditor might believe that the same issue is of moderate or mild concern. Such measurements also lack transparency; a qualitative measure on its own gives you no information about how it was determined. Another significant problem with measurements derived from personal opinions is that they are labor intensive, requiring a person to perform analysis and make a decision for each measurement.

SCAP provides capabilities to help automate and quantify certain aspects of measuring risk. CVSS, included with all versions of SCAP, provides a standardized set of measures for software flaw vulnerabilities, as well as formulas that are applied to the measures to derive an overall severity score for each vulnerability. The severity score is not an exact measure of severity, but is a reasonable estimate intended to be used to help prioritize vulnerability

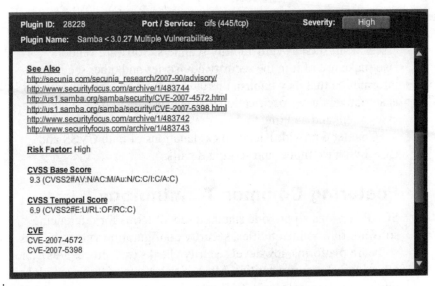

| Plugin ID: | 28228 | Port / Service: | cifs (445/tcp) | Severity: | High |

Plugin Name: Samba < 3.0.27 Multiple Vulnerabilities

**See Also**
http://secunia.com/secunia_research/2007-90/advisory/
http://www.securityfocus.com/archive/1/483744
http://us1.samba.org/samba/security/CVE-2007-4572.html
http://us1.samba.org/samba/security/CVE-2007-5398.html
http://www.securityfocus.com/archive/1/483742
http://www.securityfocus.com/archive/1/483743

**Risk Factor:** High

**CVSS Base Score**
 9.3 (CVSS2#AV:N/AC:M/Au:N/C:C/I:C/A:C)

**CVSS Temporal Score**
 6.9 (CVSS2#E:U/RL:OF/RC:C)

**CVE**
CVE-2007-4572
CVE-2007-5398

**FIGURE 2-4** Nessus vulnerability example with CVSS score

remediation efforts, such as which vulnerabilities need to be patched most quickly. Figure 2-4 shows an example vulnerability from a commercial assessment product (Nessus) and the associated base and temporal CVSS scores. A security manager might choose to prioritize on all vulnerabilities that are categorized as "High" based on a threshold CVSS score.

The ability to convey the characteristics of software flaw vulnerabilities consistently allows organizations to institute repeatable mitigation policies throughout the enterprise. For example, an organization could establish a policy that specifies how quickly vulnerabilities must be mitigated based in part on their measures or scores, such as patching the most severe vulnerabilities within a certain amount of time after patches become available.

SCAP version 1.2 also includes CCSS, designed specifically for measuring and scoring the severity of security misconfiguration. CCSS can be used when selecting the security configuration options for a given application and for performing a risk assessment of a full system. Both CVSS and CCSS can be customized for a specific organization or a portion of an organization to reflect its security nature and technical composition.

The CVSS specification has been in use for several years. It is supported by a range of tools used for software flaw vulnerability assessment, such as vulnerability scanners. Software vendors also make use of it in the security advisories and other security information that they publish on flaws in their own products. CCSS is a relatively new specification that is expected to be adopted by assessment and auditing tools.

Chapter 6 provides detailed explanations of both CVSS and CCSS with examples and scoring details.

## Fostering Common Terminology

SCAP versions all provide standard sets of terms for referencing software flaw vulnerabilities, security configuration vulnerabilities, software platforms, low-level security checks (test procedures), and other logical security entities. Most of these sets of terms are globally unique. For example, each CVE identifier specifies one software flaw vulnerability, and any reference by any organization or tool to that identifier is always referencing the same vulnerability. Some terms are organizationally unique, such as an organization creating CPE identifiers for its own custom software that is used only internally. Any references to organizationally unique identifiers are authoritative within that organization only, but they have no meaning outside that organization.

The common terminology provided by SCAP is widely used. A variety of security management tools, such as vulnerability scanners, patch management utilities, intrusion detection systems, and log management software, often make use of terms from SCAP component specifications. Using consistent terms supports interoperability and data exchange among products and enables those terms to be reliably used in product security advisories and other security-related documentation and communications. The use of standardized terms is also helpful for incident response, enabling faster decision-making and ensuring consistency for incident reporting throughout an organization, as well as promoting clearer incident communications between an organization and other organizations (for example, reporting to an external Computer Incident Response Team about which vulnerabilities are being exploited).

Now that you have a basic understanding of SCAP and of security automation in general, we're ready to begin working on some real SCAP content. Chapter 3 will provide more detail on the various SCAP languages and will show how they are properly bundled into an automated checklist.

# Part II
## Using SCAP

# Chapter 3

**SCAP Checklist and Check Languages**

This chapter will introduce you to the basics of SCAP's checklist language, XCCDF, and check languages, OVAL and OCIL. Each of these three specifications stands on its own and has value, but they have much more value when used together, and they are frequently used together in checklists, with XCCDF referencing OVAL and/or OCIL checks. That's why we are covering all three in this chapter. First we'll look at XCCDF, then OVAL, and finally OCIL.

# EXTENSIBLE CHECKLIST CONFIGURATION DESCRIPTION FORMAT

Extensible Checklist Configuration Description Format (XCCDF) provides a common format for the representation of configuration checklist documents. It is designed to be a platform-independent representation suitable for inclusion in both manual and automatic processes. Initially authored and supported by Neal Ziring of the Department of Defense, its initial purpose was to facilitate the transmission, distribution, and automated use of security checklists. XCCDF has since expanded to represent a wide variety of checklists and other sets of security requirements.

Before the advent of XCCDF, checklists were authored by individuals in various document formats such as text documents and spreadsheets. These formats were often standardized to some extent within an organization, but there were no standards among organizations. Even if one organization desired to use another organization's checklist, the adopting organization often had to convert the checklist into a format that was compliant with the organization's existing checklists. Having security checklists in the proper, organizationally approved format did not assist in automating compliance assessments with the checklist. The checklist had to be converted into proprietary formats for use in assessment tools. The entire conversion exercise would be repeated at each organization and as assessment tools changed.

XCCDF enables sharing of checklists among organizations and enables the use of those checklists within various assessment tools through the use of a standard, open format for representing security checks to be performed. The format is vendor- and platform-independent and is freely available for anyone to implement. XCCDF uses an XML file format for presenting configuration requirements, which are referred to as *rules* in XCCDF parlance. Furthermore, XCCDF provides the capability to define *values* for configuration rules. XCCDF *profiles* allow an end user to customize which portions of a checklist are applicable in a given situation. Each of these pieces, along with others, will be discussed in more detail later in this section.

XCCDF has undergone several revisions during its lifetime, but a few major versions have been released and used widely. The initial version of the XCCDF specification, 1.0, was released in January 2005. Version 1.1.4 (the first version included in SCAP) was released in January 2008, and the latest edition, version 1.2, was finalized in September 2011. In addition to their traditional use to inform checking languages (such as OVAL and OCIL) regarding assessments to perform, XCCDF documents may also be combined with style tags to produce a printed or prose version of the document that is easier for most people to read than XML.

The following section will explain the core capabilities provided by XCCDF and the use cases that have driven its design. We will also describe the components that make up an XCCDF file, provide examples of tools that utilize XCCDF, present a sample XCCDF document, and provide a list of additional resources you may use to learn more about XCCDF and its potential uses.

## Data Model and Syntax

The XCCDF data model defines what content is allowed in an XCCDF document, what format restrictions exist for data, and any other constraints that might exist in a single XCCDF document (such as uniqueness, required or optional). In addition to a data model are syntactical requirements that govern the expression of XCCDF documents. Both the data model and XML schema information can be found in the XCCDF schema definition (XSD) and the XCCDF specification document. Links to both of these documents can be found at http://scap.nist.gov/specifications/xccdf. The XML samples presented here are reproduced from the sample XCCDF file in Appendix B of XCCDF 1.1.4 specification, available at that location.

# Benchmark

The *benchmark* is the top-level element of an XCCDF document. Only one benchmark element can exist in an XCCDF document. All other XCCDF content exists inside the benchmark element. A benchmark is identified by a combination of an ID and version. The ID can be any alphanumeric string the author wants to assign to the benchmark. The version is usually represented by a two- to four-part numeric identifier, with the parts separated by a period. The parts are used to identify the extent of changes made during a revision, with the leftmost part indicating major changes to requirements and guidance, and the rightmost parts indicating minor cosmetic revisions such as the removal of whitespace. It is important that these values be descriptive and up to date.

The output of an SCAP-validated tool must contain a reference to the benchmark ID and version number at a minimum, although the entire benchmark document may be included. As we will discuss later on, specific requirements are represented by *rules* in an XCCDF document. There is no requirement that these rule names be globally unique, so it is possible for the same rule name to exist in multiple benchmarks. If you have two results that reference the same rule name, and you need to know the specifics of the requirement that was tested, you need to identify the benchmark of which the rule was part in order to determine the root requirement. Without distinct, up-to-date benchmark IDs and version numbers, this is almost impossible.

The *status* of a benchmark is used to indicate its relative maturity. The allowed values for status are *deprecated*, *incomplete*, *draft*, *interim*, and *accepted*. A status of deprecated means the document should no longer be used. Incomplete and draft usually indicate works in progress. Interim guidance is usually intended to be used as a stopgap measure while other policies, procedures, or equipment are put in place. Accepted content is the most mature content and should be used whenever possible.

Legal notices are often included as part of security guidelines. These notices can include copyright information, trademark notices, disclaimers, and terms of use as well as other information. All legal notices should be placed inside a *notice* element so that special processing can be applied during document generation or processing. Examples of special processing might include displaying the content to the user during evaluation or applying special formatting when creating a print version of the document.

The benchmark contains several areas for other types of general text. These include *front-matter* text to be included at the beginning of a printed document, *rear-matter* text to be included at the end of a printed document, and *reference* elements to include bibliographical references. Text that does not fall into one of these general categories, for example, the description of a specific security requirement, is associated with other elements in the benchmark.

Document metadata is information about the document itself and is contained in the *metadata* element. The most common information found here includes the author's name and the identity of the publishing organization; however, much more information may be present in this section, such as version number, release date, and description. The metadata is primarily used when you are searching for XCCDF documents in a repository.

The last of the major components that make up the basic benchmark information are the *platform* and *platform-specification* elements. These elements use names from the Common Platform Enumeration (CPE) specification to indicate when the benchmark is applicable. Platform elements are used to indicate simple applicability conditions—for example, applicable to Windows 7. Platform specification elements can be used to represent more complex applicability rules, such as Windows Server 2008 systems running SQL Server 2008 SP1.

Although several other entities are allowed in a benchmark element, we will not discuss them at this time because they have little to no impact on interpreting the intent of the benchmark, but are intended to aid in processing, document generation, or authoring of the benchmark.

The XML sample that follows shows an XCCDF benchmark document with an ID of "ios-test-1", with a version of 0.1.15. The benchmark entered draft status on 10/09/2007. It includes a title and a description, as well as a legal notice covering the terms of use of the guideline. Two references are provided, and some general assumptions about the target systems are stated in the front matter. The benchmark uses the platform tag to identify the fact that it is intended to run on Cisco IOS 12.3, and the platform specification is more specific and indicates it is intended for Cisco IOS 12.3 on a Catalyst 6500.

```
<cdf:Benchmark id="ios-test-1" resolved="0" xml:lang="en" style="sample"
  xmlns:cdf="http://checklists.nist.gov/xccdf/1.1"
  xmlns:cpe="http://cpe.mitre.org/language/2.0"
  xmlns:dc="http://purl.org/dc/elements/1.1/"
  xmlns:xsi="http://www.w3.org/2001/XMLSchema-instance"
  xmlns:htm="http://www.w3.org/1999/xhtml"
  xmlns:dsig="http://www.w3.org/2000/09/xmldsig#"
  xsi:schemaLocation="http://checklists.nist.gov/xccdf/1.1
  xccdf-1.1.4.xsd http://cpe.mitre.org/language/2.0 cpe-language_2.0.xsd">

  <cdf:status date="2007-10-09">draft</cdf:status>
  <cdf:title>XCCDF Sample for Cisco IOS</cdf:title>
  <cdf:description>This document defines a small set of rules for securing
Cisco IOS routers. The set of rules constitute a <htm:i>benchmark</htm:i>.
A benchmark usually represents an industry consensus of best practices. It
lists steps to be taken as well as rationale for them. This example benchmark
is merely a small subset of the rules that would be necessary for securing an
IOS router.</cdf:description>
  <cdf:notice id="Sample-Terms-Of-Use" xml:lang="en">
    This document may be copied and used subject to the NIST terms of use
    (http://www.nist.gov/public_affairs/disclaim.htm) and the NSA Legal
    Notices (http://www.nsa.gov/notices/notic00004.cfm?Address=/).
  </cdf:notice>
  <cdf:front-matter>
    <htm:p>
      This benchmark assumes that you are running IOS 11.3 or later.
    </htm:p>
  </cdf:front-matter>
  <cdf:reference href="http://www.nsa.gov/ia/">
    NSA Router Security Configuration Guide, Version 1.1c
  </cdf:reference>
  <cdf:plain-text id="os-name">
    Cisco Internet Operating System (tm)
  </cdf:plain-text>
  <cpe:platform-specification>
    <cpe:platform id="">
      <cpe:title>Cisco IOS 12.3 on Catalyst 6500 platform</cpe:title>
      <cpe:logical-test operator="AND" negate="0">
        <cpe:fact-ref name="cpe:/o:cisco:ios:12.3"/>
        <cpe:fact-ref name="cpe:/h:cisco:catalyst:6500"/>
      </cpe:logical-test>
    </cpe:platform>
  </cpe:platform-specification>
  <cdf:platform idref="cpe:/o:cisco:ios:12.3"/>
  <cdf:version>0.1.15</cdf:version>
  <cdf:model system="urn:xccdf:scoring:default"/>
```

```
<cdf:model system="urn:xccdf:scoring:flat"/>
<cdf:model system="urn:testing.com:scoring:relative">
  <cdf:param name="floor">0.0</cdf:param>
  <cdf:param name="ceiling">1000</cdf:param>
</cdf:model>
...
```

Now what we have introduced the information included as part of the core XCCDF benchmark, we will start exploring some of the other constructs that make up the remainder of an XCCDF file.

## Items

*Items* are an abstract concept in XCCDF. This means you will not see an item element in a benchmark; what you will see are elements that are based on items. Elements that are based on items will have all the item properties that we talk about here in addition to specific properties unique to that element type.

Every item must have an ID that is unique within a benchmark. Each item also has a version indicator to track revisions. Since item IDs are unique only within a benchmark, the results from an evaluation performed on a benchmark use the item IDs to identify various items. The IDs are not globally unique, so you often need to combine the benchmark ID, benchmark version, item ID, and possibly item version to positively identify a specific item.

A text *title* and *description* are provided both to assist the author in maintaining the document and for use if a printed version of the document is generated. *Warnings* may be provided with the item to provide cautionary notes, and *references* may be provided. The *status* of the item can be set just as the status of the benchmark can. This allows subcomponents of a benchmark to identify their relative maturity in relation to the overall benchmark. In general, an item should never have a status indicating that it is less mature than the benchmark in which it is contained.

We now conclude our discussion of the item type and will move on to discussing specific types such as group, value, and rule that are based on items. As we delve into specific types, remember that everything mentioned here is applicable to the specific type even if not explicitly called out. Figure 3-1 shows the individual components of an XCCDF benchmark.

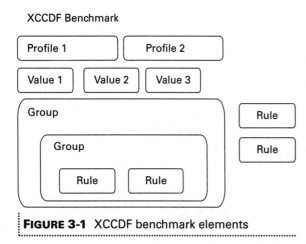

XCCDF Benchmark

**FIGURE 3-1** XCCDF benchmark elements

## Group

Group elements are the primary organizational structure of an XCCDF document. They are based on the item type and inherit all of the components that were discussed in the item type section. Groups may contain other groups, rules, and values. This allows document authors to use groups to control the logical structure of a document. For example, if you are writing a guide with several sections and subsections, you can create a group for each major section, and inside that group create additional groups to represent subsections. The ability to nest content allows the creation of document sections and subsections that can be used in a printed version of the document or in tools to organize the graphical user interface (GUI) that is associated with the document.

Many guides focus on the overall system and address specific components or variants of that system as *sections* of the larger document. For example, you might have a guide on Windows Server 2008, and inside that guide you have specific sections dealing with Member Server, Domain Controller, File Server, and Web Server security and configuration requirements. To support this type of document, while still allowing specific guidance to be applied if desired, groups have a *selected* member that can be either true (1) or false (0). If a group is not selected, then that group and all of the items it contains are not processed when the tool or application processes the XCCDF document.

If multiple components or conflicting sections exist, the document author may need to indicate that one group is dependent on another group. The author might do this by indicating that it *requires* the other group. In other cases, two groups may exist that contain contradictory information, and the author might indicate that the groups *conflict*. All requirements and conflicts must be resolved before the document can be successfully processed.

In addition to the title and description that a group may contain, there is also a specific place where the author can indicate the *rationale* for following the guidance provided in this group. Several other options can be used to control the display and processing of a group, and the XCCDF specification document provides a discussion of these. The following XML example shows a sample of a group object. This group has an ID of **"mgmt-plane"**. The group is *selected*, meaning that it will be included when the benchmark is processed. The title and description of the group are provided, and we can see that this group also requires the group with an ID of **"no-directed-broadcast no-tcp-small-servers"** also to be selected and processed for the mgmt-plane group to process successfully.

```
<cdf:Group id="mgmt-plane" selected="1" prohibitChanges="1" weight="3">
  <cdf:title>Management Plane Rules</cdf:title>
  <cdf:description>Services, settings, and data streams related to setting
up and examining the static configuration of the router, and the
authentication and authorization of administrators/operators.
  </cdf:description>
  <cdf:requires idref="no-directed-broadcast no-tcp-small-servers"/>
...
```

## Value

XCCDF provides the Value object, which is based on the item type, to allow customization of the benchmark through the specification of different valid values for a rule. This allows an organization to tailor the content to its specific needs without having to re-create the content if the only change is to the value. For example, many security guides recommend a minimum password length for use on a system, but the specific length required often varies among organizations. If the organization needs to modify only the minimum password length number and all other parts of the check remain the same, the Value object can be modified and other changes to the XCCDF document are not required.

Every Value object must have an ID that is unique within the benchmark, a type, and an operator. The type and operators are used when comparing the value as part of the technical evaluation. The allowed types are **"number"**, **"string"**, and **"boolean"**, and the available operators will vary based on the type of the value. The XCCDF specification should be referenced to determine which operators are allowable with a given value type.

Each Value object must have at least one value element that defines the number, string, or Boolean to be used. Note that the Value object makes use of an uppercase "V," whereas the value element makes use of a lowercase "v." Each value element is composed of an ID and a string that represent the value setting. These can be used to customize or define the setting to be used when the rule is evaluated. If no value element is defined, the default element is used when the rule is evaluated.

In the next example, the Value is **"exec-timeout-time"** and is of type **"number"**. This means that in any comparison, the value should be treated as a number instead of a string. The default for this object is 15, and a value of *10* has been defined because the default value of 15 was not desired. In this case, if the system being evaluated has a timeout duration equal to 10 minutes or less, this rule would pass. This sample also includes upper and lower limits for the value. In this case, **1** is the minimum value and **60** is the maximum value.

```
<cdf:Value id="exec-timeout-time" type="number" operator="less than or equal">
  <cdf:title>IOS - line exec timeout value</cdf:title>
  <cdf:description>The length of time, in minutes, that an interactive
session should be allowed to stay idle before being terminated.
  </cdf:description>
  <cdf:question>Session exec timeout time (in minutes)</cdf:question>
  <cdf:value>10</cdf:value>
  <cdf:default>15</cdf:default>
  <cdf:lower-bound>1</cdf:lower-bound>
  <cdf:upper-bound>60</cdf:upper-bound>
</cdf:Value>
```

## Rule

A rule in an XCCDF benchmark represents a specific requirement that is being levied as part of the guidance. Rules are usually included inside groups that organize and consolidate similar rules into logical sections. For example, all rules for password policy settings (that is, minimum password length, maximum password length, password complexity, and so on) may be organized into one group. Rules are based on items, so they inherit all of the components of the item type discussed previously.

Rules are similar to groups in that they can be selected, they can assert that they require or conflict with other items, and they may provide a rationale for why the rule should be followed. Although it is also legal in XCCDF for the rule to use the *platform* element to specify when it is applicable, this is not valid in SCAP content prior to SCAP version 1.2.

One of the most important capabilities of a rule is the ability to link to an external language that can evaluate the state of a system for compliance with the rule. XCCDF uses the *check* element to link to an external system. The check element has a *system* attribute that identifies the external checking system; this may be OVAL in SCAP 1.0 and OVAL or OCIL in SCAP 1.2. (Both OVAL and OCIL are discussed later in this chapter.) In addition to the check system, the check element includes a *check-content-ref* element that identifies the file that contains the external check and the identifier of the check inside that file.

Many rules are written in ways that allow benchmark users to tailor the content for their specific environments. For example, many guidelines require a minimum password length, but the actual length varies from organization to organization. In this case, values are used to customize the password length without requiring changes to any other content. The value (password length number in this example) is passed to the external checking system through the use of *check-export* statements. The check-export specifies the value from the XCCDF document to export and the name that it should be given when it is exported.

The technical checking mechanism returns a result that is then converted into an XCCDF result and reported in the XCCDF results. The rules for translating these technical check results into valid XCCDF results vary based on the content type.

In addition to providing methods to evaluate compliance with the rule, instructions for bringing a system into compliance may be provided. These instructions, if available, are included in the *fix* and *fixtext* elements that may support a tool's capability for automated or interactive remediation.

The next example shows the **"enabled-buffered-logging-at-level"** rule. This rule is selected; therefore it will be evaluated when the XCCDF document is processed. A title, description, and instructions for fixing the problem are provided. The rule links to OVAL checks and exports the **"buffered-logging-level"** value as **"var-4"**. The result of this OVAL check would be used to determine the result of this XCCDF rule after processing is complete.

```
<cdf:Rule id="enabled-buffered-logging-at-level" selected="1"
prohibitChanges="0" weight="8.5">
  <cdf:title xml:lang="en">Ensure buffered logging enabled at proper level
  </cdf:title>
  <cdf:description>Make sure that buffered logging is enabled, and that the
buffered logging level to one of the appropriate levels, Warning or higher.
  </cdf:description>
  <cdf:question>Check buffered logging and level</cdf:question>
  <cdf:fix>
    logging on
    logging buffered
    <cdf:sub idref="buffered-logging-level"/>
  </cdf:fix>
  <cdf:complex-check operator="AND" negate="1">
    <cdf:check system="http://oval.mitre.org/XMLSchema/oval">
      <cdf:check-export value-id="buffered-logging-level" export-name="var-4"/>
      <cdf:check-content-ref href="iosDefns.xml"
        name="org.cisecurity.cisco.ios.logging.buf.level"/>
    </cdf:check>
    <cdf:check system="http://oval.mitre.org/XMLSchema/oval">
      <cdf:check-content-ref href="iosDefns.xml"
        name="org.cisecurity.cisco.ios.logging.enabled"/>
    </cdf:check>
  </cdf:complex-check>
</cdf:Rule>
```

## Profile

We have mentioned customization of a benchmark several times so far, and it is finally time to look at how you would go about doing that. There are two customization methods: changing the selected state of groups and rules and refining the value that is selected for a given Value object. Both of these changes are made in a *profile*, which is a section of the document that specifies which groups and rules are to be processed and which values are to be used. You may select or deselect every group, rule, and value in a benchmark as part of a profile, and you may have multiple profiles per benchmark.

Each profile must have an ID that is unique within the benchmark. When a benchmark is processed, a profile may be specified to apply customizations. Profiles have a title and a description, and a profile can *extend* another profile. In cases of extension, the profile that is doing the extension gains all the selections and refined values from the profile being extended, and can then make additional selections and refinements.

The *select* element is used to change the selected state of a group or rule. Each select element specifies the group or rule ID to modify and the new state of the selected member of the item. Values are modified through the use of *refine-value* elements. In the refine-value, you specify the ID of the Value object you want to change and the ID of the value element you want to be used.

In the following sample, the profile has an ID of **"profile1"**. It changes the selected status of some rules and groups and refines the value of the **"buffered-logging-level"** Value object to the value (lowercase v) element with an ID of **"lenient"**.

```
<cdf:Profile id="profile1" prohibitChanges="1" note-tag="lenient">
  <cdf:title>Sample Profile No. 1</cdf:title>
  <cdf:select idref="mgmt-plane" selected="0"/>
  <cdf:select idref="ctrl-plane" selected="1"/>
  <cdf:select idref="finger" selected="1"/>
  <cdf:set-value idref="exec-timeout-time">30</cdf:set-value>
  <cdf:refine-value idref="buffered-logging-level" selector="lenient"/>
</cdf:Profile>
```

## TestResult

Processing a benchmark without being able to view the results would not be of much use. The *TestResult* element is used to hold the result of an evaluation of the benchmark on a specific system.

The TestResult includes a reference to the benchmark that was used, or the entire benchmark, with the version, may be included in the result file. Timestamps indicate the start and end of the evaluation. Information identifying the target of the evaluation such as a network address, DNS name, or MAC address is also included. The profile used, if applicable, is included in the TestResult element.

The specific results for individual rules are included in *rule-result* elements. The rule-result element includes the ID of the rule to which the result is applicable, the time that the rule was evaluated, and the result of the rule evaluation. The result may be one of the following values: **"pass"**, **"fail"**, **"error"**, **"unknown"**, **"notapplicable"**, **"notchecked"**, **"notselected"**, **"informational"**, or **"fixed"**. The rule result may also include a diagnostic message to indicate why the evaluation engine encountered problems, or it may include a check element that contains detailed information from the evaluation system.

The TestResult sample that follows shows that the results are for an evaluation performed using the **"ios-sample-v1.1.xccdf.xml"** benchmark run against the lower.test.net system. The system had the IPv4 address of 192.168.248.1, an IPv6 address of 2001:8::1, and a MAC address of 02:50:e6:c0:14:39. Specific results would be in the rule-result elements. The sample rule-result element shows the result for the **"req-exec-timeout"** rule. In this case, the rule resulted in a **pass**.

```
<cdf:TestResult id="ios-test-5" end-time="2004-09-25T13:45:02-04:00">
  <cdf:benchmark href="ios-sample-v1.1.xccdf.xml"/>
  <cdf:title>Sample Results Block</cdf:title>
  <cdf:remark>Test run by Bob on Sept 25</cdf:remark>
  <cdf:organization>U.S. Government</cdf:organization>
  <cdf:organization>Department of Commerce</cdf:organization>
  <cdf:organization>National Institute of Standards and Technology
  </cdf:organization>
  <cdf:identity authenticated="1"privileged="1">admin_bob</cdf:identity>
  <cdf:target>lower.test.net</cdf:target>
  <cdf:target-address>192.168.248.1</cdf:target-address>
  <cdf:target-address>2001:8::1</cdf:target-address>
  <cdf:target-facts>
    <cdf:fact type="string" name="urn:scap:fact:asset:identifier:mac">
    02:50:e6:c0:14:39</cdf:fact>
    <cdf:fact type="string" name="urn:scap:fact:asset:identifier:host_name">
    lower</cdf:fact>
    <cdf:fact type="string" name="urn:scap:fact:asset:identifier:ipv4">
    192.168.248.1</cdf:fact>
    <cdf:fact type="string" name="urn:scap:fact:asset:identifier:ipv6">
    2001:8::1</cdf:fact>
  </cdf:target-facts>
  <cdf:set-value idref="exec-timeout-time">10</cdf:set-value>
...
<cdf:rule-result idref="req-exec-timeout" time="2004-09-25T13:45:06-04:00">
  <cdf:result>pass</cdf:result>
  <cdf:override time="2004-09-25T13:59:00-04:00" authority="Neal Ziring">
    <cdf:old-result>fail</cdf:old-result>
    <cdf:new-result>pass</cdf:new-result>
    <cdf:remark>Test override</cdf:remark>
  </cdf:override>
  <cdf:instance context="line">console</cdf:instance>
  <cdf:fix>
    line console
    exec-timeout 10 0
  </cdf:fix>
</cdf:rule-result>
```

# OPEN VULNERABILITY AND ASSESSMENT LANGUAGE

The Open Vulnerability and Assessment Language (OVAL) is a standard, nonproprietary specification to represent the technical aspects of evaluating compliance with a security guidance line item such as the installation of a specific patch. Security guidance line items expressed as OVAL checks are intended to be used by automated assessment tools to evaluate a system's compliance without requiring user input or intervention. OVAL can be used to assess a system's compliance with a configuration setting, perform an inventory of software that is installed on a system, identify missing patches on a system, and determine when a system has a specific vulnerability present.

The OVAL Advisory Board provides input to the OVAL Moderator (currently the MITRE Corporation), collaborating with the security automation community to provide input into OVAL's strategic direction and specific technical decisions. The board currently comprises OVAL-knowledgeable individuals from 28 entities including security product vendors, security researchers, government agency representatives, and interested individuals. Membership is open to those with sufficient OVAL understanding as described at http://oval.mitre.org.

OVAL has undergone several revisions during its lifetime. It started as a SQL-based language that could be used to query system information, but it was changed to an XML-based representation in version 3. OVAL versions 5.3 and 5.4 were officially adopted as part of SCAP 1.0. SCAP 1.1 allows the use of OVAL versions 5.3 to 5.8, and SCAP version 1.2 supports OVAL 5.10.

NOTE

*In early 2012, the OVAL Board approved version 5.10.1 of the OVAL language to provide several bug fixes to the OVAL schema constraints and associated documentation. Although the SCAP specification and Derived Test Requirements (DTR) refer to OVAL version 5.10, it is recommended that consumers use the new 5.10.1 version to take advantage of these corrections.*

OVAL is backward-compatible for non-major version changes. For example, an OVAL-compliant engine that can process OVAL 5.8

should be able to process OVAL 5.4 content without a problem. This section will explain the different components that make up an OVAL document, the tools that can be used with an OVAL document, and present a sample XML document.

## Data Model

OVAL is divided into multiple schemas, a set of common schemas, and schemas based on the specifics of the platform against which the OVAL content is intended to be used. Three common schemas are used, core, common, and independent, which define the common capabilities, data structures, and evaluation types that are platform-independent. Operating system schemas exist to provide operating system–specific capabilities.

The OVAL data model is defined in the schema files for the specific version of OVAL in which you are interested. Figure 3-2 shows some of the high level components within OVAL. Detailed descriptions are available at http://oval.mitre.org/languge. Currently, no official specification document is available for OVAL, but there is a reference interpreter that was created and is maintained by MITRE, which is available at http://sourceforge.net/projects/ovaldi/.

The root-level document element of an OVAL file is the *oval_definitions* element. Inside this element is information about the document, definitions, tests, objects, states, and variables. Together these constructs provide the information needed for an assessment engine to evaluate the technical aspects of the system and produce a result indicating the compliance status of an asset with a given element.

We will first discuss sections of the document that contain general information before moving into the specifics of performing assessments.

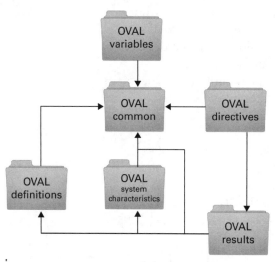

**FIGURE 3-2** OVAL components

XML samples in this section are taken from the USGCB content for Red Hat Enterprise Linux 5 (RHEL5) desktops, available at http://usgcb.nist.gov/usgcb/rhel/download_rhel5.html.

## Generator

The *generator* element contains data about the file itself. This information includes the name of the *product* that was used to create the OVAL file, the *schema_version* with which the content was built, and the *timestamp* indicating when the file was created. The schema_version is the most important, as it controls which OVAL constructs are allowed to be used in the document and allows a document consumer to determine whether it can properly process the document.

The following sample is a generator sample from an OVAL document. It shows an OVAL file that was created by hand using a variety of editors. It uses the OVAL schema version 5.4 and was created on 06-08-2010.

```
<generator>
  <oval:product_name>
    A mixture of Notepad++, Oxygen, and Visual Studio
  </oval:product_name>
  <oval:schema_version>5.4</oval:schema_version>
  <oval:timestamp>2010-06-08T12:00:00-04:00</oval:timestamp>
</generator>
```

## Definition

The *definition* is the starting point for an evaluation action and is the OVAL construct that is referenced by an external system. For example, when an XCCDF document links a rule to an OVAL item it identifies the OVAL definition in the OVAL file. OVAL definitions return true or false to indicate the result of the evaluation. The interpretation of the returned result is dependent on the *class* of the definition.

Each definition provides a unique ID and a version number. The ID must be in the following format: **oval:*<your domain>*.*<your namespace>*:def:#**. You would substitute your DNS name in reverse order for *<your domain>* and provide an appropriate namespace for the *<your namespace>* elements. The **#** is any number you want to use for identifying this definition inside this namespace. For example, an ID may look like this: oval:com.g2-inc.windows8:def:1—where g2-inc.com is the domain name. Domain names and namespaces are included to help ensure that OVAL IDs are globally unique. You should not use someone else's domain when creating content, but you should use a domain name in the form of *yourname.priv* if you do not have an actual domain name that you can use. The version number provides a quick indicator that some portion of the definition has changed.

Each definition identifies its *class*. The class provides a hint as to how to write or interpret the content. The available classes are inventory, vulnerability, compliance, patch, and miscellaneous. Inventory definitions should be written to return true if the software of interest is present or false if it is absent. Vulnerability definitions should return true if the system is subject to a given vulnerability and false if it is not. Compliance definitions should return true if the system is compliant with a given requirement and false if it is not. Patch definitions should return true if a patch is missing from a system and false if it is present. Miscellaneous tests are those that do not fall into one of the other categories. No default interpretation is associated with a miscellaneous test type, and you should avoid using them.

A *title* is used to provide a human-readable indication of the intent of the definition. This assists in both evaluating and maintaining the OVAL file. The *affected* tag can be used to provide a list of platforms on which the definition is applicable.

Multiple *references* may be supplied. These references can include CPE names, CCE identifiers, CVE identifiers, or others. For SCAP content, when a definition is referenced by an XCCDF rule that has either a CVE or CCE associated with it, the OVAL definition must specify that CVE or CCE in addition to any other references provided.

The actual assessment logic is contained within *criteria* blocks that contain specific *criterion* elements. Criteria blocks can be nested inside one another and can have a logical operator of **AND**, **OR**, **ONE**, or **XOR** that specifies how its contents are to be combined when calculating the final result of the definition. A criteria block can also have a *negate* attribute indicating that the definition results should be inverted. The default behavior in the absence of an explicit operator is to use the **AND** operation to combine criterion. The negate attribute defaults to false if it is not specified. The combination of nesting, operators, and negation allows complex evaluation criteria to be used to obtain an accurate result when performing an evaluation.

Individual criterion elements inside a criteria block may have the negate flag specified to indicate that the result of that element should be inverted before it is evaluated by the containing criteria. The other attribute available for criteria is a *test-ref* that provides a link to an OVAL *test* element used in the evaluation of the definition.

The next XML sample shows an OVAL definition for CCE-14113-5; this is reflected in the CCE reference element. The ID for this definition is **oval:gov.nist.usgcb.rhel:def:200783**. You can interpret this ID like this:

- **oval**   This indicates that this is an OVAL ID of some sort.

- **gov.nist**   This is produced by the organization that owns nist.gov, the National Institute of Standards and Technology (NIST) in this case.

- **usgcb.rhel**   This is in the namespace rhel.usgb that was defined by NIST.

- **def**   This is a definition ID.

- **200783**   The individual ID number for this is 200783.

This is the first *version* of this definition; subsequent changes to any part of this definition would result in increments to the version number. The title, description, and affected platform are all specified as part of the OVAL definition.

```
In order to evaluate the state of the system in regards to this requirement
run the OVAL test with an id of oval:gov.nist.usgcb.rhel:tst:200783.
<definition class="compliance"
  id="oval:gov.nist.usgcb.rhel:def:200783"
  version="1">
    <metadata>
      <title>Set Password dcredit Requirements</title>
      <affected family="unix">
        <platform>Red Hat Enterprise Linux 5</platform>
      </affected>
      <reference ref_id="CCE-14113-5" source="CCE"/>
      <description>
       The password dcredit should meet minimum requirements
       using pam_cracklib
      </description>
```

```
    </metadata>
    <criteria>
      <criterion
        comment="Conditions for dcredit are satisfied"
        test_ref="oval:gov.nist.usgcb.rhel:tst:200783"/>
    </criteria>
  </definition>
```

## Test

There are several types of OVAL test elements, and they are defined in the independent or operating system–specific schemas. Test elements usually have names like **textfilecontent54_test** or **passwordpolicy_test**. In situations where capabilities are added to a test type that break backward-compatibility, the OVAL version number in which the changes are introduced is appended to the base test name. For example, the **textfilecontent_test** was changed in OVAL 5.4 in a way that broke backward-compatibility, so the **textfilecontent54_test** was introduced, and the **textfilecontent_test** is still available for use in creation of OVAL 5.3 content.

Each test element must have a unique ID of this format **oval: <*yourdomain*>.<*yournamespace*>:tst:#**. As in the declaration of definition IDs, you would substitute your domain name in reverse representation, a specific namespace, and a number to create the element ID. A comment can be added to a test element to assist in maintenance and human comprehension, and the version number should be incremented any time the element changes to help identify revisions.

Test elements reference *object* and *state* elements that are used in the evaluation process. An object is a system artifact that is collected by the evaluation tool. There are a large number of potential object types that vary based on the family and that are defined in the specific schemas. States provide a representation of what factors of the system artifact are to be examined and in what state we want to see those factors. States may or may not be required depending on the specific test type. It is possible for a single object specifier to return multiple system artifacts.

Two additional attributes on a test element can have a profound impact on the results of a specific test.

The first is the *check-existence* attribute. This attribute may have one of the following values: **all_exist**, **any_exist**, **at_least_one_exist**,

**none_exist**, or **only_one_exist**. These values specify how many artifacts that meet the specified state must be found for the test to return true. For example, if **none_exist** is specified, then the presence of any artifacts would indicate failure of the test.

The *check* attribute may have one of the following values: **all**, **at least one**, **none exist**, **none satisfy**, or **only one**. This value is used to control how the results from multiple artifact and state comparisons are to be combined into a final result for the test.

- **all**   Indicates that every object must pass the given test

- **at least one**   Means that at least one of the objects must pass the test

- **none exist**   Has been deprecated and should not be used

- **none satisfy**   Means that if none of the artifacts meet the state requirement, the test should return true; otherwise, it should return false

- **only one**   A value of "only one" means that a final result of true is given if one and only one of the individual results under consideration are true.

In the next sample, a test item shows a textfilecontent54_test test. It has an ID of **check- "oval:gov.nist.usgcb.rhel:tst:200783"**. Since the **check attribute** is **"all"**, any object that is returned by the object will be compared to the specified state. Since **check** is set to **"all"**, that means that every object returned must meet the state specified in order for the test to return true. The **check_existence** attribute is **"all_exist"** meaning that every object specified must exist on the system or the check will not pass. This is the first version of this test, and it has a comment. Evaluation of this test involves querying the system for instances of object 100004 and comparing it to state 100004.

```
<ind-def:textfilecontent54_test
  id="oval:gov.nist.usgcb.rhel:tst:200783"
  version="1"
  check="all"
  check-existence="all_exist"
  comment="check the configuration of /etc/pam.d/system-auth">
    <ind-def:object object_ref="oval:gov.nist.usgcb.rhel:obj:100004"/>
    <ind-def:state state_ref="oval:gov.nist.usgcb.rhel:ste:100004"/>
</ind-def:textfilecontent54_test>
```

## Object

An OVAL *object* is used to specify a system artifact to be retrieved during an evaluation. A wide variety of object types exist, and they vary based on the platform schemas that are used to create and use the content. The specific elements of each object type also vary, so we will confine our discussion to the common properties of all objects as well as a specific discussion of the **textfilecontent54_object** since it is in the independent schema and is applicable to many platforms. To learn more about the other object types, you should refer to the appropriate schema documents.

All objects must have a unique ID of the form **oval:*<your domain>.<namespace>*:obj:#**. Once again, you substitute the reverse representation of your domain name, a namespace, and a number to create a globally unique identifier. Objects may also have a comment that will aid in understanding and maintaining the content and a version number to track changes. These are really the only common object properties, so we will now turn to a specific discussion of the **textfilecontent54_object**.

The **textfilecontent54_object** is used to retrieve text from within files to be used for comparison against a state. Many operating systems and applications use a settings file to store their configuration, so this object type is applicable in many environments. The object specifies a path to a file, the filename of the file, a regular expression pattern to identify what text to retrieve from the file, and an optional instance that identifies what capturing group from the pattern to use in the evaluation against the state.

The next sample shows a **textfilecontent54_object** expressed in XML. The object ID is **"oval:gov.nist.usgcb.rhel:obj:100004"**, it is version 1 of the object definition. The content is looking in the file /etc/pam.d/system-auth, which you can build from the path and filename elements. Inside that file it is searching for any text that matches the specified pattern; this pattern in particular is matching a line that describes the password requirements and in particular is looking for the value of the **dcredit** setting. The value of the **dcredit** parameter is captured in a regex capturing group, in this case the first and only capturing group (-?\d+). The capturing group to be used as the object is specified in the instance element, even though it is redundant to specify it in this case, with only one capturing group, but it must be done.

```
<ind-def:textfilecontent54_object
  id="oval:gov.nist.usgcb.rhel:obj:100004"
  version="1">
  <ind-def:path>/etc/pam.d</ind-def:path>
  <ind-def:filename>system-auth</ind-def:filename>
  <ind-def:pattern operation="pattern match">
    ^[\s]*password[\s]+(?:(?:required)|(?:requisite))[\s]+
    [\w_\.\-=\s]+[\s]dcredit=(-?\d+)(?:[\s]|$)
  </ind-def:pattern>
  <ind-def:instance operation="less than or equal"
datatype="int">
    1
  </ind-def:instance>
</ind-def:textfilecontent54_object>
```

## State

The *state* element provides a view of how we want the collected
artifact to look. As with the object element, specific variants are based
on the object type, so we will limit our discussion to the common
components and a discussion of the **textfilecontent54_state**.

All state elements must have a unique ID of the form **oval:<*your
domain*>.<*namespace*>:ste:#**. As with all other IDs in an OVAL
document, you substitute your domain name, custom namespace, and
a numeric identifier in the appropriate sections of the ID. The other
two common elements are the *comment* and *version* fields, which
serve the same purpose as they do in other OVAL constructs.

The **textfilecontent54_state** contains one element, *subexpression*.
This element specifies the *datatype* with which the contents should
be treated, for comparison purposes. The *operation* to be used
during the comparison is also specified. There are many potential
operation values, but not all of them make sense for every datatype.
The operations include standard mathematical comparisons, bitwise
comparisons, string comparisons, and regular expression pattern
matching. Also specified are the entities to check from the associated
object to compare to this state.

The last piece of information included in the **textfilecontent54
_state** is the actual value to be used in the comparison against the
object. When evaluating an OVAL, the artifacts returned by the
object portion of the state are then compared to the state components
specified as part of the test and a result is returned.

In the sample that follows, the state has an ID of **"oval:gov.nist .usgcb.rhel:ste:100004"** and is version 1. The instance that is used from the object is again specified. The subexpression, or capturing group, should be treated as an **int** and compared to see if it is less than or equal to the variable with the ID of **"oval:gov.nist.usgcb .rhel:var:200783"**.

```
<ind-def:textfilecontent54_state
  id="oval:gov.nist.usgcb.rhel:ste:100004"
  version="1">
    <ind-def:instance datatype="int">1</ind-def:instance>
    <ind-def:subexpression datatype="int"
      operation="less than or equal"
      var_ref="oval:gov.nist.usgcb.rhel:var:200783" />
</ind-def:textfilecontent54_state>
```

## Variables

OVAL variables allow you to customize the assessment at runtime, instead of relying on decisions made at content creation time. This provides a lot of flexibility and power to the checking system, but it does add a layer of complexity. There are two types of variables, *local* and *external*. We will talk about the differences between local and external variables and then explain a few of their potential uses.

Every variable has a unique ID of the format **oval:<*your domain*>.<*namespace*>:var:#**. This format should be very familiar by now, but once again you would substitute your domain in reverse representation, a namespace, and an identifier. The variable would also have a *version* and *comment* and would specify the *datatype* such as string, integer, or Boolean. The datatype specified here should match the datatype (if specified) of any component that references the variable. A variety of operations may be applied to variables to refine their value before they are referenced, or they may just be used as simple substitutions.

Local variables are defined within the OVAL document itself, while external variables are passed in from an external source such as an XCCDF document. Other than the source of the variable, there are no significant differences between the two variable types. They can be used in the same ways and have the same operations applied to them. Variables can be referenced as part of object and state definitions, and they can also be referenced by other variables.

Variables can also reference objects to retrieve and use system information as part of the variable.

The simplest use case for variables is as a simple substitution. In many cases, the same OVAL content can be used with just a simple value change. For example, the requirement of minimum password length will vary among organizations, but the OVAL content to check that value is identical except for the specific value to be checked for. Using a variable to control the value used in the tests allows reuse of the rest of the OVAL content, and specifically using an external variable in this situation allows the XCCDF to be used to control the value without requiring any changes to the OVAL.

A more complex use case for variables is to use system information to build dynamic test content. For example, the Windows install directory location is not a static value: it may vary from system to system. However, within the Windows directory, the directory structure is well defined. To write content that can dynamically perform assessments within the Windows directory and subdirectories, you can build a variable that represents the appropriate path. You can do this by using a variable that references a registry object that retrieves the location of the Windows directory.

Let's assume, for example, that the registry object returns "c:\ windows". You can then reference this variable in another variable and use the string concatenation functions to add the "\system32" string to the base directory string, resulting in "c:\windows\ system32". This final variable can then be used in an object definition to retrieve files from the Windows\System32 directory no matter where the base Windows installation directory is located.

The external variable shown next is used in a simple substitution for the state object used in the preceding section. The ID of this variable is **"oval:gov.nist.usgcb.rhel:var:200783"**, it is version 1, and it should be treated as having a datatype of integer. Since this is an external variable, the actual value of this variable is passed in from an external system.

```
<external_variable
  id="oval:gov.nist.usgcb.rhel:var:200783"
  version="1"
  datatype="int"
  comment="External variable for definition 20078"/>
```

## OVAL Results

An OVAL test can return the following results: true, false, unknown, error, not evaluated, and not applicable.

Return values of *true* and *false* are the most straightforward return types. True indicates that the conditions specified by the test have been met. False indicates that the conditions have not been met.

An *unknown* return value essentially indicates that the object specified as part of the test could not be collected. Not collected is different from not found. For example, the evaluation software would put a "not found" entry in the system characteristics file if it tried to gather information about a file that was not on the system. If the evaluation system was not capable of gathering file system information, it should put a "not collected" entry in the system characteristics.

An *error* result is an indication that an error occurred while the evaluation was being performed. Errors could include missing external variables or technical problems encountered while gathering information from the system.

*Not evaluated* means that no attempt was made to evaluate the given definition, usually because it was not selected for evaluation by whatever is controlling the evaluation process.

*Not applicable* results indicate that a given test is not applicable on the given system. This might occur, for example, if you were attempting to run a registry test on a UNIX system or running a RPM test on a Windows system.

The results of all tests are calculated and then combined using the Boolean logic defined in the criteria sections of the definition to return a final result for the definition itself.

# OPEN CHECKLIST INTERACTIVE LANGUAGE

The Open Checklist Interactive Language (OCIL) is a check language that was created for developing these questionnaires to people, and collecting and analyzing their answers. Unlike OVAL, which is designed to perform technical checks on systems in a fully automated manner, OCIL was designed to be interactive with people, essentially automating the process of collecting information from them. This can involve virtually any type of information—from answering true/false or multiple choice questions to submitting electronic copies of system configuration files. Although the motivation for creating OCIL was to collect security information, absolutely nothing in OCIL is specific to security, so it can be used for any type of questionnaire. After learning more about what OCIL can do, you might be surprised when you realize how many uses it can have for your organization.

The MITRE Corporation led the efforts to create the original versions of OCIL. OCIL version 1.0 was finalized in late 2008, and version 1.1 followed in mid-2009. Work on OCIL version 2.0, a major update to the OCIL specification, was led by NIST with assistance from MITRE and others. NIST released version 2.0 as final in April 2011. OCIL 2.0 is the first version of OCIL to be included in SCAP, and this is the version we will cover herein. Links to all of the specifications, XML schemas, and other supporting information for all OCIL versions are publicly available at http://scap.nist.gov/specifications/ocil/.

## OCIL Data Model

The OCIL data model defines the syntax requirements for writing OCIL questionnaires and the processing requirements for using the questionnaires. The data model is formally and primarily defined by the official OCIL XML schema, with secondary information on requirements provided by the official OCIL specification, NIST Interagency Report (IR) 7692, "Specification for the Open Checklist Interactive Language (OCIL) Version 2.0."

All OCIL content is stored in an XML element simply called *ocil*. This element contains metadata regarding the OCIL document where it's stored, as well as all other pieces of OCIL content. The highest level logical structure in an ocil element is a *questionnaire*, which defines the questions to be asked, the actions to be performed based on responses to questions (also known as *test actions*), and other information needed to pose the questionnaire to people. Each *question* comprises the text of a question, at a minimum, and can also include instructions to help a person formulate a response to a question. For example, if you ask a user to provide her laptop's serial number, you might also want to provide instructions on how to find the serial number.

OCIL can also be used to collect *artifacts*, which are pieces of evidence such as copies of files or blocks of text, to support an answer provided by the person answering a questionnaire. If an auditor needs to confirm that a system has a security plan, the questionnaire could ask the system owner if a security plan exists, and if the owner answers "yes," the questionnaire could then prompt the owner to submit a copy of the security plan. Finally, the results of someone answering an OCIL questionnaire are recorded in the OCIL *results*.

The next several parts of this chapter discuss these major OCIL concepts in more detail: questions, test actions, questionnaires, artifacts, and results.

## Questions

Each OCIL document contains definitions for one or more questions. There are four types of questions, differentiated by the kind of answer they can accept: *boolean_question* (yes or no), *choice_question* (multiple choice), *numeric_question* (number), and *string_question* (text). Regardless of type, each question has two mandatory properties in common: a unique identifier for the question and the text of the question. Here's an example of a boolean_question with just the mandatory properties:

```
<boolean_question id="ocil:org.orgname:question:45">
  <question_text>Does each system administrator have a unique account
dedicated to administering the system?</question_text>
</boolean_question>
```

In this example, the question's unique identifier is specified in the first line by the **id** attribute. The value of this attribute has four fields, separated by colons. The value of the first field is always **ocil**. The second field should indicate the identity of the organization (or the part of the organization) that is creating the question. There's no mandatory format for that identification, but the OCIL specification recommends using a Domain Name System (DNS) name, and listing it inverted (in reverse order, from most general domain to most specific domain). So, for example, if a government agency wanted to use the DNS name ocil .myagency.gov to identify its OCIL questions, it would specify gov .myagency.ocil for the second field. The value of the third field is always **question** to denote that this is a question identifier. The fourth field is set to a positive integer, 1 or higher. You can assign any such numbers that you want to your questions—they don't have to be consecutive—but you have to make sure that you don't define two questions with exactly the same identifier (all four fields) in the same OCIL document.

The question_text element in the second line of the example defines the text to be shown to the respondent when asking the question. The boolean_question tags at the beginning and end of the example are used to declare this as a boolean question and to indicate the beginning and end of the question's declaration.

This example shows only the two mandatory properties that all the question types have in common. All four question types also support three of the same optional properties: instructions to help someone understand how to answer the question, notes that provide additional information regarding the question (intended for questionnaire authors, editors, or administrators, not the people responding to the questionnaire), and a default answer for the question. In addition to the mandatory and optional properties that all question types support, boolean and choice questions support additional properties. Let's look at examples of all four types of questions with optional properties.

## Boolean Questions

The next example is a different version of the previous boolean example, highlighting the optional *model* property, which is valid only for boolean questions. Compare the question text in this new example to the previous example. Both examples are really asking the same question, but the next example is phrasing it as a statement and expecting a true or false answer, while the previous example is asking a direct question and expecting a yes or no answer. By default, OCIL questions expect yes or no answers. Question writers can override this by setting the model attribute to **"MODEL_TRUE _FALSE"**. The other possible setting for this attribute is the default **"MODEL_YES_NO"**; question writers can state that explicitly, but it's assumed if no model attribute is specified. There's no advantage to using one model or the other; question authors should choose the model they prefer.

```
<boolean_question id="ocil:org.orgname:question:101" model="MODEL_TRUE_FALSE">
  <question_text>Each system administrator has a unique account dedicated
to administering the system.</question_text>
</boolean_question>
```

### Choice Questions

The next example shows a choice question. Notice that after the question text, there are four *choice* elements, which specify four possible answers from which the respondent can choose. Each choice element has a unique identifier, similar in syntax to the question identifier, but with **choice** in the third field instead of **question**. The value for each choice element's **id** attribute must be unique within the OCIL document. The first line in the example includes a **default _answer_ref** attribute, which is an optional property valid only for choice questions. In this example, it specifies that the choice with identifier **"ocil:org.orgname:choice:121"** is the default answer to this question.

```
<choice_question default_answer_ref="ocil:org.orgname:choice:121"
id="ocil:org.orgname:question:20">
  <question_text>Approximately how many years of security administration
experience do you have?</question_text>
    <choice id="ocil:org.orgname:choice:121">Less than 2</choice>
    <choice id="ocil:org.orgname:choice:122">2 to 5</choice>
    <choice id="ocil:org.orgname:choice:123">6 to 10</choice>
    <choice id="ocil:org.orgname:choice:124">11 or more</choice>
</choice_question>
```

Instead of specifying each possible answer in a unique choice element, you have the option of using a *choice_group* element in place of some or all of the choice elements. The choice_group element allows you to specify a group of choices and refer to them with a single choice_group identifier. This is very useful when you want to use the same group of choices for multiple-choice questions. For example, suppose that you want people to rank several of your security services on the same scale. Instead of defining the same choices over and over for each question, you could just define the choices once in a choice_group element, such as the following example:

```
<choice_group id="ocil:org.orgname:choicegroup:1">
    <choice id="ocil:org.orgname:choice:101">Excellent</choice>
    <choice id="ocil:org.orgname:choice:102">Good</choice>
    <choice id="ocil:org.orgname:choice:103">Fair</choice>
    <choice id="ocil:org.orgname:choice:104">Poor</choice>
    <choice id="ocil:org.orgname:choice:105">N/A</choice>
</choice_group>
```

Then you simply refer to this choice_group element from your choice questions by specifying a choice_group_ref:

```
<choice_question id="ocil:org.orgname:question:25">
  <question_text>How do you rate our password reset portal?</question_text>
  <choice_group_ref>ocil:org.orgname:choicegroup:1</choice_group_ref>
</choice_question>
<choice_question id="ocil:org.orgname:question:26">
  <question_text>How do you rate our security awareness training?
  </question_text>
  <choice_group_ref>ocil:org.orgname:choicegroup:1</choice_group_ref>
</choice_question>
```

You can mix choice and choice_group_ref elements in a single choice question. No matter which type or types of elements you use to list the choices, the people answering the questionnaire will see the choices in the order that you specify. The OCIL specification requires that all products that present OCIL questionnaires to preserve the sequence of possible choices when presenting them to people.

## Only One Choice

In OCIL version 2.0, a person answering a choice question can select only one of the possible answers. Imagine that the question is, What type of mobile device do you use for work? and the possible answers are laptop, smartphone, and tablet. There's no way for a person to select more than one of these answers. Instead, the question author needs to design the question and possible answers to handle this. One option is to break this question into three separate questions, such as, Do you use a laptop for work?, Do you use a smartphone for work?, and Do you use a tablet for work? Alternatively, the question author could keep the question but expand the possible answers by listing the combinations: laptop only, smartphone only, tablet only, laptop and smartphone, smartphone and tablet, laptop and tablet, and all three.

### Numeric Questions

The third type of question is the numeric question. The next example is straightforward, similar to the original example except for the addition of the *default_answer* attribute. The default_answer attribute specifies the default value for the answer. This attribute is optional for all question types other than choice questions, which use the *default_answer_ref* attribute instead.

```
<numeric_question default_answer="0" id="ocil:org.orgname:question:8">
  <question_text>During a typical work day, approximately how many times do
you type in a password?</question_text>
</numeric_question>
```

In some cases, it might make more sense to use a choice question instead of a numeric question. A numeric question should be used when you need a precise answer and there are more than a few possibilities. A choice question can be used instead if you don't need a precise answer and can group the answers into a small number of ranges. For example, the preceding question is perfectly fine as a numeric question, but it could also be expressed as a choice question if precise answers aren't needed:

```
<choice_question default_answer_ref="ocil:org.orgname:choice:121"
id="ocil:org.orgname:question:20">
  <question_text>During a typical work day, approximately how many times do
you type in a password?</question_text>
  <choice id="ocil:org.orgname:choice:121">Less than 5</choice>
  <choice id="ocil:org.orgname:choice:122">5 to 9</choice>
  <choice id="ocil:org.orgname:choice:123">10 to 24</choice>
  <choice id="ocil:org.orgname:choice:124">25 or more</choice>
</choice_question>
```

### String Questions

The last type of question is the string question. As the next example shows, it is very similar to the numeric question in terms of structure. And, similar to the previous discussion about using a choice question instead of a numeric question, in some cases it makes sense to use a choice question instead of a string question. If respondents would supply only a small number of predictable strings (and no unpredictable strings), you could create a choice question instead that lists each possibility. This makes it faster for people to answer the question, and it eliminates problems with people typing in variations on the same string, such as misspellings.

```
<string_question id="ocil:org.orgname:question:13">
  <question_text>What is your job title?</question_text>
</string_question>
```

### Variables

Question writers can customize the text of various OCIL elements, such as any type of question or any choice, by using a *variable*, which is an element containing a single value. There are three types of variables:

- *constant_variable*, which is defined directly within the OCIL document
- *external_variable*, which is defined by an external source
- *local_variable*, which is defined dynamically based on the answer that a respondent gives to a particular question

Let's look at an example of the simplest type of variable: a *constant_variable*. The example that follows shows all the mandatory properties of a constant_variable. The variable has a unique ID, similar to those used for questions, choices, and choice groups. The variable also has a declared datatype, which must be set either to TEXT or NUMERIC. The datatype defines how the value in the value element is to be treated. In this example, the value is **2011** and the datatype is **TEXT** because the OCIL document author wants 2011 to be treated as text (representing the current year) and not a numeric value.

```
<constant_variable id="ocil:org.orgname:variable:1" datatype="TEXT">
  <value>2011</value>
</constant_variable>
```

The author could then refer to this variable instead of hard-coding the current year into each question, choice, or other text element that needs to list the year.

An *external_variable* has the same mandatory and optional properties as a constant_variable, except that the value for an external_variable isn't specified within the OCIL document. Here is an example:

```
<external_variable id="ocil:org.orgname:variable:2" datatype="NUMERIC">
  <description>Minimum password length</description>
</external_variable>
```

## Question_Test_Action Elements

Now that we've got the basics of questions, let's look at the mechanism that actually calls questions: the *question_test_action* element. A question_test_action specifies the identifier of a question to ask, and then defines how the answer provided for the question is to be handled. There are four types of question_test_action elements, corresponding to the four types of questions:

- A *boolean_question_test_action* is used for questions answered by YES/NO or TRUE/FALSE.

- A *choice_question_test_action* is used when the user is presented with a list of possible responses and selects a single answer from the list.

- A *numeric_question_test_action* is used for questions answered with a numeric value.

- A *string_question_test_action* is used for questions answered with an alphanumeric string of characters.

All four types of question_test_action elements have several common properties. The two mandatory properties are a unique ID (similar to the other identifiers) and a *question_ref*, which specifies the unique identifier of the question to be asked. Each also has one or more "when" elements, which define the action to be taken based upon the question response.

### boolean_question_test_action

The next example is a simple instance of a boolean_question_test_action. This example specifies both "when" elements that are available for a boolean_question_test_action: the *when_true* element, which specifies the action to perform when the respondent gives an answer of true, and the *when_false* element, which specifies the action to perform when the respondent gives an answer of false.

```
<boolean_question_test_action id="ocil:org.orgname:testaction:31">
  <when_true>
    <result>PASS</result>
  </when_true>
  <when_false>
    <result>FAIL</result>
  </when_false>
</boolean_question_test_action>
```

In this example, the action taken for a true answer is to return a PASS result and for a false answer a FAIL result. The result is returned to whatever called the test_action: either a questionnaire or another test_action. Here's an example of how a test_action can call another test_action, snipped from a larger boolean_test_action:

```
<when_true>
  <test_action_ref negate="false">ocil:org.orgname:testaction:53
  </test_action_ref>
</when_true>
```

In this excerpt, if an answer of true is given, the test_action_ref element specifies that the next action is to call the test_action with the identifier ocil:org.orgname:testaction:53. The result of that test_action is returned to the test_action_ref element. Notice the **negate** attribute within that element. If it is set to true, then the result returned to the test_action_ref element is inverted—changed from false to true, or true to false. We'll come back to these logical values in the "Questionnaires" section of this chapter a bit later.

## Choice test_actions

The next example shows a *choice_question_test_action*, which defines how to handle the results of answering a choice question. Like the boolean_question_test_action, it includes **question_ref** and **id** attributes. But instead of using the when_true and when_false elements of a boolean_question_test_action, the choice_question_test_action uses when_choice elements. Look at the first when_choice portion of the example that follows. It means that if the person answering the specified question (ocil:org.orgname:question:45) selects one of the choices defined by ocil:org.orgname:choice:11 and 14, that the test_action will return the result FAIL. If the person selects one of the other choices (specified as 12 and 13), the test_action will return the result PASS.

```
<choice_question_test_action question_ref="ocil:org.orgname:question:45"
id="ocil:org.orgname:testaction:33">
  <when_choice>
    <result>FAIL</result>
    <choice_ref>ocil:org.orgname:choice:11</choice_ref>
    <choice_ref>ocil:org.orgname:choice:14</choice_ref>
  </when_choice>
  <when_choice>
    <result>PASS</result>
    <choice_ref>ocil:org.orgname:choice:12</choice_ref>
    <choice_ref>ocil:org.orgname:choice:13</choice_ref>
  </when_choice>
</choice_question_test_action>
```

### Numeric test_actions

Next, let's look at the *numeric_question_test_actions*, which work with a numeric_question. The "when" elements available for a numeric_question_test_action are when_range and when_equals. In the next example, two when_range elements define the answer ranges that correspond to PASS and FAIL results. An answer in the range 0 to 20 generates a PASS, while an answer in the 21 to 50 range causes a FAIL result.

```
<numeric_question_test_action question_ref="ocil:org.orgname:question:22"
id="ocil:org.orgname:testaction:44">
  <when_range>
    <result>PASS</result>
      <range>
        <min>0</min>
        <max>20</max>
      </range>
  </when_range>
  <when_range>
    <result>FAIL</result>
      <range>
        <min>21</min>
        <max>50</max>
      </range>
  </when_range>
</numeric_question_test_action>
```

The example doesn't include a when_equals element, but it's used in a similar fashion to when_range to specify a single answer value that corresponds to a PASS or FAIL result. Questionnaire writers can use combinations of when_equals and when_range elements in a single numeric_question_test_action; however, there are some rules you must follow. The when_equals elements must all be listed before the when_range elements. Also, if there are two or more elements that handle the same values, the first element listed is the one that will be used. So, for example, if you had a when_equals that treated an answer of 10 as a PASS, followed by a when_range that treated answers in the range 0 to 20 as FAIL, an answer of 10 would generate a PASS result because it would be handled by the first matching "when" element—in this case, the when_equals.

### String test_action

The final type of question_test_action is the *string_question_test_action*. It uses one or more when_pattern elements to define patterns as regular expressions. The string answer entered by a questionnaire respondent is compared against these patterns, in the order that the patterns are specified, and the first pattern that matches is used to choose the result. So, in the example shown next, since the question referenced requires the response to include a number ("At least how many characters must be changed before the information system allows the creation of new passwords?"), any response that does not include a number will result in a FAIL.

```
<string_question_test_action question_ref="ocil:mitre.org:question:11"
id="ocil:mitre.org:testaction:11">
<when_pattern>
<result>PASS</result>
<pattern>^[0-9]+$</pattern>
</when_pattern>
<when_pattern>
<result>FAIL</result>
<pattern>^[a-zA-Z\s,\.]+$</pattern>
</when_pattern>
</string_question_test_action>
```

## Questionnaires

So far we've looked at the composition of individual questions and the test_actions that reference those questions. Now it's time to look at the OCIL *questionnaire* element, which is the framework that calls the test_actions. A questionnaire can be extremely simple, such as the following example that includes only the mandatory properties:

```
<questionnaire id="ocil:org.orgname:questionnaire:4">
  <actions>
    <test_action_ref>ocil:org.orgname:testaction:6</test_action_ref>
  </actions>
</questionnaire>
```

The first line contains the unique questionnaire identifier ID, in the same general format we've seen for every other type of OCIL identifier. The other required property is the *actions* element, which contains one or more *test_action_ref* elements, each of which lists the identifier for a particular test_action element. In this example, the questionnaire is calling a single test_action. To determine what that test_action does, including which questions it asks, we'd have to look at the definition of the test_action itself.

Here's the same example questionnaire elements, but with several optional properties and test_action_ref elements added:

```
<questionnaire id="ocil:org.orgname:questionnaire:4">
  <title>Physical Security for Teleworker Laptops</title>
  <description>This questionnaire asks teleworkers a series of questions
  related to the physical security measures in place for the laptops
  they use for telework.</description>
  <actions negate="false" operation="AND">
    <test_action_ref>ocil:org.orgname:testaction:6</test_action_ref>
    <test_action_ref>ocil:org.orgname:testaction:7</test_action_ref>
    <test_action_ref>ocil:org.orgname:testaction:8</test_action_ref>
  </actions>
</questionnaire>
```

The *title* and *description* elements provide an explanation of the purpose of the set of test_actions, reducing the need to look through the individual test_actions to figure out what the questionnaire does. In the actions element, there are two attributes: **negate** and **operation**. The **operation** attribute defines how the results of the individual test_action_ref elements are to be logically combined. In this case, the **"AND"** means that all the test_action_ref PASS or FAIL results should be ANDed together. This results in PASS if all the individual results are PASS, and it results in FAIL if any of the individual results are FAIL. The **negate** attribute in the actions element works just like the one for test_action_ref elements; it takes the result calculated through the operation setting and inverts it if set to true. When **negate** is set to false, the result is unchanged.

OCIL takes a modular approach to questionnaires. Although it's perfectly fine to have one questionnaire element that calls all the test_actions, which in turn call all the questions, OCIL is designed to have multiple, smaller questionnaires in a single OCIL document. Questionnaires can call other questionnaires. This approach is beneficial because the questionnaires are simpler to write and understand, and the modular approach promotes reuse, such as using the same questionnaire module for several purposes.

## Result Values

In the question_test_action discussion, we looked at several "when" elements that specify how to handle answers. The examples provided illustrated PASS and FAIL results, two of the six possible result types. Each test action evaluates to one result type which will be one of the following:

- **PASS**   The objective (of the questionnaire or question_test_action) has been fully met.

- **FAIL**   The objective has been refuted; some condition required to meet the objective has been shown not to be present.

- **UNKNOWN**   The objective was neither met nor refuted. Suppose, for example, that a person is asked several questions, but she leaves some of them blank because she doesn't know the information being requested.

- **ERROR**   There was either an unacceptable answer to a question or another error condition that could not be handled gracefully. Examples include a user providing unexpected text as an answer to a string question, or a questionnaire-asking application having a failure while asking a question.

- **NOT_APPLICABLE**   The objective is not applicable in this case. For example, suppose that the objective is to confirm that telework laptops are secured properly, and a person indicates (through an answer to a question) that he doesn't use a laptop for telework. Subsequent questions relating to the security of telework laptops would not be applicable for this particular person.

- **NOT_TESTED**   The objective has not yet been evaluated. An example is when a person suspends answering a questionnaire partway through.

## Putting It All Together

Using the OCIL components described here, you can create an OCIL document. For each check (or set of checks) to be performed, create the questionnaire elements (such as title, description, references). For each questionnaire element, create a boolean, multiple choice, numeric, or string-based question (with ID and text elements), and then create the appropriate test_actions based upon the anticipated answer to those questions.

We provide a number of examples of OCIL documents at our web site, and OCIL questionnaires are also available to review on the National Checklist Program site.

# Chapter 4

**Asset Management**

All of the security automation components we have described thus far are based on understanding the state of individual entities that have some value to the organization. The National Institute of Standards and Technology (NIST) defines these entities as "assets," and each could refer to any resource, whether a person, a device, a network, a real or virtual software component, a physical location, or even the organization itself. The asset is the foundation around which security automation is built, since each of the automation components is describing a state or a finding about "something." Following are some example cases that demonstrate how an assessment might relate to an asset:

- A network is discovered and its devices are inventoried.

- Hosts are reviewed as to whether they exhibit vulnerability to a given threat.

- Data centers are assessed to determine compliance with a given policy.

- People are interviewed with an Open Checklist Interactive Language (OCIL) questionnaire regarding management controls.

- Software is reviewed for indicators of suspicious malware activity.

In these examples and in Figure 4-1, you can see that asset management impacts many IT management components, such as inventory, configuration, and vulnerability management capabilities, plus ongoing situational awareness and continuous monitoring of those services.

Each of these examples describes the consideration of security around a given type of asset, so the ability to identify assets, report findings, and summarize those reports effectively are important to security automation. For this reason, SCAP 1.2 includes the addition of Asset Identification (AI) and Asset Reporting Format (ARF) specifications, each of which addresses an aspect of security asset management. A third specification, Assessment Summary Results (ASR), has been presented by the U.S. Department of Defense in draft form and provides a means to communicate the collective results of findings from compatible data sources.

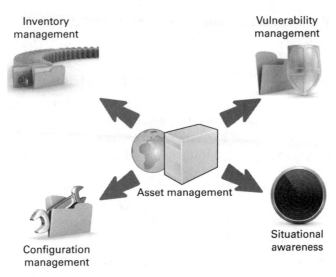

Inventory
management

Vulnerability
management

Asset management

Configuration
management

Situational
awareness

**FIGURE 4-1** Asset management supports many IT management functions.

# ASSET IDENTIFICATION

NIST Interagency Report 7693, "Specification for Asset Identification," defines an asset as anything that has value to an organization. It proceeds to describe a finite list of asset types that are defined by the AI specification:

| | | |
|---|---|---|
| Person | Organization | System |
| Software | Database | Network |
| Service | Data | Computing device |
| Circuit | Web site | |

The AI model is intended to help uniquely identify the asset, and, if applicable, to help point to a reference that contains more information about the asset. For example, while AI will identify a specific system, AI will not indicate any security details about that asset such as its compliance or vulnerability state. By providing a common reference identifier, however, additional information about the results of assessments may be derived (as described in detail in the following section.)

The AI specification provides a core set of fields that aid in the identification of each of the 11 asset types. One or more of each field can be used to identify the asset uniquely through the use of "identifiers," as described next.

## Literal and Synthetic Identifiers

The AI specification lists four identifier types to help represent information in the data model: literal identifiers, relationship identifiers, synthetic identifiers, and extension identifiers. The following examples are from the specification.

- ■ **Literal identifiers**    Predefined fields containing literal values that may identify an asset. For example, a Media Access Control (MAC) address is an example of a literal identifier for a computing device.

- ■ **Synthetic identifiers**    Meant to be used when a database or process assigns an identifier. For example, an employee is often assigned an employee identifier, which may be used to track him or her across the organization. These identifiers should be represented using the synthetic identifier construct: the namespace denotes the management domain for which the identifier is valid, and the identifier contains the identifier itself.

- ■ **Relationship identifiers**    Used when an asset may be identified based on a relationship to another asset. For example, a system may be identified based on the fact that it is named "System 1" and it is connected to network "INTERNAL." Relationship types are represented as a controlled vocabulary.

- ■ **Extension identifiers**    Provided to allow for additional values that are outside of the AI controlled vocabulary.

## Correlation

One valuable function of AI is the ability to correlate information from disparate data sources about a given asset. Though these specific references pertain to a given asset, an asset database can gain important information about that entity, such as a collection of information that will aid in understanding its security state.

The AI specification does not prescribe how asset information will be managed, and it leaves it to the system owner to define the key record by which an asset will be referenced. AI information may be used to track relationships among assets, recording that the computing-device with **hostname:meteor** belongs to a person with **PersonName:John**, for example.

## AI Elements

The AI data model defines how to store and reference identifying information about an asset. The model contains element names and their descriptions and may include one or more properties that further define the identification element. Each literal data element may also have a "timestamp" attribute associated with it. If populated, the timestamp attribute indicates when the data was last known to be correct for that element.

The following AI elements are included within the model:

| Element Name | Descriptions and Properties |
|---|---|
| **ai:asset** | An abstract element that may contain a synthetic ID, locations (location information where the asset resides), extended information, and timestamp (date and time when the information was last known to be correct). |
| **ai:it-asset** | An abstract element that extends from the asset element. **it-asset** is a placeholder element to carry common attributes related to IT assets. |
| **ai:circuit** | Captures identifying information about a circuit, potentially including the circuit name. |
| **ai:computing-device** | Captures identifying information about a computing device, such as the following potential identifiers:<br><br>**distinguished-name**   The X.500 distinguished name of the computing device being identified.<br>**cpe**   The Common Platform Enumeration name for the hardware computing device being identified.<br>**connections**   Information about a network interface on the computing device being identified.<br>**fqdn**   The fully-qualified domain name for the computing device being identified.<br>**hostname**   The hostname of the computing device.<br>**motherboard-guid**   The motherboard globally unique identifier (GUID) of the computing device. |

| Element Name | Descriptions and Properties |
|---|---|
| **ai:data** | A generic element to describe any type of data. |
| **ai:database** | Captures identifying information about a database, including:<br><br>**instance-name**  The name of the database instance. |
| **ai:network** | Captures identifying information about a network:<br><br>**network-name**  The name of the network being identified.<br>**ip-net-range**  The starting and ending IP addresses for the range of IP addresses for the network being identified.<br>**cidr**  The Classless Inter-Domain Routing (CIDR) information for the network being identified. |
| **ai:organization** | Captures identifying information about an organization:<br><br>**xnl:OrganizationNameDetails**  The name of the organization being identified. See OASIS Extensible Name Language (xNL) specification for details on populating this element.<br>**email-address**  An e-mail address associated with the organization being identified.<br>**telephone-number**  A phone number associated with the organization being identified. For a North American number, the number *must* be valid and the format *must* be *XXX-XXX-XXXX*.<br>**website-url**  A web site associated with the organization being identified. |
| **ai:person** | Captures identifying information about a person:<br><br>**xnl:PersonName**  The name of the person being identified. The element type is defined in [xNL] and *shall* be used as documented in that specification. See OASIS xNL specification for details on populating this element.<br>**email-address**  An e-mail address associated with the person being identified.<br>**telephone-number**  A phone number associated with the person being identified.<br>**Birthdate**  The birth date of the person being identified. |

| Element Name | Descriptions and Properties |
|---|---|
| **ai:service** | Captures identifying information about a service running on a computing-device:<br><br>**Host**   The IP address or fully qualified domain name of the host of the service.<br>**Port**   The port number to which the service is bound. Restricted to $0 <= x <= 65535$.<br>**port-range**   The lower and upper bound (inclusive) of the range of ports to which the service is bound.<br>**Protocol**   The protocol used to interact with the service (e.g., HTTP, JMS, SSH, and FTP). |
| **ai:software** | Captures identifying information about a class of software or a software instance:<br><br>**installation-id**   Any identifier for a software instance (installation).<br>**Cpe**   The Common Platform Enumeration (CPE) name for the class of software being identified.<br>**License**   The license key associated with the software instance. |
| **ai:system** | Captures identifying information about a system:<br><br>**system-name**   The name of the system being identified.<br>**Version**   The version of the system being identified. |
| **ai:website** | Captures identifying information about a web site:<br><br>**document-root**   The absolute path to the document root location of the website on the host.<br>**Locale**   The locale of the web site represented as an RFC 5646 language, and, optionally, region code. |

# Helper Elements

Additional elements are specified to provide more details about the identification and attributes of identified assets. The following table describes these additional elements:

| Helper Element Name | Description and Properties |
|---|---|
| **ai:connections** | Contains a list of **ai:connection** elements:<br><br>**Connection**   Information about a network interface on the computing device being identified. |
| **ai:connection** | Contains information relevant to a single connection to a network. If multiple IP addresses map to the same MAC address, each **ai:connection** *shall* represent a single MAC address-IP address pair.<br><br>**ip-address**   The IPv4 or IPv6 address for the connection.<br>**mac-address**   The MAC address for the network interface.<br>**url**   A universal resource locator address for the network interface.<br>**subnet-mask**   The subnet mask for the connection.<br>**default-route**   The IP address for the default gateway for the connection. |
| **ai:locations** | Contains a geographic coordinate system point:<br><br>**Location**   **ai:location** is an abstract element that is the root of the substitution group for the elements listed in the type field. |
| **ai:location-point** | Contains a geographic coordinate system point: latitude, longitude, elevation in meters, radius. |
| **ai:location-region** | Contains region information:<br><br>**region-name**   The name of the region. |
| **ai:ip-net-range** | Contains a start and end IP address to create a range:<br><br>**ip-net-range-start**   The start IP address of the range.<br>**ip-net-range-end**   The end IP address of the range. |
| **ai:ip-address** | Contains an IP address:<br><br>**ip-v4**   An IP v4 address.<br>**ip-v6**   An IP v6 address. |

| Helper Element Name | Description and Properties |
|---|---|
| **ai:port-range** | Contains a start and end port number to create a range: |
| | **lower-bound**   The lower bound (inclusive) of the range of ports. Restricted to $0 <= x <= 65535$. |
| | **upper-bound**   The lower bound (inclusive) of the range of ports. Restricted to $0 <= x <= 65535$. *Must* be greater than lower-bound. |
| **ai:host** | Holds a fully-qualified domain name or an IP address: |
| | **Fqdn**   The fully-qualified domain name of the host. **ip-address**   The IP address of the host. |
| **ai:cpe** | A CPE 2.2 URI [CPE22] or CPE 2.3 formatted string [CPE23]. |

# ASSET REPORTING FORMAT

ARF is used to provide detailed results about one or more assets, leveraging the AI specification. Through this standardized format, you can aggregate or correlate reports about results and findings (such as a collection of assessment information checks about a particular set of assets, or perhaps a series of instances of the same review over a period of time).  Since ARF provides information about specific assets or groups of assets, it helps to track changes over time.

Consider the following two cases in which information may be correlated, considered, and tracked:

- A continuous monitoring dashboard receives information from a vulnerability scanner, a host-based intrusion detection product, and a system configuration management utility. Although each of these products is likely to maintain an internal reference identifier for a particular device (such as GUID, IP address, or hostname), the use of AI enables the information to be integrated for a more comprehensive understanding.

- A vulnerability scanner reviews a network segment every three days. Although each vulnerability assessment report will document a point-in-time state of vulnerability, you may track the results over time for each of the assets assessed; for example, you might do this to determine the efficacy of a flaw remediation solution.

ARF is used to provide aggregate reporting, correlating, and fusing of asset information and findings from a broad range of assessments, including inventory, vulnerability, and compliance reviews. As a data exchange standard, it is intended to be vendor-neutral, supporting interoperability among assessment products to enhance security information reporting.

Organizational security situational awareness often comprises an integrated view from a broad range of assessment products, such as inventory, systems management, intrusion detection, vulnerability assessment, and anti-virus systems. For those products that leverage the AI specification, ARF reports can be correlated and the reports can be fused, contributing to the continuous monitoring of the enterprise security posture.

As described in the NIST Interagency Report 7694:

The intention of the ARF data model is to capture and encapsulate information about assets in a structured manner. The format is broken into four main sections:

1. The asset section includes asset identification information for one or more assets. The asset section simply houses assets independent of their relationships to reports. The relationship section can then link the report section to specific assets.

2. The report section contains one or more asset reports. An asset report is composed of content (or a link to content) about one or more assets.

3. The report-request section contains the asset report requests, which can give context to asset reports captured in the report section. The report-request section simply houses asset report requests independent of the report which was subsequently generated.

4. The relationship section links assets, reports, and report requests together with well-defined relationships. Each relationship is defined as {subject} {predicate} {object}, where {subject} is

the asset, report request, or report of interest, {predicate} is the relationship type being established, and {object} is one or more assets, report requests, or reports.

The following tables describe the ARF elements and the associated properties for each. The detailed schema is available for download at NIST's SCAP web site.

| Element Name | Description and Properties |
| --- | --- |
| **arf:asset-report-collection** | The top-level container element that holds all of the information in an ARF report.<br><br>**id**   The ID for the collection of asset reports.<br>**report-requests**   A container element that, when it exists in the **arf:asset-report-collection**, holds one or more **report-request** elements.<br>**assets**   A container element that, when it exists in the **arf:asset-report-collection**, holds one or more asset elements.<br>**reports**   A container element that contains one or more report elements. |
| **arf:report-requests** | Contains a collection of **report-request** elements.<br><br>**report-request**   Contains an asset report request for at least one of the reports on this ARF report. |
| **arf:report-request** | Contains a report request for at least one of the reports on this ARF report collection.<br><br>**id**   An ID that must be unique among all IDs within this **asset-report-collection**.<br>**content**   XML content related to the assessment or results in the report. If content is not provided, **remote-resource** should be specified to identify where the content may be obtained.<br>**remote-resource**   If actual content is not provided, this element provides the link to an XML element representing a report request. |
| **arf:assets** | Contains a collection of asset elements.<br><br>**asset**   Contains an **arf:asset** element that describes a unique **ai:asset** as described earlier. |

| Element Name | Description and Properties |
|---|---|
| **arf:asset** | Contains an **ai:asset** that represents an asset to be identified. |
| | **id**  An ID that must be unique among all IDs within this **asset-report-collection**. This ID must be referenced at least once in a relationship in this ARF report.<br>**asset**  An **ai:asset** that represents an asset to be identified.<br>**remote-resource**  A link to an **ai:asset** element. This element should be used when the asset identifying information is external to this ARF report collection. |
| **arf:reports** | Contains a collection of report elements. |
| | **report**  Contains the content of a report. |
| **arf:report** | Contains the content of a report. |
| | **id**  An ID that must be unique among all IDs within this **asset-report-collection**.<br>**content**  XML content related to the assessment or results in the report. If content is not provided, **remote-resource** should be specified to identify where the content may be obtained.<br>**remote-resource**  If actual content is not provided, this element provides the link to an XML element representing a report request. |
| **core:relationships** | Contains a collection of relationships between the report content and assets, report requests, and other reports. |
| | **relationship**  Contains a relationship between a subject and object(s) assets. |

## Relationship Terms

ARF defines relationships among the reports described and asset(s) to which the report refers. Each relationship is defined as {subject} {predicate} {object}, where {subject} is the principal asset, report request, or report of interest; {predicate} is the relationship type being established; and {object} is one or more of the following: assets, report requests, or reports. As defined in the data model, the predicate (that is, the value of the type field on the relationship element) must be a qualified name that refers to a term in a controlled vocabulary.

The following table specifies the terms defined in a controlled vocabulary for ARF. It is not required that content producers use these terms, but all ARF-compliant implementations must be capable of processing all of the terms defined in this section.

| Term | Domain | Range | Description |
|------|--------|-------|-------------|
| **isAbout** | **arf:report** | **ai:asset** | The data in the report is about the asset. |
| **retrievedFrom** | **arf:report** | **ai:asset** | The data in the report was retrieved from the asset. |
| **createdBy** | **arf:report** | **ai:asset** | The data in the report was created by the asset. |
| **hasSource** | **arf:report** | **ai:asset** | The report contains knowledge from the asset. This relationship refers to the asset that supplied the knowledge to create the report content. |
| **recordedBy** | **arf:report** | **ai:asset** | The information in the report was recorded by the asset. This relationship will usually be used when the report content is data about a digital event that is captured by an asset. |
| **initiatedBy** | **arf:report** | **ai:asset** | The information in the report was initiated by the asset. This relationship will usually be used when the report content represents a digital event and that digital event is initiated by the asset. |
| **createdFor** | **arf:report** | **ai:report-request** | The report was created because of the report request. This relationship will usually be used to associate request and response type data. |
| **hasMetadata** | **arf:report** | **ai:report** | The subject report has additional metadata that is represented in the object report. |

## ARF Example

The following sample demonstrates the use of ARF to assess a host using SCAP:

```
<?xml version="1.0" encoding="UTF-8"?>
<asset-report-collection xmlns:ai="http://scap.nist.gov/schema/asset-
identification/1.1"
xmlns="http://scap.nist.gov/schema/asset-reporting-format/1.1"
xmlns:core="http://scap.nist.gov/schema/reporting-core/1.1"
xmlns:xlink="http://www.w3.org/1999/xlink"
xmlns:xsi="http://www.w3.org/2001/XMLSchema-instance"
xsi:schemaLocation="http://scap.nist.gov/schema/asset-reporting-format/1.1
http://scap.nist.gov/schema/asset-reporting-format/1.1/asset-reporting-
format_1.1.0.xsd">
<core:relationships
xmlns:arfvocab="http://scap.nist.gov/vocabulary/arf/relationships/1.0#">
        <core:relationship type="arfvocab:isAbout" subject="report_1">
                <core:ref>asset_1</core:ref>
        </core:relationship>
        <core:relationship type="arfvocab:createdFor" subject="report_1">
                <core:ref>report_request_1</core:ref>
        </core:relationship>
</core:relationships>
<report-requests>
    <report-request id="report_request_1">
        <content>
        <Benchmark id="minimal-xccdf" xml:lang="en-US"
        xmlns="http://checklists.nist.gov/xccdf/1.1"
        xmlns:cpe=http://cpe.mitre.org/dictionary/2.0
xmlns:dc="http://purl.org/dc/elements/1.1/"
        xmlns:xhtml="http://www.w3.org/1999/xhtml">
        <status date="2009-12-01">draft</status>
        <title>Test Title</title>
        <description>
            <xhtml:strong>Test Description</xhtml:strong>
        </description>
        <notice id="test-notice">Test Notice</notice>
        <reference href="http://testreference1">
            <dc:publisher>Test Publisher1</dc:publisher>
            <dc:identifier>Test Identifier1</dc:identifier>
        </reference>
        <platform idref="cpe:/o:microsoft:windows_vista"/>
        <version>Test Version</version>
        <metadata>
            <dc:creator>Test Creator</dc:creator>
            <dc:publisher>Test Publisher</dc:publisher>
```

```
            <dc:contributor>Test Contributor</dc:contributor>
            <dc:source>http://scap.nist.gov/</dc:source>
        </metadata>
        <Profile id="test_profile1">
            <title>Test Title for Profile 1</title>
            <description>Test Description for Profile 1</description>
            <select idref="test_rule1" selected="true"/>
        </Profile>
            <Rule id="test_rule1" selected="true" weight="10.0">
                <title>Test Title for Rule 1</title>
                <description>Test Description for Rule 1</description>
                <ident system="http://cce.mitre.org">CCE-2466-1</ident>
        <check system="http://oval.mitre.org/XMLSchema/oval-definitions-5">
                <check-content-ref href="minimal-oval.xml"
                name="oval:gov.nist.test.compliance:def:1"/>
                </check>
            </Rule>
        </Benchmark>
    </content>
    </report-request>
</report-requests>


<assets>
    <asset id="asset_1">
        <ai:computing-device>
            <ai:connections>
                <ai:connection>
                    <ai:ip-address>
                        <ai:ip-v4>192.168.2.10</ai:ip-v4>
                    </ai:ip-address>
                </ai:connection>
            </ai:connections>
                <ai:fqdn>comp1234.tempuri.org</ai:fqdn>
        </ai:computing-device>
    </asset>
</assets>


<reports>
    <report id="report_1">
    <content>
    <TestResult xmlns="http://checklists.nist.gov/xccdf/1.1"
        id="minimal-xccdf-1280857747215"
        version="Test Version" test-system="cpe:/a:nist:scap_scanner:1.0"
        start-time="2010-08-03T13:44:07.657-04:00"
        end-time="2010-08-03T13:49:07.657-04:00">
    <benchmark href="minimal-xccdf"/>
```

```
<title xml:lang="en-US">SCAP automated assessment for checklist
 minimal-xccdf performed at    Tuesday, August 3, 2010</title>
<organization>National Institute of Standards and Technology</organization>
<identity authenticated="1" privileged="1">administrator</identity>
<profile idref="test_profile1"/>
<target>0:0:0:0:0:0:0:1</target>
<target>127.0.0.1</target>
<target>host.domain.tld</target>
<target-address>0:0:0:0:0:0:0:1</target-address>
<target-address>127.0.0.1</target-address>
<target-address>192.168.222.1</target-address>
<target-facts>
    <fact name="urn:xccdf:fact:asset:identifier:host_name"
type="string">0:0:0:0:0:0:0:1</fact>
    <fact name="urn:xccdf:fact:asset:identifier:fqdn"
     type="string">0:0:0:0:0:0:0:1</fact>
    <fact name="urn:xccdf:fact:asset:identifier:ipv6"
     type="string">0:0:0:0:0:0:0:1</fact>
    <fact name="urn:xccdf:fact:asset:identifier:host_name"
     type="string">127.0.0.1</fact>
    <fact name="urn:xccdf:fact:asset:identifier:fqdn"
     type="string">127.0.0.1</fact>
    <fact name="urn:xccdf:fact:asset:identifier:ipv4"
     type="string">127.0.0.1</fact>
    <fact name="urn:xccdf:fact:asset:identifier:mac" type="string"/>
    <fact name="urn:xccdf:fact:asset:identifier:host_name"
type="string">host.domain.tld</fact>
    <fact name="urn:xccdf:fact:asset:identifier:fqdn"
     type="string">host.domain.tld</fact>
    <fact name="urn:xccdf:fact:asset:identifier:ipv4"
     type="string">192.168.222.1</fact>
    <fact name="urn:xccdf:fact:asset:identifier:mac"
     type="string">00:50:56:c0:00:01</fact>
</target-facts>
<rule-result idref="test_rule1" time="2010-08-03T13:49:07.650-04:00"
    weight="10.0">
    <result>pass</result>
    <ident system="http://cce.mitre.org">CCE-2466-1</ident>
    <instance>host.domain.tld</instance>
    <check system="http://oval.mitre.org/XMLSchema/oval-definitions-5">
    <check-content-ref href="minimal-oval-res.xml"
      name="oval:gov.nist.test.compliance:def:1"/>
    </check>
</rule-result>
<score maximum="1" system="urn:xccdf:scoring:flat-unweighted">1</score>
<score maximum="10" system="urn:xccdf:scoring:flat">10</score>
```

```
    </TestResult>
</content>
</report>
</reports>
</asset-report-collection>
```

# ASSESSMENT SUMMARY RESULTS

The ASR format is an emerging data exchange model for documenting the results of one or more automated assessments. Leaders in the automation community discovered that sometimes a simple summary (such as a pie chart contrasting patched versus non-patched IT systems) is necessary, rather than the detailed results of a compliance assessment or software inventory request. ASR was drafted as a means to address this need, drawing on work with ARF to provide a way to communicate counts or device lists. Because the specification is still in draft, and because it can be used to quantify assets from an asset information source, it has also been referred to as an Asset Summary Report format.

Although the primary use of ASR is to convey the results of a given assessment (for example, to convey a list of operating systems discovered by CPE and a count of each), ASR has also been used to support query-response web services. Both models are useful for asset management and are expected to be an important aspect of growing continuous security-monitoring capabilities in the future. As the security automation community continues to refine the schemas and model for ASR, the protocol will greatly improve the ability to gather necessary result data from a wide array of assessment products.

## System-Ident Model

The primary report format consists of a consecutive stream of information, each beginning with a **System** tag that indicates the high level entity being reported, followed by an **Ident** identifier that describes a more detailed tag. Each is then followed by metadata about the results themselves.

The ultimate format of ASR results is still under formation. A simple tabular result is easily read and integrated into common database models but is not necessarily extensible for more complex result requests. XML-encoded results provide additional information, but interpretation is relatively more complex.

The following example illustrates a tabular report, by suborganization, of the number of systems that have been reviewed per the U.S. Federal Information Processing Standard 199 as exhibiting risk categorization of "low," "medium," and "high":

```
System=OrgUnit; Ident=Accounting
System=FIPS199; Ident=High; Count=1
System=FIPS199; Ident=Med; Count=1
System=FIPS199; Ident=Low; Count=1

System=OrgUnit; Ident=Sales
System=FIPS199; Ident=High; Count=2
System=FIPS199; Ident=Med; Count=0
System=FIPS199; Ident=Low; Count=1

System=OrgUnit; Ident=Engineering
System=FIPS199; Ident=High; Count=2
System=FIPS199; Ident=Med; Count=0
System=FIPS199; Ident=Low; Count=1
```

This example demonstrates a similar report using XML encoding:

```
<asr:summary-report xmlns:asr="http://scap.nist.gov/schema/asset-summary-
reporting/1.0"
    xmlns:ai="http://scap.nist.gov/schema/asset-identification/1.1"
    xmlns:xsi="http://www.w3.org/2001/XMLSchema-instance"
    xsi:schemaLocation="
    http://scap.nist.gov/schema/asset-summary-reporting/1.0 summary_res.xsd">
        <asr:population-characteristics population-size="500000">
        <asr:resource>site1.org</asr:resource>
    </asr:population-characteristics>
    <asr:system-ident system="http://cce.mitre.org/#">
        <asr:ident>CCE-2009</asr:ident>
        <asr:result count="235" parameter="set"/>
        <asr:result count="23" parameter="not_set"/>
        <asr:result count="512" parameter="not applicable"/>
    </asr:system-ident>
</asr:summary-report>
<asr:summary-report xmlns:asr="http://scap.nist.gov/schema/asset-summary-
reporting/1.0"
    xmlns:ai="http://scap.nist.gov/schema/asset-identification/1.1"
    xmlns:xsi="http://www.w3.org/2001/XMLSchema-instance"
```

```
    xsi:schemaLocation="
    http://scap.nist.gov/schema/asset-summary-reporting/1.0 summary_res.xsd">
    <asr:population-characteristics population-size="250">
        <asr:resource>VulnDb.site1.org</asr:resource>
    </asr:population-characteristics>
    <asr:system-ident system="http://cve.mitre.org/#">
        <asr:ident>CVE-2009-0001</asr:ident>
        <asr:result count="50" cve-finding="true"/>
        <asr:result count="170" cve-finding="false"/>
        <asr:result count="30" cve-finding="not applicable"/>
    </asr:system-ident>
</asr:summary-report>
```

# Chapter 5

## Enumerations

In the context of security automation, enumerations provide consistent identifiers for specific entities, such as commonly referenced vulnerabilities, hardware/software platforms, and configuration settings. Enumerations improve data correlation and product interoperability, enabling automated processes and simplifying the aggregation and correlation of security metrics. Without standardized enumeration, security products and procedures depend upon proprietary or specialized names and formats, reducing interoperability and diminishing the ability to automate security processes. In contrast, common enumerations remove that ambiguity and ensure that tools and procedures are consistently referencing the intended security elements. These common references make it possible to describe a desired configuration state, consistently assess compliance, and report security assessment results in a repeatable manner.

## AUTOMATION ENUMERATIONS AND THEIR PURPOSES

Many of the Security Content Automation Protocol (SCAP) specifications themselves are quite complex, and they need to be to support the automated decisions and communications they are built for. The use of enumerations can help provide specificity and help categorize disparate results. Although ensuring a common definition is important in many ways, such definition specificity is especially critical for automation. Enumerations let us reliably instruct products how to perform in accordance with standardized instructions, such as occurs through an SCAP checklist.

Consistent enumeration is intended to solve several key impediments to automating security assessment and reporting. Among those challenges addressed by enumerations are the following:

- **Correlation and aggregation**   There is a need to correlate and aggregate information from disparate sources. Consider the challenge of aggregating vulnerability scans from several vendors' applications. A security review team often uses multiple utilities to leverage differing capabilities from each product but must aggregate the results to identify the full list of security flaws. Although each product will present a broad range of findings, without common references it will be difficult for users to understand when tools are referring to the same issue. For example, Nessus's plug-in 28228 refers to a vulnerability within the Samba software product. McAfee reports an issue with a Windows Internet Name Service (WINS) server. If we use the Common Vulnerabilities and Exposures (CVE) enumeration, such as CVE-2007-4572, we can confirm that these are both in fact the same potential flaw and apply the appropriate remediation procedures. While the lack of a common identifier makes manual report integration difficult, it renders automated correlation nearly impossible.

■ **Proprietary naming conventions** Similar to the correlation and aggregation challenge, even when two products are referencing the same flaw, the lack of a standard naming convention prevents automated comparison and correlation. Even within a single product line (such as Microsoft Office), variance in names and versions can result in mismatches that prevent effective patch-checking, software updates, or configuration-compliance assessment. Since various organizations use their own identifiers (for example, DISA's Vulnerability Management System [VMS] ID), either everyone must map to every other proprietary name or everyone can simply reference common identifiers, such as those provided in the Common Platform Enumeration (CPE).

■ **Need for authoritative nomenclature** An official data source providing an exhaustive and comprehensive enumeration of security data (such as that provided by the Common Configuration Enumeration [CCE]), enables a security manager to review the capabilities of a given process or product or a given scan policy within an application. Such a comprehensive repository, often managed by a trusted authority that has vetted and verified the relevant security information, provides a powerful tool to ensure that security products are assessing the right elements and reporting findings consistently.

# ENUMERATIONS INCLUDED IN SCAP

In Chapter 2, we introduced SCAP, which includes three important enumerations to accomplish its purpose of automating vulnerability management and compliance evaluation: CCE, CPE, and CVE (see Figure 5-1).

The use of these standardized enumerations allows security products to perform the functions for which they are designed (such as checking system attributes, identifying applications in use to populate software inventory records, and discovering vulnerabilities) in a consistent and standard manner.

NOTE    *We use the word "platform" a lot throughout this chapter. In the context of security automation, a platform is simply a way to describe a particular component of the enterprise computing environment, whether it is a type of application, an operating system, or a firmware version on a hardware device.*

Several environmental factors are leading to the evolution and improvements of SCAP's base enumerations: expanded use of common enumerations in commercial products, new innovations in their use, and new challenges that require interoperability. Enumerations are now being integrated into common security products such as McAfee's Policy Auditor and Microsoft's System Center Configuration Manager; this integration in turns aids in harmonization of results and reduces any duplication that may occur from disparate naming conventions.

Security automation languages use these enumerations to provide specificity to the products they support. For example, if you want to identify your organization's exposure to a specific vulnerability in the Windows Server Service (as described in Microsoft's Security Bulletin MS08-067), you could create an SCAP data stream to provide as input to a set of vulnerability scanners. The data stream would contain a CPE value that specifies the particular operating system you want the scanner to focus on, such as Windows XP systems, as well as a CVE value to represent the flaw you want to locate (in this case, CVE-2008-4250). An effective workaround for

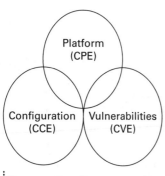

**FIGURE 5-1** Enumerations included in SCAP 1.2

| Specification | Description |
|---|---|
| Common Configuration Enumeration (CCE) | Enumeration for software security configuration issues |
| Common Platform Enumeration (CPE) | Enumeration for IT product names and versions (such as operating systems, applications, and hardware) |
| Common Vulnerabilities and Exposures (CVE) | Enumeration for software flaw vulnerabilities |

**TABLE 5-1** SCAP Enumeration Components

this flaw is to disable the host's "browser service," so the CCE to assess whether that service has been disabled on a given XP system (CCE-2880-3) could be included in the appropriate checklist in the data stream. The use of consistent enumerations ensures that this SCAP content can be provided as input to several vendors' vulnerability scanners, with confidence that each will assess the appropriate platforms for existence of the specified vulnerability and for evaluation of the correct configuration setting. This security automation model enables organizations consistently to perform security operations, increase repeatability, and improve interoperability.

Table 5-1 lists the enumerations SCAP uses, each described in this chapter. Additional enumerations and reference information are evolving and improving, with details available at many of the common web sites we have described in this book, such as those for the MITRE Corporation, the U.S. Department of Homeland Security, and the U.S. National Institute of Standards and Technology (NIST).

# COMMON CONFIGURATION ENUMERATION

In a computing environment, many applications, processes, and operating systems depend upon configuration settings to specify how they should operate. Individual settings within those files and registries often specify security-relevant conditions such as background services to start, permissions to grant specific groups of users, or instructions regarding what information should be logged.

Because these settings have significant impact on the secure operation of a platform, organizations often specify detailed implementation policies describing how a platform must be configured to maintain an appropriate level of risk (as defined by that organization's risk management authority). Security configuration guidance (for example, the U.S. Department of Defense's Security Technical Implementation Guide, or STIG) includes specific configuration guidance statements that prescribe preferred or required settings for a given platform. Such configuration guidance statements (or configuration statements) include these:

- Security permissions (for example, the required permissions for the directory %SystemRoot%\System32\Setup should be assigned to the Administrator account only)

- Configuration values to implement security controls (for example, the account lockout threshold setting should be set to 3)

- Services or modules that should be enabled or disabled for secure operation (for example, the startup type of the remote Shell service should be set to disabled)

The CCE provides a consistent model for describing those specific configuration statements and the technical mechanism(s) by which each configuration statement may be assessed. CCE assigns a unique, common identifier to each particular security-related configuration setting on a platform, providing the basis for assessing compliance in a standard way, permitting you to create a checklist that states the desired value for each configuration specified, and supplying a consistent reference for the assessment tool to compare the settings observed to the desired values.

## CCE History

CCE was designed to help security practitioners apply guidance about how a given platform should be securely configured. Sometimes that guidance will be in the form of formal, organizational security implementation criteria (such as the DISA STIG). Other sources provide important security requirements and recommendations as well, such as:

- Configuration guidance from the software vendor

- Recommendations from oversight organizations (such as Payment Card Industry requirements or the U.S. Government's Configuration Baseline [USGCB] settings)

- Knowledgeable industry experts such as those at SANS Organization and the Center for Internet Security

As the availability of security guidance providers increased in the early 21st century, and as more computing platforms became available, the security community identified a growing need for common configuration reference identities.

Although CCE was originally part of CVE enumeration (described in detail in the next section), CVE focused primarily on software flaws. Citing the importance of addressing the misconfiguration issues and the need for a complimentary enumeration, NIST's Steve Quinn and MITRE's Dave Mann began the work to create the CCE. Starting small and expanding, they worked with a consortium of security assessment product vendors (including ArcSight, Configuresoft, Center for Internet Security, Citadel, eEye, nCircle, TriSixty, Microsoft, Sun, Symantec, and ThreatGuard), to establish a Common Configuration Enumeration Working Group in 2006. The group reviewed existing configuration criteria from commercial and government references for the Microsoft Windows 2000, Windows XP, and Windows Server 2003 platforms, creating a draft list of approximately 500 configuration statements that constituted the initial CCE entries. The Working Group designed the model for ongoing management of the list, establishing MITRE as the host of the CCE list and moderator of CCE submissions and changes.

## The Purpose of CCE

CCE does not describe a security policy, or even a checklist, but simply enumerates the potential configuration items from which you might choose. It is noteworthy that although information security was the first use case, CCE is not limited to security settings. For example, the USGCB settings use CCE to reference environmental configuration such as power-saving settings.

Security policy is necessarily broad and comprehensive, describing security roles and responsibilities and the requirements for the fulfillment of those responsibilities. For example, an excerpt from a U.S. Department of Justice information security policy states that "[the] agency shall approve individual access privileges and shall enforce physical and logical access restrictions associated with changes to the information system; and generate, retain, and review records reflecting all such changes." The policy does not, and likely should not, describe the individual settings to accomplish the requirement. From that policy, however, security personnel can derive configuration guidance on the means to implement and maintain specific platforms to comply with the high-level policy. Compliance checklists, in turn, provide a means to step through individual configuration settings to verify that the configuration items are properly set in accordance with the guidance provided to accomplish the given policy.

Effective implementation and assessment of security guidance require comprehensive and authoritative lists of the possible items that may be configured. CCE provides such lists, drawing upon knowledgeable practitioners and custodians to describe the potential security configuration items and the method(s) to review them. In a security automation context, CCEs enable the automation of both implementation and assessment, working in concert with checklists (such as an XCCDF file) and supporting languages (such as OVAL definitions). Using these building blocks, a security manager can create an assessment checklist for use as input to an automated product (for example, ThreatGuard's Secutor Prime), describing both what to check and what settings to confirm. Note that the CCE does not describe the required state, just the configuration item itself. Standardizing assessment and reporting through CCE enables you to aggregate information, correlate information across organizational boundaries, and support important security reporting tasks such as continuous monitoring of residual risk.

# CCE Entries

CCE assigns a unique, common identifier called a *CCE entry* (also called CCEs, CCE identifiers, and CCE IDs) to a particular security-related configuration issue. CCE identifiers associate the human description of a given security configuration control (for example, Account Lockout Duration) with the technical mechanisms used by automation processes such as those used within configuration audit tools.

Every CCE entry consists of a textual description of the configuration element (with no specific recommendation) and the logical parameter values that might be associated with the control. For example, logical parameters might include **enabled** or **disabled**, but not the actual storage values associated with these conceptual values. Each CCE entry also includes links to associated technical mechanisms (files, users, registry keys, and permission bits), and references (prose statements, XCCDF, and audit checks).

Specifically, each entry on the CCE list contains the following:

- **CCE identifier number**   A unique identifier that is random and non-descriptive, used to provide the reference to the record in the CCE list, followed by a single check digit. The check is produced according to the Luhn Check Digit Algorithm, designed to protect against accidental errors such as common transcription errors and transposed digits.

- **Description**   A humanly understandable description of the configuration issue referenced by the CCE entry (for example, "The minimum password length should be set appropriately"). CCE descriptions functionally operate as the "name" of a CCE entry.

- **Conceptual parameters**   Parameters that would need to be specified in order to implement a CCE on a system (for example, Automatic, Manual, and Disabled for a CCE describing an executable service of an operating system).

- **Associated technical mechanisms**   One or more methods to implement (or assess) the desired configuration result. (For example, in Windows, the setting of "The Autoplay feature should be set correctly for all drives" can be configured either through a direct registry key edit or by way of a Group Policy Object if the system participates in an Active Directory domain.)

■ **References**   Pointers to published configuration guidance documents that point to the specific sections of the documents or tools in which the configuration issue is described in more detail. Each CCE must provide at least one publically accessible reference document that demonstrates the requirements and recommendations for the associated configuration guidance statement.

## CCE Submission Process

Platform vendors are the primary submitters of new CCEs, requesting CCE entries for various security configuration settings in a new or updated product. The vendor has a unique and detailed understanding of the technical mechanisms and configuration entries available to implement the product's security model as designed. Other entities also submit CCE entry requests, including the following:

■ **Security guidance authors**   Inclusion of CCE IDs enables a security guidance author to augment prose instructions with specific references both to the configuration guidance statement and the technical mechanisms to achieve the security requirements. Ensuring that CCE IDs exist for relevant technical guidance in the document will help the author's consumer implement the guidance and assess compliance.

■ **Security guidance implementers**   Organizations or individuals implementing specific configuration guidance statements may choose to submit these for consideration as CCE entries to ensure that a broad range of products are able to assess and report compliance with those requirements.

■ **Configuration scan product vendor**   To support end users' implementation of a configuration scanning product, the product's vendor may find it valuable to ensure that CCEs are available for the technical components being assessed.

As the number of participants has grown and as the number of supported platforms has increased, the CCE list is well over 10,000 entries. Each submission is carefully considered for inclusion in the CCE repository and enables automated products to assess and report the security configuration setting named in the description. Because these identifiers are relied upon by dozens of products and thousands of users, the details of each submission are crucial. To aid the submitter in providing useful CCE entries, MITRE provides detailed style guidance, discussed in the following sections.

## Counting (Delineation of Entries)

CCE IDs are associated with the lowest level controls (most granular) of the human comprehensible abstract security model of the system. This statement attempts to capture the tension involved with creating CCEs at the correct level of abstraction. On the one hand, it is common for analysts to talk and write in a way that naturally groups individual configuration controls together. Examples include "strong passwords" or "install and configure FTP." For CCE, these statements are at too high of a level of abstraction, and they should be decomposed into more granular individual statements. This is what is meant in saying that CCE IDs are associated with "the lowest level controls (most granular)."

On the other hand, a system will typically provide multiple technical mechanisms by which the same conceptual configuration control can be applied. For example, the same configuration control might be applied via a selection in a graphical user interface (GUI), a variable defined in a configuration file, or a function call in the system's application programming interface (API). Because all three of these technical mechanisms achieve the same conceptual effect, CCE considers them to be comparable at the level of the "human comprehensible abstract security model." For this reason, different CCE IDs are not associated with these individual technical mechanisms, and, instead, a single CCE ID is associated with the conceptual security control that unites them (relative to the conceptual security model for the system).

CCE IDs tend to be associated with selection controls in commonly used GUIs. This is because GUIs tend to be designed to present the conceptual security model to the user. For this reason, create CCEs in a manner consistent with prior, related CCEs.

When creating CCEs for a new major release of a system, you should review all CCEs for prior major versions of the system. It is common for security models (or portions of security models) to be reused across major releases, and CCE IDs must be consistently created across these major releases. CCEs should be assigned differently only when there has been a significant change in the security model between major releases. CCEs for applications tend to be similar for CCEs for the operating systems (OSs) they are designed to run on.

It is also common, but not universal, for applications to use security models that are native to the underlying OS that the application is expected to be installed on. For example, an application may manage user accounts and rights by utilizing native OS account constructs. In these cases, CCEs for the application should be assigned in a manner that is consistent with those assigned to the base OS. For this reason, when creating CCEs for an application, you should review associated OS CCEs carefully.

Some applications have security models that are truly cross-platform, and in those cases OS-level CCEs may not provide helpful guidance. Authors are advised to consult previous CCE content decisions. Over the years, many difficult and recurring counting issues have been encountered and discussed by the CCE Working Group. The lessons learned from these discussions are reflected in these CCE editorial policies. The CCE Working Group, experienced in helping create CCEs that are recognizable for a broad range of constituents, helps answer CCE creation questions on the CCE mailing list and seeks input and guidance from industry peers.

## CCE Entry Contents

CCE entries contain correct and well-formatted information for five fields: ID, Description, Parameters, Technical mechanisms, and References, as shown in Figure 5-2. MITRE's criteria for these fields are outlined in the following sections.

**CCE Identifier Number (CCE ID)**    The ability for an organization to assign CCE IDs is dependent on that organization demonstrating a mastery of the basics of CCE content creation, particularly with respect to counting (that is, level of abstraction) issues. CCE maintains a centralized ID-generation capability that

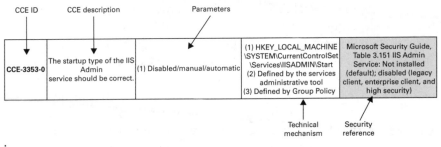

**FIGURE 5-2** A sample CCE entry

guarantees the generation of unique IDs with correct check digits. No other organization is authorized to generate CCE IDs, as doing so will destroy the uniqueness of IDs, and with them, the integrity of the CCE system. Organizations that have demonstrated mastery of CCE content authoring and that want to assign CCE IDs as a part of their CCE content creation process can obtain blocks of pre-generated CCE IDs from the CCE Content Team.

Three options are available for populating the CCE ID column in a CCE spreadsheet when submitting new content:

- *Leave the CCE ID column blank.* It is acceptable for this column to be left blank entirely. This is the most common approach used for initial submissions.

- *Use a proprietary ID.* If the authoring organization has a preferred proprietary identifier system or internal key for individual proposed CCE entries, and if it would be helpful to have those identifiers associated with the proposed entries during the authoring or review process, it is acceptable to populate this column with those IDs.

- *Assign pregenerated CCE IDs.* If your organization has been approved by CCE to assign CCE IDs, the CCE Content Team will provide your organization with a block of official CCE IDs that can be used to populate this column at your discretion. Your organization is also free to begin utilizing these CCE IDs in products and publications on a provisional basis. It must be emphasized that review of proposed CCE IDs by the CCE Working Group and the CCE Content Team may reveal deficiencies in the proposed content that may require entries to be modified and for proposed CCE ID assignments to be deprecated. Managing such deprecations is costly for both CCE authors and CCE users, and for this reason, we urge CCE authors to exercise due care when assigning CCE IDs. In particular, if the entries involved are at all potentially controversial in terms of counting (that is, level of abstraction issues), we strongly advise authors to seek guidance and input from both the CCE Working Group and CCE Content Team prior to assigning IDs.

**Description**    CCE entries contain a human-understandable description of the configuration control. This description is intended to describe the control in terms of the conceptual security model. Arguably, the description is the most important field in allowing analysts to recognize an entry quickly and accurately and to distinguish it from other entries. Because selection controls in GUIs tend to reflect the security model of the system and are so formative in terms of CCE counting, it is considered best practice for the description to reflect the language associated with the names or strings from the most common GUI associated with the control. With the advent of configuration management capabilities that are not locally installed on end systems (for example, Microsoft Active Directory Group Policy Objects or XCCDF benchmarks), it is not uncommon for different GUI controls to be associated with different names or strings, despite the fact that they both are associated with the same conceptual control or CCE ID. In such cases, the author must use discretion and choose wording that is most likely to be recognizable to users of all associated GUIs. In this light, CCE descriptions functionally operate as the "name" of a CCE entry. CCE IDs are used to identify a control that can be configured.

Users often expect CCE entries to provide guidance on how a setting should be configured, but CCE entries never make an assertion as to what particular configuration should or should not be made. For this reason, CCE has adopted the convention of authoring descriptions in a way that emphasizes and makes clear that CCE remains agnostic on how a particular control should be configured. It is critical that CCE descriptions be recognizable by analysts, and consistency is important to achieve this goal. When creating a CCE entry for a control in a new major release of a system for which there exists CCEs for prior versions of that system, it is expected that CCEs for "the same" control will use the same description.

**Parameters**   CCE entries contain a list of conceptual parameters that would be needed to be specified in order to configure a CCE on a system. For example, for the CCE associated with "The start-up permissions on telnet should be set appropriately" (for Windows), there is a single conceptual parameter of "start up type" that has the possible values: Automatic, Manual, and Disabled. CCE entries distinguish between such human-understandable conceptual parameters and machine-understandable parameters such as the specific registry key values that might be associated with the conceptual notions of "Automatic," "Manual," and "Disabled." Established practice for CCE parameters is to list all possible conceptual values of the parameter. Although most controls are defined by a single parameter (which may have many possible values), some controls are defined by multiple parameters. In these cases, the accepted practice is to provide a list of possible values for each parameter and to delimit the lists in the spreadsheet cell with leading "(1)," "(2)," "(3)," and so on, as needed. As with descriptions, consistency across associated platform groups (that is, major releases) is important. For this reason, it is expected that CCE content authors review associated platform groups and reuse parameter descriptions when possible.

**Technical Mechanisms**   For any given configuration issue, there may be more than one way to implement the desired result. For example, in Windows the issue of "The Autoplay feature should be set correctly for all drives" can be set either with a direct registry key edit or by way of a Group Policy Object (GPO) if the system participates in an Active Directory domain. And in most forms of UNIX and Linux, the issue of "The FTP service should be enabled or disabled as appropriate" can be achieved in multiple ways. The listing of technical mechanisms for a CCE entry serves two purposes. First, it augments and enriches the description of the CCE. While the "Description" field describes the issue at a conceptual (that is, GUI) level, the associated technical mechanisms describe the issue at a more technical level. Second, they help clarify the relationship between comparable technical mechanisms that achieve the same configuration goals and the CCE ID and description that unites them. It is common for CCEs to have multiple technical mechanisms. Each should be listed in the associated cell and should be delimited with a leading "(1)," "(2)," "(3)," and so on, as needed. In cases where a technical mechanism is described by a navigation path (for example, Microsoft registry keys or GPO settings), the accepted practice is to provide the full path.

**References**   Each CCE entry has a set of references from published configuration guidance documents such as the NSA Security Guides, the Center for Internet Security Benchmarks, and DISA STIGS, that point to the specific sections of the documents or tools in which the configuration issue is described in more detail. These references provide a logical linkage to more detailed information, validate the need for a CCE ID for any given configuration issue, and validate that the CCE ID is described at a level of abstraction that is used and accepted within the community.

The submission spreadsheet should contain a single column for each reference document. The top cell of each column should contain the name of the reference document and, if it exists, a URL where the document can be accessed. For each proposed CCE entry, provide the most granular internal identifier that is associated with the proposed CCE. Ideally, the document has a set of proprietary identifiers that map 1:1 with the proposed CCE IDs, but in practice this is often not the case. Often, the best possible index that can be used is a section heading or page number.

Security controls that are not documented in publicly accessible documents are problematic for the CCE Working Group, especially when CCE authors are from organizations other than a producer of the platform. There is a real problem of who has the authority to definitively say that a configuration control exists. On numerous occasions, CCEs have been proposed by third parties and were disputed by the platform vendor and ultimately rejected. For this reason, it is essential that the necessity for proposed CCEs be established by the inclusion of at least one reference. CCE will not accept submissions for new CCEs without at least one publically accessible reference document for each proposed entry.

### Submission to CCE Content Team and Working Group

With the CCE entries drafted, content can be submitted using the spreadsheet template hosted on the CCE web site. CCEs are organized by platform with new entries separated from updates to previous entries. Newly proposed CCE content is reviewed by the CCE Content Team and then distributed to the CCE Working Group for comment prior to being accepted as official CCE content. Submissions should be sent directly to the CCE Content Team at cce@mitre.org to begin this review and comment process.

## CCE and the National Vulnerability Database

Beginning in 2012, the National Vulnerability Database (NVD) added a CCE console to provide additional value-added data that supplements the official CCE list. This console provides a dynamic, web-based reference to each CCE entry, the relevant description and technical mechanisms behind it, and the source references that prescribe the configuration entry. It provides one or more severity scores for each CCE (see the description of the Common Configuration Scoring System, CCSS, in Chapter 6). A useful aspect of this interface is the ability to compare similar CCEs of differing platforms—for example, how to compare a similar setting across several versions of the Windows operating system. The console is available at http://nvd.nist.gov.

# COMMON PLATFORM ENUMERATION

The automation processes we've described depend heavily on a product's ability to determine what assets to act upon. Confirming patch application, identifying vulnerability to a given software flaw, and assessing compliance with a configuration standard all first require the ability to specify the platform itself. It was for this reason that CPE was created.

CPE is a standardized method of describing and identifying classes of applications, operating systems, and hardware devices present among an enterprise's computing assets. It is used extensively to identify the platforms (and families of platforms) on which languages should operate, so it must accurately inform those languages regarding automated actions to be performed. CPE helps bridge the gap between the necessary generality of policy frameworks (for example, a mandate to ensure that all systems remained patched) and the detailed technical mechanisms we described through CCEs.

Identifying software names seems simple; a simple glance at our workstation desktop or observing an application starting will quickly identify its version. In fact, common systems management tools do a good job of maintaining current inventory of installed software and they are increasingly including CPE information in that inventory. Unfortunately, software manufacturers are inconsistent in naming and assigning versions for their products, and updates add to that complexity. For reliable security automation functions, automated data feeds and web services need precision identification and versioning for matching; inconsistency makes such matching difficult when even a character's difference can invalidate an operation.

A common example of the challenge is shown in Figure 5-3 through variance in the naming for Microsoft's Windows 2000 product line. A query through the Windows interface for the name of the OS of what we might call a Win2K machine may return "Microsoft Windows 2000," while a registry check may show "Windows 5.0.2195." Then there are various editions of Windows 2000 for different markets and business needs: Professional, Server, Advanced Server, and Datacenter Server. Add to this various language packages and Service Pack updates, and you can see that just figuring out the OS and consolidating with the results of other

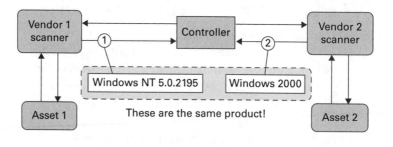

**FIGURE 5-3** IT product naming confusion (from Brant Cheikes, MITRE)

assessments can be challenging without a common way to reference the platform.

CPE resolves this issue by enabling products to record results in the standardized convention, so that either of the two product names in Figure 5-3 would resolve to the CPE version of Windows 2000. In addition, the latest version of CPE enables users to record a great deal of information about the version of a platform, as we describe next.

## The New CPE 2.3 Stack

Beginning with version 2.3, the single CPE specification was separated into four components that operate in harmony as a "stack" (similar to the way networking protocols work) to share information and operations with interoperability.

Figure 5-4 shows the separate components, Applicability Language, Dictionary, Name Matching, and Naming, which are used together to accomplish the intended goal. In the following sections, we'll explore each component working our way up the stack from the base to the top.

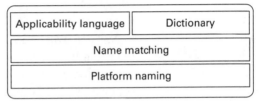

**FIGURE 5-4** CPE 2.3 stack

### CPE Naming

The foundation of CPE is the naming convention, providing a standardized and repeatable means of specifying the name and version of a particular platform. Detailed in NIST Interagency Report 7695, "Common Platform Enumeration: Naming Specification, Version 2.3," CPE naming defines standardized methods for assigning names to IT product classes. An example is the following name representing Microsoft Internet Explorer 8.0.6001 Beta:

> wfn:[part="a",vendor="microsoft", product="internet_explorer", version="8\.0\.6001",update="beta"]

Describing a product involves identifying each of a set of distinguishing attributes and their values. The NIST spec uses the following example: "Joe might describe his car as a '2004 Subaru Outback with a black leather interior'. Conceptually, this description could be modeled as a set of attribute/value pairs: [year=2004, maker=subaru, model=outback, interior_color=black, interior_material=leather]."

Version 2.3 brings significant changes to the way CPE names are formed. CPE 2.2 recorded entries in the generic format specified for Uniform Resource Identifiers (URIs), which worked well for several years but limited the amount and type of data that could be included. Experience has shown the need for the naming convention to provide both agility and growth potential. Just when the designers of the next generation of CPE needed more flexibility, the RFC specifying URI construction became more restrictive, so a new type of string seemed necessary. There are numerous potential replacement formats, and the Security Automation Community members are exploring new methods to identify products and transport the necessary information among automated tools, but the solution had to support backward compatibility with both existing applications and SCAP files and enable future expansion as envisioned for CPE versions 3 and beyond. For this reason, the community decided that a stage should be added in between, what NIST refers to as an "interlingua," making it possible to lay out the attributes and values necessary to describe a particular application or device. This foundation for providing the capability to create both URI-compatible names and future-compatible "formatted strings" is simply called the *Well-Formed Name (WFN)*. WFNs, in turn, may be bound either to URI or formatted string constructs, and potentially to other structures in the future.

**CPE Naming Through WFN** CPE WFNs are used to describe and identify classes of IT products, such as Microsoft Internet Explorer or Sun Solaris. The CPE naming specification permits the user to determine the identifiers and descriptions that make the entry unique, so that all names constitute descriptions of product classes, and a description becomes an identifier when it contains sufficient information to select a single entity from the universe of possibilities.

WFNs are used solely for product classes. The official specification states that CPE *cannot* be used to represent the following:

- A single product instance (for example, a particular installation such as a specific licensed and configured installation of Microsoft Office installed on a user's workstation)

- Relationships (for example, part of, bundled with, released before/after, same as) between products

- User-defined configurations of installed products

- Entitlement/licensing information about products

Because WFN is used to create the machine-readable CPE data, but is not itself a data format, attribute-value pairs can be named in any order. The following CPE attributes are permitted for use in version 2.3:

- **part** The **part** attribute is one of these three string values:

  - The value **"a"** when the WFN is for a class of applications

  - The value **"o"** when the WFN is for a class of operating systems

  - The value **"h"** when the WFN is for a class of hardware devices

- **vendor** The person or organization that manufactured or created the product.

- **product** The most common and recognizable title or name of the product

- **version** Vendor-specific name characterizing the particular release version of the product update; vendor-specific name characterizing the particular update, service pack, or point release of the product

- **edition** No longer used, but permitted for backward-compatibility with version 2.2, which used this attribute to capture edition-related terms applied by the vendor

- **sw_edition** How the product is tailored to a particular market or class of end users

- **target_sw** The software computing environment within which the product operates

- **target_hw** The instruction set architecture (for example, x86) on which the product being described or identified by the WFN operates

■ **language**   Valid language tags as defined by [RFC5646] and used to define the language supported in the user interface of the product being described

■ **other**   Any other general descriptive or identifying information that is vendor- or product-specific and that does not logically fit in any other attribute value; values should not be used for storing instance-specific data

So, putting together a sample Well-Formed Name for HP Insight Diagnostics, version 7.4.0.1570 Online Edition for Windows 2003 x64, would look like this:

```
wfn:[part="a",vendor="hp",product="insight_diagnostics",
version="7\.4\.0\.1570",sw_edition="online",
target_sw="windows_2003",target_hw="x64"]
```

> **NOTE**   *Restrictions exist on unusual or special characters. CPE users should refer to sections 5 and 6 of the IR 7695 for details about what's permitted in specific attribute-value pairs.*

**Binding the WFN to URI**   As we described, URI binding is being phased out but provides for backward-compatibility with prior CPE versions. A CPE 2.2 style name is a name that is encoded with a Generic-style URI (see RFC3986), with each name having the URI scheme name **cpe:**. The CPE Naming specification v2.3 defines specific procedures for creating a URI binding based on the values provided in the WFN. It also provides a means to "pack" in some of the extra attributes that have been added to the new version, such as sw_version, hw_version, and the contents of the "other" attribute.

Following the procedures outlined in NIST IR 7695, binding the preceding WFN example for HP Insight Diagnostics produces this URI CPE:

```
cpe:/a:hp:insight_diagnostics:7.4.0.1570:-:~~online~win2003~x64~
```

The specification also provides for converting URI names back to WFN for matching and for conversion to the new *formatted string binding*, covered next.

**Formatted String Binding**   The NIST CPE Naming Specification points out that the new formatted string binding is constructed similar to the old-style names, "but is defined simply to be a 'formatted string' rather than a URI in order to relax the requirements that typically apply to URIs as specified in RFC3986." The format is a colon-delimited list of fields prefixed with the string **cpe:2.3:**. The formatted string binds the attributes in a WFN in a fixed order, separated by the colon character, like so:

```
cpe:2.3: part : vendor : product : version : update : edition
: language : sw_edition : target_sw : target_hw : other
```

In a formatted string binding, the alphanumeric characters plus hyphen (-), period (.) and underscore (_) appear unquoted. When used alone, the asterisk (*) represents the logical value **ANY**, and the hyphen (-) represents the logical value **NA**. All other non-alphanumeric characters, if used, *must* be quoted (preceded by the backslash). The special characters asterisk and question mark may appear without quoting, in which case they are open to special interpretation by other CPE specifications. Note that all 11 attribute values *must* appear in the formatted string binding. Using this model, the example WFN binds to the following formatted string:

```
cpe:2.3:a:hp:insight:7.4.0.1570:-:*:*:online:win2003:x64:*
```

## CPE Name Matching

One of the biggest changes to CPE is the added methodology for matching CPE names with the IT products targeted. Previous versions of CPE provided little ability for you to search for ranges of software or to match particular conditions. Although many security bulletins contain instructions such as, "This flaw affects versions 8 and previous," software products had to enumerate the possible versions and work backward in a game of "Go Fish," asking, "Do you have version 8 installed? Do you have version 7 installed?" Although some product vendors created internal workarounds, the need for a standard method for stating the matching criteria was evident. Similar challenges existed for the broad range of marketing names applied to software products, such as the various "editions" we mentioned for Windows 2000: Professional, Server, Advanced Server, and Datacenter Server. The ability to indicate that any or all of the above apply provides greater capability for the security automation content author.

The CPE matching engine provides the ability to compare one WFN with another, enabling a product that leverages the matching

| No. | Definition |
|-----|------------|
| 1 | The source is a superset of the target. |
| 2 | The source is a subset of the target. |
| 3 | The source and target are equal. |
| 4 | The source and target are mutually exclusive or disjoint. |

**TABLE 5-2** CPE Name-Matching Set Relations

capability to determine one of four conditions for the relationship of the source to the target: superset, subset, equal, or disjoint. Based on the result of analysis (as shown in Table 5-2), the matching engine returns the appropriate result that may be used to enable the automation software to proceed as appropriate.

Matching in this way, working in harmony with the underlying naming conventions and supporting both the Dictionary and Language components, CPE can support machine-to-machine decision support for a broad range of security automation uses.

## CPE Dictionary

The fourth CPE NIST Interagency Report, IR 7697, describes the CPE Dictionary model. NIST maintains the "Official CPE Dictionary," where automation users can search for and find existing CPE identifier names.

CPE 2.3 permits organizations to create their own extended CPE dictionaries to store and maintain identifier names not present in the "Official CPE Dictionary." Sometimes an organization will have internal software names that are meaningless outside of the enterprise, or a developer might want to support a CPE for a product that is not yet released and therefore wouldn't yet be included in the official dictionary.

The organization can also operate a formal, extended dictionary for use by other entities. Both procedural and architectural rules should be followed to permit this extension—remember that automated tools will be basing significant security decisions on the information these will store. The specification describes the data model for storage and interface, including the process for removing outdated or deprecated information. It also requires two CPE Dictionary Management Documents: Dictionary Content

Management and Decisions Document. Dictionary maintainers must either create or reference a Dictionary Content Management and Decisions Document for each dictionary that they maintain to ensure compliance with procedures for name creation, versioning, matching, and provenance (the authority by which the entries were created).

# COMMON VULNERABILITY AND EXPOSURES

The oldest and most pervasive of these three enumerations is CVE. CVE began when a vulnerability had multiple names, often references provided by the multiple dedicated teams that identified and tracked them, or worse yet, simply by whatever name the media assigned it. This included the misconfiguration exposures described earlier in the chapter, compounding the issue.

The CERT Coordination Center (CERT/CC) at Carnegie Mellon University was a major clearinghouse for tracking new bugs, along with commercial groups such as Internet Security Systems' X-Force and noncommercial vulnerability hunters like BugTraq. Add to that the actual vendor information provided (at times), and you can see that the potential reference information for a single flaw became a cloud of confusion. From a security automation standpoint, although the human correlation challenge was tough, automation was impossible. In Table 5-3, an example from early CVE efforts

| Organization | Vulnerability Identifier |
|---|---|
| CERT | CA-96.06.cgi_example_code |
| CyberSafe | Network: HTTP "phf" attack |
| ISS | http-cgi-phf |
| AXENT | phf CGI allows remote command execution |
| BugTraq | PHF Attacks |
| BindView | #107 – cgi-phf |
| Cisco | #3200 – WWW phf attack |
| IBM ERS | Vulnerability in NCSA/Apache Example Code |
| CERIAS | http_escshellcmd |

**TABLE 5-3**  Disparate Vulnerability References

illustrates the problem: a single flawed web server application exhibited a vulnerability that was referenced at least nine disparate ways. Such a condition discouraged information exchange and rendered automation impractical.

## The Birth of CVE

Emerging incident detection system (IDS) product vendors and incident responders wanted to create a means to share the results of research performed and to provide "indicators and warnings" of recognized attacks. The lack of a structured system to describe them, however, prevented such an exchange. In 1999, a broad array of government and academic organizations, network/security tool vendors and incident response teams began to circulate a proposal to create a "Common Vulnerabilities and Exposures list." The list would provide pointers to the source data others produced, but it would ensure a common method of identifying a particular strain of vulnerability and a way to track progress among the various research groups. Drawing on data from the various advisory sites, the initial draft contained more than 600 vulnerabilities. CVE went public later that year and continues to provide a common reference point for tens of thousands of software flaws.

To achieve the goal of enabling IDS sensors, assessment tools, and incident responders to communicate, especially in an automated manner, a reliable identifier was critical. The team developed a method by which a submitter could provide the details about a vulnerability, or a reference to a site that did, and have the bug considered for addition to the list. To maintain reliability, the list had to be accurate, and avoiding duplication was a critical component for success, so the team created an editorial board to maintain integrity.

## CVE Editorial Board

The CVE editorial board comprises numerous participants from the security community, many of them well-respected veterans of the network security world. Drawing on members of academia, research institutions, and government agencies, the board considers submissions to the CVE list and reviews them for potential addition. Many of the original CVE supporters still serve on the board and in many other ways to support security automation, such as through participation in periodic working group sessions. Primarily, this board's purpose is to ensure that candidate submissions are carefully reviewed and meet the requirements for permanent addition.

## CVE Identifiers

Upon first submission to the board, CVEs are considered "candidates" and are provided candidate status in the database. Candidates are those vulnerabilities or exposures under consideration for acceptance into CVE but not yet approved for addition. Each CVE identifier has the following items associated with it:

- CVE identifier number (for example, "CVE-1999-0067")

- Indication of "entry" or "candidate" status

- A brief description of the security vulnerability or exposure

- Any pertinent references (that is, vulnerability reports and advisories or OVAL-ID)

If the candidate is accepted, it is entered into CVE and is published via the site. However, assignment of a candidate number is not a guarantee that it will become an official CVE entry.

To help speed the time to create candidate numbers, and to enable the use of CVE numbers for issues that have not yet been publicly announced, the CVE Initiative created subsidiary Candidate Numbering Authorities (CNAs), specified organizations or individuals permitted to "reserve" candidate numbers from MITRE, the primary CNA. These CNAs then include the candidate number in their initial public announcement. Although this method of providing "blocks" of candidates to key parties (for example, major OS vendors) requires close coordination across all the parties involved, it helps streamline the process and encourages the use of CVE identifiers throughout the life cycle of a vulnerability. The process has worked well enough that the MITRE Corporation has begun similar practices for CCE, providing common participants' blocks of CCEs to pre-assign for new software's configuration.

## Common Vulnerability Scoring System

As the list of CVE entries has grown, and as the need for a method to categorize them became more critical, the community developed a means to rate the severity of each vulnerability. The Common Vulnerability Scoring System (CVSS), described in detail in Chapter 6, was commissioned by the National Infrastructure Advisory Council (NIAC) and was originally chartered as a joint effort involving many groups including CERT/CC, Cisco, DHS, MITRE, eBay, IBM/ Internet Security Systems, Microsoft, Qualys, and Symantec.

At a high level, CVSS enables a consistent way to establish a base severity score for a given flaw, drawing on the attack criteria and potential impact to identify the general severity of a vulnerability. Although the base score provides a general idea of the risk presented by one vulnerability compared with another, temporal and environmental factors enable an organization to derive a risk score more accurately.

Today, many security products rely upon the CVSS base score for an initial categorization and leverage the CVSS temporal and environmental factors to customize the risk. Effective security automation and continuous monitoring activities depend upon the ability to report results based on business risk. Enterprise customers have found little value from stacks of raw vulnerability findings with little risk context, and they need real risk data to understand security posture, prioritize remediation, and track the results of security investment; CVSS helps accomplish those goals.

# OTHER RELATED ENUMERATIONS AND EXPRESSIONS

In addition to those enumerations discussed so far are several security-related enumerations that are beginning to emerge. The following enumerations are not part of the SCAP suite of protocols but serve important roles. We also describe "evolving expressions," data exchange methods that aren't a central dictionary or reference list but that provide a common way to describe something that's going on.

## Common Weakness Enumeration

Common weakness enumeration (CWE) is a comprehensive list that describes the root causes of vulnerabilities, examining the common errors that result in the individual vulnerabilities described in CVE.

Observing that preventing vulnerability is easier and less costly than remediation, the MITRE CVE team began to explore the underlying issues behind the vulnerabilities described by CVE. Clear patterns emerged, showing those root causes (for example, developer errors, compiler issues, and implementation mistakes) that led to the vulnerable conditions discovered.

CWE provides an effective security education opportunity; the U.S. Department of Homeland Security leverages the list of weaknesses to help teach the conditions that cause vulnerability in the first place. DHS and members of the Software Assurance Forum work with programming instructors and corporate development organizations to teach developers how to avoid the mistakes that lead to common vulnerabilities. To this end, to increase awareness of the way programmers can prevent software weaknesses and to help highlight the relationship between insecure development practices and hacking incidents, MITRE and the SANS Organization have created the "CWE/SANS Top 25 Most Dangerous Software Errors" list.

To further their objective of helping to shape and mature the code security assessment industry and to accelerate the use and utility of software assurance capabilities for organizations in reviewing the software systems they acquire or develop, the SWA team works with vendors of products that perform automated software code reviews. These applications (for example, HP Fortify) review source code for the conditions that are exploited by adversaries, with CWE providing the standard and repeatable enumeration with which to reference those flaws. A broad list of those products implementing CWE is available at http://cwe.mitre .org/compatible/organizations.html.

MITRE provides the CWE list in three methods:

- High-level dictionary view of enumerated weaknesses

- Classification tree view that provides access to individual weaknesses with more simplicity to various potential users through classification layering

- Graphical view of the classification tree that allows a user better to understand individual weaknesses through their broader context and relationships

## Common Software Weaknesses

MITRE has provided a list of some common types of software weaknesses:

- Buffer overflows, format strings
- Structure and validity problems
- Common special element manipulations
- Channel and path errors
- Handler errors
- User interface errors
- Pathname traversal and equivalence errors
- Authentication errors
- Resource management errors
- Insufficient verification of data
- Code evaluation and injection
- Randomness and predictability

## Common Attack Pattern Enumeration and Classification

Common attack pattern enumeration and classification (CAPEC) works alongside CWE to provide an index of the common ways attackers exploit the weaknesses in software. For example, CAPEC-48 describes the methods hackers use for "Passing Local Filenames to Functions that Expect a URL." Understanding how hackers find and exploit those flaws helps to provide developer training to prevent the mistakes in the first place, enables developers and risk assessors to conduct better threat modeling, and enables vulnerability detectors to do a better job of discovering issues. Many developers have been surprised to hear about exploit methods from a hacker's perspective, and when they learned how crafty an adversary can be, they are surprised by their own failure of imagination. CAPEC works to educate developers and risk reviewers about exploitation, enabling preventive measures and countermeasures early in the development life cycle.

## Common Malware Enumeration

Similar to the challenges addressed by CVE, common malware enumeration (CME) is intended to help provide a central index for the growing list of virus threats (aka malicious code, or malware). Although the worst outbreaks of malicious code are often referenced by names provided by anti-virus product teams (for example, Melissa and CodeRed), a central, common index helps everyone ensure that they point to a single reference. The efforts helped lead to the Malware Attribute Enumeration and Categorization (MAEC) described in Chapter 3. Also managed and maintained by the MITRE Corporation, CME is not as fully implemented as CVE, but it remains part of an ongoing effort by the software assurance community to improve information sharing about attacks occurring through malicious code.

## Common Event Expression

Common event expression (CEE) standardizes the way computer events are described, logged, and exchanged. Many electronic systems (for example, computers, routers, and firewalls) create logs when they observe activities, perhaps a network connection or a logon event. Although many software platforms create log entries for similar types of events, the actual log syntaxes are rarely the same. For instance, a workstation, a web server, and a firewall all log a network session differently, but with a common event expression, these events can align and assist with security monitoring and incident detection. CEE enables a common framework for representing events and sharing that data. CEE is designed to be flexible and extensible to support a broad array of platforms. By providing a common language and syntax, like other enumerations described in this chapter, important security processes such as correlation, aggregation, and monitoring become more effective.

The CEE profile consists of three components (Figure 5-5):

- CEE event (base event and user extensions)

- Event taxonomy

- Field dictionary

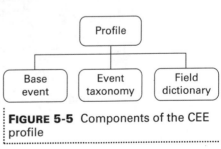

**FIGURE 5-5** Components of the CEE profile

## Event Header Fields

A CEE event block includes some or all of the following fields to record information about a single event. The first three (**p_proc**, **p_sys**, and **time**) are required. The remaining fields are optional but recommended if the information is available. The following table describes the purpose of each element. This information comes from the CEE web site, cee.mitre.org, which provides more detail in the CEE specifications.

| Field Name | Description |
| --- | --- |
| **p_proc** | The name of the process that produced the event. The process should belong to the application identified by the **p_app** field. If necessary, the process ID (pid) can be included via the **p_proc_id** field. |
| **p_sys** | The hostname of the system that generated the event. |
| **time** | The time the event occurred. This timestamp should have microsecond granularity (1E-6 seconds) and include the time zone GMT offset. |
| **id** | The event message ID. Events generated by the same producer and having the same **id** value must be of the same event type. |
| **p_proc_id** | The process identifier (pid) of the process that generated the event. |
| **crit** | A relative indication of the criticality, or impact, of an event. Events with a higher **crit** value have a potential for greater impact. For example, a hard disk failure is more critical than a user login. |
| **pri** | The event priority, expressed as an integer value. A higher **pri** value indicates a higher processing or transmission priority. Systems that produce or process event logs should use the **pri** field to prioritize their processing queues. |
| **p_app** | The application that is responsible for generating the event. Where applicable, the **p_app** identifier should uniquely identify the application using the application name, version, and vendor information. |
| **uuid** | The event identifier. The value of the **uuid** field is used to identify uniquely this individual event instance. |

Users and developers can define their own event structures and customize various plug-ins by extending the CEE event schema to define their own event profiles.

## Event Taxonomy

The event taxonomy provides a listing of tags that can be used to classify and identify similar events. The event type is indicated through CEE taxonomy tags placed in the event's **<Type>** block. This block consists of fields representing the seven tag fields, described in the following table. Full details of their use are available in the specification.

| Field Name | Description |
|---|---|
| **action** | The primary type of action that was undertaken as part of the event. The status or result of the action should be detailed in the **status** field. |
| **domain** | The environment or domain of the event. Typical event domains include network, operating system, and application. |
| **object** | The type of object that is targeted or otherwise affected by the event. |
| **status** | The end result or status of the event action identified by the **action** field. |
| **subject** | The type of object that initiated or started the event action identified by the **action** field. |
| **service** | The service the event involves. The **service** field value provides context to the event action or more precision to the event domain. |
| **tags** | A list of uncategorized CEE taxonomy tags. |

## Field Dictionary

The field dictionary is a listing of fields that should be used to represent common event data. It consists of the schema (a URI that resolves to the location of an XML schema that profiles the CEE event structure) and the **schema_ver** (the version of the schema that was used to construct the CEE event).

## Distributed Audit Service

A parallel and comparable event and audit automation enumeration is instantiated in the Open Group's Distributed Audit Service (XDAS) protocol. It shares some points of similarity with CEE, working to help provide auditability and reporting in the enterprise. In today's distributed computing platforms, especially with modern distributed and virtual cloud computing environments, much of our data is spread around the globe. To maintain effective security monitoring and to fulfill audit requirements, a distributed event–management capability is crucial. This need is complicated by the vast array of servers, workstations, network devices, and other types of information technology. Just collecting the logs from that vast number of devices doesn't solve the problem—risk managers need to be able to correlate the events to provide context and to support suitable alerts to provide proactive security.

Event and log management requirements are also mandatory for many federal, state, or industry regulations. The Payment Card Industry Data Security Standard (PCI DSS), for example, states the following, in part: "Implement automated audit trails for all system components to reconstruct the following events... use of identification and authentication mechanisms." Clearly, to gather all the various authentication logs manually from operating systems, databases, and applications and provide them to the PCI auditor in readable form will be a difficult and expensive task.

XDAS specifies the nature and structure of real-time activity and event records that are generated by IT components. To help normalize event records, permitting them to be collected and analyzed centrally, the XDAS standard defines a data model that can be used to describe how enterprise resources interact. Details of the data model are available at www.opengroup.org/projects/security/xdas/, but we'll provide an outline here.

The data model begins with a definition of a resource:

■ **Resource**   A discrete component of the IT infrastructure such as people, hosts, network devices, and applications.

The highest level objects within the XDAS data model are described next and shown in Figure 5-6:

- **Initiator** The resource(s) that caused the event to occur; that which caused the interaction that is recorded in the event record

- **Action** The interaction or transaction that occurred and is recorded in the event record

- **Target** The resource(s) affected by the action recorded in the event record

- **Observer** The resource(s) that detected that the event occurred and generated an event

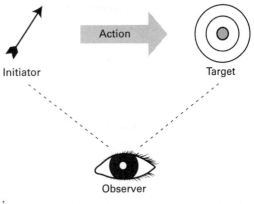

**FIGURE 5-6** XDAS event record contents

## Common Remediation Enumeration

An exciting future expansion for security automation is the potential to enable remediation of the flaws detected, or implement the configuration settings described in a checklist. While some commercial products can accomplish these tasks today, standardizing this capability and enabling interoperability is a continuing goal for security practitioners. Common remediation enumeration (CRE) lets you assign a common identifier to the set of actions that must be performed to accomplish a distinct remediation objective (for example, install Java Version 6 Update 26, or set file *abc.exe* to read-only permissions). The security automation community continues to evolve the remediation use case and provide additional capabilities, so this and the Open Vulnerability Remediation Language (OVRL) will certainly share an important role in the future of information security.

CRE is described in NIST Interagency Report (IR) 7831 (currently in draft), "Common Remediation Enumeration." CRE describes remediation as "a set of actions that result in a change to an IT asset's configuration that bring it into compliance with policies, correct discovered vulnerabilities or misconfiguration, change settings or controls in response to events, or to install, remove or disable software which include patches." CRE enables automation and enhanced correlation of enterprise remediation activities.

The CRE data model uses the following terminology for remediation concepts:

- **Remediation method** The specific steps or actions taken to perform a remediation.

- **Remediation effect** The result of successfully applying a remediation method. This includes not only the changes to an IT asset's configuration state (for example, settings and software), but also other aspects such as the delay or required action (for example, reboot) before the change becomes effective, the duration for which the change is effective, and other side effects above and beyond making the change.

- **Remediation instance** The conceptual combination of a specific remediation method and its remediation effect, including platform and (optionally) parameters.

- **Remediation location** The system on which the remediation is ultimately applied. Note that this may be different from the system on which the remediation method is performed.

It uses the following terminology for remediation artifacts:

- **Remediation statement** A prose description of a remediation instance, including its method and effect.

- **Remediation implementation** The creation of a script, software module, or set of detailed, human-oriented instructions that enable the application of a specific remediation.

And it uses the following terminology for CRE artifacts:

- **CRE-ID** A globally unique formatted string that is associated with a single CRE entry.

- **CRE entry** A set of fields that describe a specific remediation instance and whose structure conforms to the CRE XML schema.

- **CRE producer** An organization or individual that issues new CRE-IDs and CRE entries.

- **CRE publisher**  An organization or individual that maintains a CRE repository.

- **CRE consumer**  A product that uses a CRE entry as a key resource. Typical CRE consumers are tools that directly perform, manage, or report remediation actions.

- **CRE referrer**  A product or data that contains or cites CRE-IDs.

- **CRE repository**  A collection of CRE entries maintained by a single CRE publisher. Documentation provided as part of the CRE repository must include the processes and content decisions that guide the publication of CRE entries within that repository.

The following sample CRE code from the NIST IR illustrates how the XML structure looks:

```
<cre:cre_entry>
<cre:id>cre:com.example:10521-3</cre:id>
<cre:description>Using the RegSetKeyValue API function set the
        ScreenSaveActive entry in the registry
(HKEY_CURRENT_USER\Software\Policies\Microsoft\Windows\Control Panel\Desktop)
        to either enabled(1) or disabled(0).</cre:description>
    <cre:parameters>
     <cre:parameter name="ScreenSaveActiveValue">
        <cre:description>Enable (1) or disable (0) the screen saver password.
                Valid values are 0 or 1.</cre:description>
     </cre:parameter>
    </cre:parameters>
    <cre:platform id="1701">
       <cpe:title> Microsoft Windows 7</cpe:title>
       <cpe:logical-test operator="AND" negate="0">
       <cpe:fact-ref name="cpe:2.3:o:microsoft:windows_7:*:*:*:*:*:*:*:*"/>
       </cpe:logical-test>
    </cre:platform>
    <cre:supporting_references>
     <cre:reference>
       <cre:date>2011-09-30</cre:date>
       <cre:title>Microsoft System Administration Guide</cre:title>
       <cre:section>Microsoft System Administration Guide,
                         Section 12.5.3</cre:section>
     </cre:reference>
    </cre:supporting_references>
```

```
<cre:metadata>
<cre:creationDate>2011-09-15T16:00:00.377-04:00</cre:creationDate>
<cre:modificationDate>2011-09-15T16:00:00.377-04:00</cre:modificationDate>
  <cre:version>1</cre:version>
  <cre:submitter>Example Corporation</cre:submitter>
</cre:metadata>
</cre:cre_entry>
```

# Chapter 6

## SCAP Vulnerability Measurement

At the time of this writing, nearly 50,000 vulnerabilities are listed in the National Vulnerability Database; each has some impact on a given set of systems but none affects all systems within a security manager's purview. Security practitioners often need to determine the priority of addressing a given vulnerability as part of an overall vulnerability management process, such as determining the urgency of applying a workaround to mitigate risk of a vulnerability's exploitation. The ability to categorize vulnerabilities based upon their potential impact on an information system's confidentiality, integrity, or availability can help the organization determine the priority of assigning resources to test and deploy a given patch, or to implement a hardware or software update. By tracking vulnerabilities and understanding each one's severity, a security automation process can significantly improve an organization's ability to manage and monitor residual risk across a broad range of information systems.

## Patches and Vulnerabilities

Most organizations manage patches rather than individual vulnerabilities. Vendors typically release patches that cover a multitude of vulnerabilities (individual Common Vulnerabilities and Exposures, or CVEs), and vulnerability-related Open Vulnerability and Assessment Language (OVAL) tests are designed to confirm that patches are installed or "up to date."

In most cases, OVAL doesn't provide the capabilities to test specific flaws. For example, if Patch #123 fixes a buffer overflow in a piece of software, the SCAP content tests for the presence of Patch #123 and assumes you are susceptible to the buffer overflow if the patch is missing or protected if it is installed. The SCAP content does not try to exploit the buffer overflow itself.

Security automation components such as those in the Security Content Automation Protocol (SCAP) enable security practitioners to use automation products (such as commercial vulnerability scanners and intrusion detection applications) to correlate lists of identified vulnerabilities, rank those by severity based on potential impact to an organization, and prioritize the actions taken in response to those vulnerabilities. To support that automation, security industry professionals created the Common Vulnerability Scoring System

(CVSS) to provide a common, consistent method for describing the relative severity of each vulnerability.

# COMMON VULNERABILITY SCORING SYSTEM

The CVSS is designed to provide users with an open, transparent model for measuring and communicating the characteristics and impacts of IT vulnerabilities. CVSS consists of three groups, each measured with a numeric score ranging from 0 to 10 and a description of the potential attack characteristics (vectors) that were used to derive the numeric score. CVSS values are based upon the following:

- A base group that represents the intrinsic qualities of a vulnerability

- A temporal group that reflects the characteristics of a vulnerability that change over time

- An environmental group that represents the characteristics of a vulnerability that are unique to a given organizational environment

## CVSS History

The need for CVSS was identified during a series of U.S. government studies related to the protection of critical information technology infrastructure, specifically in response to the growing list of software vulnerabilities in the early 21st century. In 2003, U.S. President George Bush asked the National Infrastructure Advisory Council (NIAC) about actions to harden information systems against attack and how security practioners were prioritizing actions against such attacks. The NIAC, composed of a broad array of government and commercial leaders, commissioned a working group that examined the methods by which information system vulnerabilities were identified and shared. The council observed that software developers, product manufacturers, and security researchers used inconsistent, proprietary methods to describe potential severity. They recognized that varying scales (ranking from 1–4, 1–5, 1–10, low/medium/high, and so on) made it difficult to correlate severity and to ensure adequate response. Their report to the president observed that severity should be measured based upon the potential impact of a successfully exploited vulnerability; recognizing the need for a common language to promote common understanding of that relative severity, the council established the CVSS.

## CVSS Version 1

The NIAC chose the international Forum for Incident Response and Security Teams (FIRST) to be the custodian of CVSS, encouraging its global adoption and improvement. As FIRST designed and deployed CVSS version 1, it did so with the following goals in mind:

- CVSS had to be freely available, adoptable, and open to use by anyone. A closed standard would not be widely implemented and would not survive.

- The scoring system had to be comprehensive, able to describe any possible vulnerability in any type of information system.

- CVSS needed to be interoperable with existing technology and infrastructures without reliance on proprietary technologies or formats.

- The system should be flexible enough to enable customization to support operational environments of differing risk profiles.

- CVSS had to be simple and straightforward to understand, implement, and use.

To conduct the documentation and maintenance activities for CVSS, FIRST sponsored and supported the Common Vulnerability Scoring System - Special Interest Group (CVSS-SIG), a diverse group of security professionals with an interest in security vulnerabilities, each using CVSS in his or her daily work. The group enjoyed success in implementing the scoring system for varying production uses within many organizations. Their experience, support, and training regarding the new scoring system established CVSS as the open framework originally envisioned, although those using it in a production capacity noticed problems with the original model.

### CVSS Version 2 (CVSS v2)

As the use of CVSS became widespread, feedback from CVSS-SIG members and other adopters indicated inconsistencies in the scoring model. The CVSS-SIG team began meeting and working on CVSS v2 in April 2005, examining a broad range of vulnerabilities to identify means for the model to provide better accuracy in measuring and scoring vulnerability severity. NIST provided a group of statisticians who reviewed scoring calculations to help reduce mathematical errors, provide a more-even distribution of scores, and increase score accuracy. In 2007, CVSS v2 was released and remains the current version supported in the Security Content Automation Protocol (SCAP).

## CVSS Use Cases

CVSS is used in many ways to help convey the potential impact of a security issue. Some of the current use cases include the following:

- Security bulletins and announcements were primary needs that drove the creation of CVSS. As part of the vulnerability's life cycle, when a security researcher identifies a flaw in a given product, or when the manufacturer of that product discovers a particular security-related defect, there is frequently a public announcement declaring the issue. Depending on the source of the information and the amount of research into the actual flaw, a repair may not be available for the vulnerability, but the announcement might include workarounds to mitigate security risks. At other times, an actual patch may be available to remediate the issue, subject to appropriate patch testing and implementation. In many cases, the entity announcing the security vulnerability will provide a CVSS score to help users prioritize their response to a given flaw. The example in Figure 6-1 demonstrates the use of CVSS base score from a 2009 Cisco security advisory for CVE-2009-2045.

- Vulnerability scanning products include CVSS scores and vectors as a method to designate the severity of one vulnerability relative to another. For example, Tenable Network Security was an early adopter of the scoring system

**CSCsj47924 - Malformed payload to xvcrman process causes reboot ( registered customers only)**

**Calculate the environmental score of CSCsj47924**

CVSS Base Score - **7.8**

| Access Vector | Access Complexity | Authentication | Confidentiality Impact | Integrity Impact | Availability Impact |
|---|---|---|---|---|---|
| Network | Low | None | None | None | Complete |

CVSS Temporal Score - **6.4**

| Exploitability | Remediation Level | Report Confidence |
|---|---|---|
| Functional | Official-Fix | Confirmed |

**FIGURE 6-1** Example vendor security announcement with CVSS

and uses CVSS to help define each flaw on a scale from low/informational to critical. Tenable's products include displays and reports that permit users to sort vulnerability findings by severity, listing the CVSS base score and how that score was derived.

- Patch management and remediation tools include CVSS references, enabling users to review patch implementation information that may be sorted by severity (as depicted by the CVSS scores). Using this model permits managers to set thresholds for reporting (such as display all "High Impact" patches in accordance with CVSS scoring criteria, or deploy all patches of CVSS base score 7 or greater). Some vendors have begun to correlate information about known vulnerabilities with asset management information. Such correlation offers users an opportunity to generate a report that describes, for example, critical business systems that are affected by those vulnerabilities with significant potential impact.

■ Government and commercial auditing professionals often conduct vulnerability and compliance assessments to determine any potential risk to major information systems, such as an organization's financial management systems. In performing such a review, an auditor will often present a list of the vulnerabilities discovered and a summary report with a count by severity category. The existence of a large percentage of vulnerabilities with severe potential impact on integrity, confidentiality, or availability may indicate to an auditor a need for additional controls (such as a more formal patch management process). In this way, CVSS supports an important aspect of information security compliance audits.

In an example of this use case, the Payment Card Industry (PCI) has built CVSS into its requirements for cardholder data protection. The PCI Data Security Standard (DSS) may require merchants, service providers, and/or financial institutions to undergo a PCI Security Scan conducted by an approved scanning vendor (ASV). Generally, to be considered compliant, a component must not contain any vulnerability that has been assigned a CVSS base score equal to or higher than 4.0.

One notable alternative to the common use of CVSS is Microsoft's Exploitability Index referenced within Microsoft's security bulletins. The Microsoft Security Research Center (MSRC) reports that, similar to these use cases, customers asked for more information to help them prioritize their deployment of Microsoft security updates each month, specifically requesting details about the likelihood of exploit code for the vulnerabilities addressed in security bulletins. As stated on the Microsoft web site, "While Microsoft's Exploitability Index is separate and not related to other rating systems, MSRC is a contributing member to the Common Vulnerability Scoring System (CVSS), and Microsoft shares its experience and customer feedback in building and releasing the Exploitability Index with the working group in order to help ensure CVSS is effective and actionable."

# VULNERABILITY CHARACTERISTICS

Much of the value in CVSS comes from its structure to assess and describe specific characteristics of a vulnerability. Rather than rely upon a researcher's simple assessment of a vulnerability as of low importance or of high criticality, CVSS enables one to describe important factors such as these:

- Does an actual, live exploit utility exist to take advantage of this vulnerability, or is it a theoretical notion that hasn't been demonstrated in the real world?

- What type of access does one need to take advantage of it? Can one exploit it remotely through the network or does it require physical access to the vulnerable resource?

- What type of damage is likely to occur should this vulnerability be successfully exploited?

- Can I determine the relative impact on my organization based upon environmental factors? For example, if the vulnerability has significant impact on an IBM AIX server, but I have no instances of AIX implemented, a moderate severity vulnerability may actually be of low impact. Similarly, if my organization depends upon the use of Portable Document Format (PDF) files for business operations, the potential collateral damage from a PDF-related vulnerability may result in a catastrophic loss of revenue or productivity, increasing the score even more.

Using these characteristics instead of a simple score on a relative scale helps each user understand how a vulnerability will impact his or her information systems. Since CVSS uses these characteristics and describes them in the score vectors, the model allows assessment of relative risk and prioritization of vulnerabilities, enabling users to focus on the vulnerability factors of most importance to their organization.

# CVSS SCORING

CVSS is composed of three metric groups, base, temporal, and environmental, each consisting of a set of metrics, as shown in

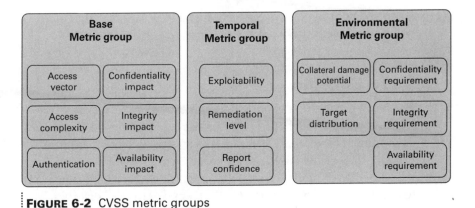

**FIGURE 6-2** CVSS metric groups

Figure 6-2. Each metric is used to calculate the potential harm likely to occur if a vulnerability is successfully exploited. Selecting the six factors affecting the base metrics produces two results: a numeric base score ranging from 0 to 10 and a textual representation of those metrics (called the "vector"). The vector is important in that it promotes immediate, visible understanding of how the score was derived by providing an abbreviated indication of the characteristics and impact information. For example, a vector of AV:L/AC:H/Au:N/C:C/I:C/A:C immediately shows a vulnerability that requires local access to the vulnerable system, a high level of complexity for the attack, and no required authentication actions; impact on confidentiality, integrity, and availability are all complete based on knowledge of the potential for harm from this flaw. Each of these metrics, its impact on scores, and the details for specifying a CVSS vector are explained here.

In addition to the base metrics group, two additional metrics groups help derive the score:

- **Temporal** Represents the characteristics of a vulnerability that change over time.

- **Environmental** Represents the characteristics of a vulnerability that are relevant and unique to a particular environment. Unlike base and temporal metrics, the environmental metrics measure a vulnerability's immediate impact on the specific conditions within a given organization or information system, enabling a user to ensure that the score accurately portrays severity.

## Base Scoring

The basic aspects of a given vulnerability remain relatively constant and do not change with the passage of time, nor from one environment to another. These are the aspects that are measured and recorded as the base metrics group, primarily focusing on the degree of difficulty of exploiting that flaw. Through extensive research and observation, the CVSS team determined that these are well represented by three measures: access vector, access complexity, and authentication. Understanding these three factors provides an effective measure of how likely an attack is to succeed; combination of these metrics with understanding of the potential impact of such success yields an effective, basic severity score. Impact is measured individually for each of the confidentiality, integrity, and availability scores, ranging for each from None (no impact) to Partial (considerable impact with mitigating factors) to Complete (total loss or disclosure).

The numeric score is based upon a scoring equation (described in detail later in this chapter) that assigns weighting factors to each of the criteria specified. By selecting the appropriate multipliers in a series of equations, based upon the answers to the Access Vector, Access Complexity, and Authentication questions, combined with the individual impact rating for Confidentiality, Integrity, and Availability, one can mathematically derive the base score value. Online CVSS score calculators, such as the one at NVD, automatically present the score based upon a user's selection of individual metric values.

The vector string is simply an abbreviation for each metric name, followed by a colon and the abbreviated metric value. The vector lists these metrics in a predetermined order, using a slash to separate each metric.

Each of the tables contained in the following sections are extracted from the NIST Interagency Report 7435, "The Common Vulnerability Scoring System (CVSS) and Its Applicability to Federal Agency Systems."

## NVD Support for Base Scores

As part of the services provided by the National Vulnerability Database (NVD), a product of the NIST Computer Security Division and sponsored by the U.S. Department of Homeland Security's National Cyber Security Division, dedicated vulnerability analysts review submissions to the Common Vulnerabilities and Exposures (CVE) enumeration to determine a base score. Analysts consider the information included with the CVE submission (including research findings, previous or existing similar vulnerability traits, and details of potential systems affected) to determine the following:

- Related exploit range (How much physical access to the vulnerable system is required to exploit the vulnerability?)

- Access complexity (How hard is it for an attacker to successfully conduct the exploit?)

- Number of authentication steps required (none, single, or multiple)

- Likely impact on confidentiality, integrity, and availability

Considering likely scenarios for how such vulnerabilities might be exploited in the real world, and based on their experience rating dozens or even hundreds of such vulnerabilities per week, NVD analysts provide the base scores that represent the innate characteristics of each vulnerability. NVD does not provide temporal scores (scores that change over time due to events external to the vulnerability) or environmental factors, since these are highly subjective and require detailed understanding of the environment in which the vulnerability will be measured.

## Access Vector (AV)

This metric specifies whether the vulnerability is exploitable locally or remotely. If a vulnerability can be exploited only locally, this may reduce the likelihood of successful attack. Although a locally exploitable vulnerability may have significant impact, in general, remote attacks are less likely to be observed and deterred, and therefore increase the severity of the issue. The following table shows the AV scoring values.

| Metric Value | Description |
|---|---|
| Local (L) | A vulnerability exploitable with only local access requires the attacker to have either physical access to the vulnerable system or a local (shell) account. Examples of locally exploitable vulnerabilities are peripheral attacks such as Firewire/USB DMA attacks, and local privilege escalations (such as sudo). |
| Adjacent network (A) | A vulnerability exploitable with adjacent network access requires the attacker to have access to either the broadcast or collision domain of the vulnerable software. Examples of local networks include local IP subnet, Bluetooth, IEEE 802.11, and local Ethernet segment. |
| Network (N) | A vulnerability exploitable with network access means the vulnerable software is bound to the network stack and the attacker does not require local network access or local access. Such a vulnerability is often deemed "remotely exploitable." An example of a network attack is an RPC buffer overflow. |

Network-based, or remotely exploitable, vulnerabilities may be successfully executed without physical access to the information system being attacked. Malicious code introduced through an attachment in an e-mail message is an example of this type of access vector. Contrast this with a type of vulnerability that leverages a weakness in the Bluetooth connection—the barrier to success is more difficult, because the attacker must be in fairly close proximity for successful exploitation, but not as difficult as an access vector that required actual hands-on access to the victim.

## Access Complexity (AC)

The tougher it is for an adversary to exploit a given vulnerability (the access complexity), either because someone else's actions are necessary or because certain conditions have to exist, the less likely the event is to occur. If the attack can be performed with a few simple steps, however, the likelihood increases, as does the score. The following table shows AC scoring values.

| Metric Value | Description |
|---|---|
| High (H) | Specialized access conditions exist. For example: |
| | ■ In most configurations, the attacking party must already have elevated privileges or spoofed additional systems in addition to the attacking system (such as DNS hijacking). |
| | ■ The attack depends on social engineering methods that would be easily detected by knowledgeable people. For example, the victim must perform several suspicious or atypical actions. |
| | ■ The vulnerable configuration is seen very rarely in practice. |
| | ■ If a race condition exists, the window is very narrow. |
| Medium (M) | The access conditions are somewhat specialized; the following are examples: |
| | ■ The attacking party is limited to a group of systems or users at some level of authorization, possibly untrusted. |
| | ■ Some information must be gathered before a successful attack can be launched. |
| | ■ The affected configuration is non-default and is not commonly configured (such as a vulnerability present when a server performs user account authentication via a specific scheme, but not present for another authentication scheme). |
| | ■ The attack requires a small amount of social engineering that might occasionally fool cautious users (such as phishing attacks that modify a web browser's status bar to show a false link, having to be on someone's "buddy" list before sending an IM exploit). |
| Low (L) | Specialized access conditions or extenuating circumstances do not exist. The following are examples: |
| | ■ The affected product typically requires access to a wide range of systems and users, possibly anonymous and untrusted (such as Internet-facing web or mail server). |
| | ■ The affected configuration is default or ubiquitous. |
| | ■ The attack can be performed manually and requires little skill or additional information gathering. |
| | ■ The "race condition" is a lazy one (that is, it is technically a race but easily winnable). |

### Authentication (AU)

The authentication metric measures the number of times an attacker must authenticate to a target in order to exploit a vulnerability. The score is not based on the strength of the authentication process, but on how many times one must authenticate to successfully exploit a vulnerability. In this case, the fewer authentication instances that are required, the higher the vulnerability score. The following table shows authentication scoring values.

| Metric Value | Description |
| --- | --- |
| Multiple (M) | Exploiting the vulnerability requires that the attacker authenticate two or more times, even if the same credentials are used each time. An example is an attacker authenticating to an operating system in addition to providing credentials to access an application hosted on that system. |
| Single (S) | One instance of authentication is required to access and exploit the vulnerability. |
| None (N) | Authentication is not required to access and exploit the vulnerability. |

### Confidentiality, Integrity, and Availability Impact: (C), (I), and (A)

To understand the true severity of the vulnerability, you must consider the potential or likely impact should a successful exploit occur. The possible values for these metrics are listed in the following tables.

The possible confidentially impact scoring evaluation values are listed here:

| Metric Value | Description |
| --- | --- |
| None (N) | There is no impact to the confidentiality of the system. |
| Partial (P) | There is considerable informational disclosure. Access to some system files is possible, but the attacker does not have control over what is obtained, or the scope of the loss is constrained. An example is a vulnerability that divulges only certain tables in a database. |
| Complete (C) | There is total information disclosure, resulting in all system files being revealed. The attacker is able to read all of the system's data (memory, files, and so on). |

The possible integrity impact scoring evaluation values are listed next:

| Metric Value | Description |
|---|---|
| None (N) | There is no impact to the integrity of the system. |
| Partial (P) | Modification of some system files or information is possible, but the attacker does not have control over what can be modified, or the scope of what the attacker can affect is limited. For example, system or application files may be overwritten or modified, but either the attacker has no control over which files are affected or the attacker can modify files within only a limited context or scope. |
| Complete (C) | There is a total compromise of system integrity. There is a complete loss of system protection, resulting in the entire system being compromised. The attacker is able to modify any files on the target system. |

The possible availability impact scoring evaluation values are listed next:

| Metric Value | Description |
|---|---|
| None (N) | There is no impact to the availability of the system. |
| Partial (P) | There is reduced performance or interruptions in resource availability. An example is a network-based flood attack that permits a limited number of successful connections to an Internet service. |
| Complete (C) | There is a total shutdown of the affected resource. The attacker can render the resource completely unavailable. |

# Temporal Scores

A vulnerability has a life cycle with varying exploitability at various points throughout its existence:

1. The vulnerability begins when the vulnerable condition itself is created and might go undiscovered for a long time.

2. At some point, the vulnerability is found, but it might go unreported for a long time thereafter.

3. Eventually, the vulnerability is disclosed and, some time later, a repair may be created.

4. At any point after step 2, an exploit may be created to take advantage of the vulnerability. The level of sophistication required to conduct that exploit has a great impact on the urgency to mitigate the risk of attack. As it becomes easier for a relatively unskilled adversary to take advantage of the flaw (or as automation becomes available, such as occurs in a malicious worm), the more urgent the issue.

5. Eventually, once many systems have been patched against the vulnerability, or the platform itself has become outdated, the flaw becomes less likely to be attacked. The likelihood rarely gets to zero, but as the number of vulnerable targets drops, so does the frequency of attempts to use that attack vector.

As you can see from these stages, certain characteristics of a vulnerability will change with time. As time progresses, patch information will become more available and more systems will be fixed. Eventually, the set of vulnerable systems will reach its low point as remediation takes place. The CVSS temporal metrics group captures these characteristics of a vulnerability that change over time. This metric measures the complexity of the exploitation process. For example, as time progresses, exploit code may become available when there previously was none. Additionally, existing exploit code may improve or be made more available.

In addition to consideration of exploitability, temporal scores also consider remediation factors as well as report confidence. As effective repairs are made available for a given vulnerability, and as they are deployed throughout the enterprise, the level of urgency may be reduced at the discretion of the organization's risk policy. For example, many network-based vulnerabilities (such as a flaw in a File Transfer Protocol [FTP] application) were highly urgent, but that urgency might be reduced with effective workarounds through network access controls or firewall rules. Urgency may be further reduced with an official fix or update from the software developer. Adjustment to the temporal scores based upon remediation levels enables a more accurate portrayal of vulnerability severity throughout the vulnerability life cycle.

Report confidence measures the degree of confidence in the existence of the vulnerability and the credibility of the known technical details. From an urgency perspective, a theoretical vulnerability is likely to exhibit a lower priority than one that is proven to exist and actively under attack. The more a vulnerability is validated by a trusted source, the higher the score.

## Exploitability (E)

Exploitability metric considers the ease of obtaining viable exploit code with which to attack a target. As a vulnerability progresses through the life cycle, the more easily a vulnerability can be exploited and the higher the vulnerability score, as described in the following table.

| Metric Value | Description |
| --- | --- |
| Unproven (U) | No exploit code is available, or an exploit is entirely theoretical. |
| Proof-of-Concept (POC) | Proof-of-concept exploit code or an attack demonstration that is not practical for most systems is available. The code or technique is not functional in all situations and may require substantial modification by a skilled attacker. |
| Functional (F) | Functional exploit code is available. The code works in most situations where the vulnerability exists. |
| High (H) | Either the vulnerability is exploitable by functional mobile autonomous code or no exploit is required (manual trigger) and details are widely available. The code works in every situation or is actively being delivered via a mobile autonomous agent (such as a worm or virus). |
| Not Defined (ND) | Assigning this value to the metric will not influence the score. It is a signal to the equation to skip this metric. |

## Remediation Level (RL)

The second temporal measure considers the availability of an official fix for the flaw described. Throughout the vulnerability life cycle, as the ability of effective countermeasures is developed, the severity of the vulnerability is decreased. The possible values for this metric are listed in the following table.

| Metric Value | Description |
|---|---|
| Official Fix (OF) | A complete vendor solution is available. Either the vendor has issued an official patch or an upgrade is available. |
| Temporary Fix (TF) | An official but temporary fix is available. This includes instances for which the vendor issues a temporary hotfix, tool, or workaround. |
| Workaround (W) | An unofficial, non-vendor solution is available. In some cases, users of the affected technology will create a patch of their own or provide steps to work around or otherwise mitigate the vulnerability. |
| Unavailable (U) | Either no solution is available or it is impossible to apply. |
| Not Defined (ND) | Assigning this value to the metric will not influence the score. It is a signal to the equation to skip this metric. |

## Report Confidence (RC)

The final temporal metric considers the confidence in the existence of the vulnerability. Many vulnerabilities are discovered in a theoretical environment and haven't been seen in general use by attackers. The urgency of a vulnerability is higher when a vulnerability is known to exist with certainty. This metric also suggests the level of technical knowledge available to would-be attackers. The possible values for the RC metric are listed next. The more a vulnerability is validated by the vendor or other reputable sources, the higher the score.

| Metric Value | Description |
|---|---|
| Unconfirmed (UC) | A single unconfirmed source or possibly multiple conflicting reports exist, but there is little confidence in the validity of the reports. An example is a rumor that surfaces from the hacker underground. |
| Uncorroborated (UR) | Multiple non-official sources exist, possibly including independent security companies or research organizations. At this point, there may be conflicting technical details or some other lingering ambiguity. |

| Metric Value | Description |
|---|---|
| Confirmed (C) | The vulnerability has been acknowledged by the vendor or author of the affected technology. The vulnerability may also be "Confirmed" when its existence is confirmed from an external event such as publication of functional or proof-of-concept exploit code or widespread exploitation. |
| Not Defined (ND) | Assigning this value to the metric will not influence the score. It is a signal to the equation to skip this metric. |

## Environmental Scores

Different user environments can have an immense bearing on the degree to which a vulnerability affects a given information system. The CVSS environmental metrics group captures characteristics of vulnerabilities in relation to the distribution of affected hosts and the network environment in which such hosts exist.

The third (Environmental) stage has the greatest influence on the final result: this is the most user-dependent component and represents the part of the equation that impacts the true severity of the vulnerability for the CVSS user. Although published CVSS scores represent an analyst's best estimate of the priority of particular CVEs, the environmental component is what completes the severity ranking. This, of course, is the case for all such rankings—what Microsoft deems "Critical" may have little impact on a Linux server farm, and a Red Hat "Moderate" flaw may be severe if a business' most critical mission depends upon a vulnerable host.

Scoring of the environmental factors is necessarily subjective; if the system were overly prescriptive, it would hamper the user's ability to tailor the severity based on local requirements. It is helpful for a user to determine the criteria that he or she will use each time to answer the scoring questions. For example, NIST's guidance recommends that vulnerabilities that give root-level access should be scored such that the result is complete loss of confidentiality, integrity, and availability, while vulnerabilities that give user-level access should be scored as causing only partial loss of confidentiality, integrity, and availability. Establishing internal criteria for scoring will help ensure that scores are consistent and will better enable the CVSS user to convey the true severity of each CVE.

## Collateral Damage Potential (CDP)

This metric measures the potential for loss of life or physical assets through damage or theft of property or equipment (or some other economic loss). For this environmental metric to be effective, each organization must establish its own criteria for the subjective thresholds herein. The possible values for this metric are listed here.

| Metric Value | Description |
|---|---|
| None (N) | There is no potential for loss of life, physical assets, productivity or revenue. |
| Low (L) | A successful exploit of this vulnerability may result in slight physical or property damage, or there may be a slight loss of revenue or productivity to the organization. |
| Low-Medium (LM) | A successful exploit of this vulnerability may result in moderate physical or property damage, or a moderate loss of revenue or productivity to the organization. |
| Medium-High (MH) | A successful exploit of this vulnerability may result in significant physical or property damage or loss, or a significant loss of revenue or productivity. |
| High (H) | A successful exploit of this vulnerability may result in catastrophic physical or property damage and loss, or a catastrophic loss of revenue or productivity. |
| Not Defined (ND) | Assigning this value to the metric will not influence the score. It is a signal to the equation to skip this metric. |

## Target Distribution (TD)

It stands to reason that the more pervasive the vulnerable targets are throughout the consumer's enterprise, the higher the severity of the underlying vulnerability. Following are the possible TD values.

| Metric Value | Description |
|---|---|
| None (N) | No target systems exist, or targets are so highly specialized that they exist only in a laboratory setting. Effectively 0% of the environment is at risk. |
| Low (L) | Targets exist inside the environment, but on a small scale. Between 1% and 25% of the total environment is at risk. |
| Medium (M) | Targets exist inside the environment, but on a medium scale. Between 26% and 75% of the total environment is at risk. |
| High (H) | Targets exist inside the environment on a considerable scale. Between 76% and 100% of the total environment is considered at risk. |
| Not Defined (ND) | Assigning this value to the metric will not influence the score. It is a signal to the equation to skip this metric |

## Security Requirements (CR, IR, AR)

These metrics enable the analyst to customize the CVSS score depending on the importance of the affected IT asset to a user's organization, measured in terms of confidentiality, integrity, and availability. That is, if an IT asset supports a business function for which availability is most important, the analyst can assign a greater value to availability, relative to confidentiality and integrity. Each security requirement has three possible values: Low, Medium, or High.

The possible values for the security requirements are listed next. For brevity, the same table is used for all three metrics. The greater the security requirement, the higher the score (remember that Medium is considered the default). These metrics will modify the score by as much as plus or minus 2.5.

| Metric Value | Description |
|---|---|
| Low (L) | Loss of [confidentiality I integrity I availability] is likely to have only a limited adverse effect on the organization or individuals associated with the organization (such as employees and customers). |
| Medium (M) | Loss of [confidentiality I integrity I availability] is likely to have a serious adverse effect on the organization or individuals associated with the organization (such as employees and customers). |

| Metric Value | Description |
|---|---|
| High (H) | Loss of [confidentiality \| integrity \| availability] is likely to have a catastrophic adverse effect on the organization or individuals associated with the organization (such as employees and customers). |
| Not Defined (ND) | Assigning this value to the metric will not influence the score. It is a signal to the equation to skip this metric. |

## Base, Temporal, Environmental Vectors

The textual descriptions (vectors) of the potential attack characteristics are critical to your understanding the severity of a flaw described in a CVE. By combining the text-based strings listed for each criteria, you can quickly and easily convey the reasons for the severity selected and tailor it for the organization's needs. Each metric in the vector consists of the abbreviated metric name, followed by a colon character, and then the abbreviated metric value. The vector lists these metrics in a predetermined order, using the forward slash character to separate the metrics. If a temporal or environmental metric is not to be used, it is given a value of "ND" (not defined). The base, temporal, and environmental vectors are shown next.

| Metric Value | Description |
|---|---|
| Base AV | [L,A,N]/AC:[H,M,L]/Au:[M,S,N]/C:[N,P,C]/I:[N,P,C]/ A:[N,P,C] |
| Temporal | E:[U,POC,F,H,ND]/RL:[OF,TF,W,U,ND]/ RC:[UC,UR,C,ND] |
| Environmental | CDP:[N,L,LM,MH,H,ND]/TD:[N,L,M,H,ND]/ CR:[L,M,H,ND]/IR:[L,M,H,ND]/AR:[L,M,H,ND] |

## CVSS Equations

As part of helping to establish CVSS version 2, NIST provided assistance with reviewing the statistical model for scoring vulnerabilities, working to achieve the community's desire for effective distribution of severity from low to high. NIST, with dedicated scientists in the development and application of statistical and analytical models, helped develop scoring equations and algorithms for the base, temporal, and environmental metric groups, which are described in the following sections. For each of the considerations, we described a condition that affects the score. (For example, the greater the proportion of vulnerable systems, the higher the Target Distribution score.) The following mathematical calculations ensure that the numeric scores reflect the severity as described in the base, temporal, and environmental vectors.

## Base Equation

The base equation is the foundation of CVSS scoring:

```
BaseScore = round_to_1_decimal(((0.6*Impact)+
            (0.4*Exploitability)-1.5)*f(Impact))
Impact = 10.41*(1-(1-ConfImpact)*(1-IntegImpact)*(1-AvailImpact))
Exploitability = 20* AccessVector*AccessComplexity*Authentication
f(impact)= 0 if Impact=0, 1.176 otherwise

AccessVector = case AccessVector of
      requires local access: 0.395
      adjacent network accessible: 0.646
      network accessible: 1.0
AccessComplexity = case AccessComplexity of
      high: 0.35
      medium: 0.61
      low: 0.71
Authentication = case Authentication of
      requires multiple instances of authentication: 0.45
      requires single instance of authentication: 0.56
      requires no authentication: 0.704
ConfImpact = case ConfidentialityImpact of
      none: 0.0
      partial: 0.275
      complete: 0.660
IntegImpact = case IntegrityImpact of
      none: 0.0
      partial: 0.275
      complete: 0.660
AvailImpact = case AvailabilityImpact of
      none: 0.0
      partial: 0.275
      complete: 0.660
```

## Temporal Equation

The temporal equation will combine the temporal metrics with the base score to produce a temporal score ranging from 0 to 10. Further, the temporal equation will produce a temporal score no higher than the base score, and no less than 33 percent lower than the base score. Here is the temporal equation:

```
TemporalScore = round_to_1_decimal(BaseScore*Exploitability
*RemediationLevel*ReportConfidence)
Exploitability = case Exploitability of
        unproven: 0.85
        proof-of-concept: 0.9
        functional: 0.95
        high: 1.00
        not defined: 1.00
RemediationLevel = case RemediationLevel of
        official-fix: 0.87
        temporary-fix: 0.90
        workaround: 0.95
        unavailable: 1.00
        not defined: 1.00
ReportConfidence = case ReportConfidence of
        unconfirmed: 0.90
        uncorroborated: 0.95
        confirmed: 1.00
        not defined: 1.00
```

## Environmental Equation

The environmental equation will combine the environmental metrics with the temporal score to produce an environmental score ranging from 0 to 10. The equation is designed to produce a score no higher than the temporal score. Here is the environmental equation:

```
EnvironmentalScore = round_to_1_decimal((AdjustedTemporal+
(10-AdjustedTemporal)*CollateralDamagePotential)*TargetDistribution)
AdjustedTemporal = TemporalScore recomputed with the BaseScore's Impact
subequation replaced with the AdjustedImpact equation
AdjustedImpact = min(10,10.41*(1-(1-ConfImpact*ConfReq)*(1-IntegImpact*IntegReq)
*(1-AvailImpact*AvailReq)))
CollateralDamagePotential = case CollateralDamagePotential of
        none: 0
        low: 0.1
        low-medium: 0.3
        medium-high: 0.4
        high: 0.5
        not defined: 0
TargetDistribution = case TargetDistribution of
```

```
        none: 0
        low: 0.25
        medium: 0.75
        high: 1.00
        not defined: 1.00
ConfReq = case ConfReq of
        low: 0.5
        medium: 1.0
        high: 1.51
        not defined: 1.0
IntegReq = case IntegReq of
        low: 0.5
        medium: 1.0
        high: 1.51
        not defined: 1.0
AvailReq = case AvailReq of
        low: 0.5
        medium: 1.0
        high: 1.51
        not defined: 1.0
```

## Your Mileage May Vary

Although CVSS is designed to help the user consider multiple factors for ranking the severity of a given vulnerability, the process is necessarily subjective and greatly depends upon a detailed understanding of the conditions under which that vulnerability might be exploited. As budgets tighten, often resulting in reduced staff available to repair vulnerabilities, this ability to prioritize the tasks is highly valuable.

Some organizations rely heavily on seasoned individuals' knowledge of which systems are important and how flaws might impact important systems. Leveraging automation to review and document environmental and temporal considerations can help reduce such reliance and improve institutional knowledge.

The factors selected for inclusion in CVSS were based on the architects' extensive experience with mitigating system vulnerability, and the scoring system was designed around the necessity for users to consider the impact on the local environment. Because these environmental considerations are so subjective, users should remember that CVSS scores help establish a relative priority of one flaw over another but do not provide an absolute ranking.

Keep in mind that conditions can change overnight, and a CVE can change to a 10.0 with the release of a single exploit script. System managers must continue to operate effective risk management practices, testing software updates and applying operational patches as soon as they can be safely implemented. Those system managers, however, are continually asked to support more diverse and complicated information systems, often with limited staff to perform all the necessary tasks. As part of the overall security automation processes, CVSS may help such a manager prioritize activities and stay abreast of how the changing vulnerability landscape affects his or her enterprise.

# COMMON VULNERABILITY REPORTING FRAMEWORK (CVRF)

One challenge in vulnerability management has been the lack of a standard framework with which to share information from vulnerability reports. Although CVE and CVSS provide some help by cataloging and categorizing the known vulnerabilities, CVRF brings a model by which security practitioners and researchers can exchange vulnerability details and other security-related documentation. Originally derived from the Internet Engineering Task Force (IETF) draft Incident Object Description Exchange Format (IODEF), CVRF is an XML-based language that will enable different stakeholders across different organizations to share critical security-related information in a single format, speeding up information exchange and digestion.

CVRF provides a standard, predictable language that can be used to generate consistent and detailed vulnerability reports. CVRF's basis in XML enables its use as part of an automated risk management solution, while also providing security practitioners with a standard format to describe security metric and vulnerability data.

Figure 6-3 describes some of the core elements within CVRF. Additional information including the schema, a dictionary, and a detailed diagram are available at http://www.icasi.org/cvrf.

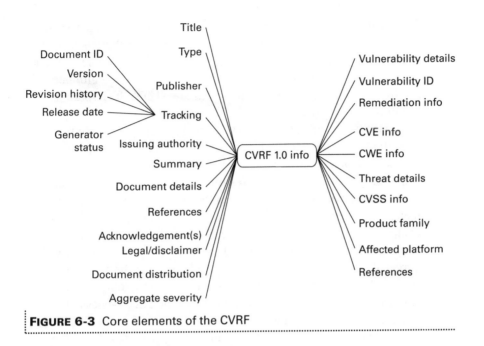

**FIGURE 6-3** Core elements of the CVRF

# COMMON MISUSE SCORING SYSTEM (CMSS)

While CVSS is the most widely adopted vulnerability scoring system, three other systems are based upon a similar model.

NIST Interagency Report 7517, "The Common Misuse Scoring System (CMSS): Metrics for Software Feature Misuse Vulnerabilities," describes the model to categorize the severity of a misuse of a legitimate feature in software. Unlike the CVSS, which describes vulnerability introduced by an unintended error in the design or coding of software, and unlike CCSS (described next), which considers vulnerability based upon a security configuration setting, CMSS provides metrics for software feature misuse vulnerability.

Consider the following example from the NIST report, "User Follows Link to Spoofed Web Site." This example of a "misuse" describes how an attacker might distribute a malicious hyperlink that surreptitiously leads a recipient of an electronic mail message to a fraudulent web site. When the user clicks the malicious link, the user's browser displays a lookalike imitation of a legitimate site. The vulnerability is that a hyperlink purporting to lead to a legitimate site instead takes the user to a malicious site. Thus, the hyperlink capability is misused.

CMSS represents a significant scoring system, similar to that described for CVSS, including a base metric group, a temporal component, and an environmental metric. The methods for calculating the vectors and scores for this model are quite similar to those described earlier in the chapter, but the CCSS and CMSS metrics are considerably more complex than those of CVSS. Target Distribution has been renamed Local Vulnerability Prevalence and two other metrics have been added to CCSS and CMSS: Perceived Target Value, which measures how attackers value the targets in a specific local environment as opposed to other environments, and Local Remediation Level, which measures the effectiveness of mitigation measures in the local environment. CCSS and CMSS also divide their environmental metrics into two groups: Exploitability and Impact. This allows Exploitability and Impact environmental subscores to be generated for CCSS and CMSS; such subscores are not available in CVSS.

For specific details regarding the scoring model for each of CVSS, CMSS, and CCSS, we commend the applicable NIST reports as well as automated calculator utilities, available in both mobile applications and at the web sites that accompany this book, www.g2-inc.com/securityautomation and www.mhprofessional.com/computingdownload.

# COMMON CONFIGURATION SCORING SYSTEM

The CCSS, the third of the vulnerability measurement and scoring specifications, is defined in NIST Interagency Report 7502, "The Common Configuration Scoring System (CCSS): Metrics for Software Security Configuration Vulnerabilities." CCSS addresses software security configuration issue vulnerabilities and is largely based on CVSS and CMSS, and it is intended to complement them to provide a comprehensive understanding of the various types of vulnerabilities. Like its predecessors, CCSS metrics are organized into three groups: base, temporal, and environmental. Base metrics describe the characteristics of a configuration issue that are constant over time and across user environments. Temporal metrics describe the characteristics of configuration issues that can change over time but remain constant across user environments. Environmental metrics are used to customize the base and temporal scores based on the characteristics of a specific user environment.

CCSS focuses more than its parallel scoring systems on the type of exploitation: active or passive. Active exploitation describes actions where an actor actively takes advantage of the vulnerable condition (such as an incorrectly set session timeout as described in CCE-2519-7). Passive exploitation refers to vulnerabilities that prevent authorized actions from occurring, such as a configuration setting that prevents audit log records from being generated for security events. The exploitability base metrics in CCSS are defined differently for active and passive exploitation because of the differences in the ease of exploitation.

# VULNERABILITY MANAGEMENT IN THE ENTERPRISE

These methods of describing and scoring vulnerability enable the security practitioner better to understand the potential flaws that place information assets at risk, whether from unintended flaws in software and systems, malicious use of legitimate components, or through misconfiguration of the applicable security settings. To perform effective vulnerability management in the enterprise, the security manager must understand as much as possible about pervasive security flaws (such as are described in the National Vulnerability Database and the Common Vulnerability Reporting Framework), as well as potential security configuration issues on important business systems. Integrating these data points with other elements of security automation will help provide a comprehensive risk management view, as you'll cover in Chapter 7.

# Part III
## Putting It All Together

# Chapter 7

# Building Automated Security Content

With the foundation laid thus far with enumerations, languages, and scoring systems, we can now move on to creating and using automated content to implement security automation. As we assemble the checklists and test definitions into meaningful arrangements, we can also use various reference implementations that are freely available to ensure that the files being built use the appropriate schemas and syntax. Examples of these are provided in this chapter, including instructions on how to obtain these from the appropriate sources.

## WORKING WITH FILES

Many of the security automation protocols are written in the eXtensible Markup Language (XML). XML, defined in the XML specification produced by the World Wide Web Consortium (W3C), provides a format that is both human-readable and machine-readable, lending itself well to the types of data exchange necessary for security automation. The following example demonstrates how the XML supports the exchange of information among information systems, yet is easily readable by a human reviewing the content. This excerpt describes several external references related to the SP 800-53 Security Control for "Configuration Settings":

```
<Group id="CM-6" hidden="true">
    <title>Configuration Settings</title>
    <reference>OMB Memoranda 07-11</reference>
    <reference>OMB Memoranda 07-18</reference>
    <reference>Priority 1</reference>
</Group>
```

### XML Editors

Because XML is a text-based language, any plain text editor can be used to manage the content. Like other markup languages, though, the proper use of tags and elements and compliance with the defined structure are critical to the suitability of the file for its intended purpose. For this reason, and simply to make editing an XML file easier, an XML-specific editor is often used to edit and maintain Security Content Automation Protocol (SCAP) and other automation files. Such editors often use color changes and provide assistance to complete tags or highlight typographical errors, and they also provide menus and buttons for common XML document tasks.

XML editors enable management of SCAP content in a user-friendly format and also help to verify that the content is compliant with the defined schema, assisting with tracing and debugging a section of the content.

Popular XML editors include the following:

- CAM editor
- Jedit XML Plugin
- Liquid XML Studio
- Oxygen XML Editor
- Quark XML Author
- Serna XML Editor
- Xerlin
- XMetaL
- XML Notepad
- XMLSpy
- XMLBlueprint XML editor

# CONTENT MAINTENANCE TOOLS

The SCAP specification describes the format for combining appropriate SCAP component specifications for a particular function or use case (such as security configuration checking), and the collective XML content used for a use case is called an "SCAP data stream." There are two types of SCAP data streams: an SCAP *source data stream* holds the input content, and an SCAP *result data stream* holds the output content. Standardizing inputs and outputs are key benefits of using the power of SCAP for tool-to-tool and tool-to-dashboard interoperability. The formats for these files are described in detail in this chapter.

Although the various automation components' requirements are straightforward, the assembly of the various sections is not trivial and requires a detailed understanding of the individual specifications and the platform(s) to be assessed. Properly integrating the checklists and checking languages can be error-prone and time-consuming. To foster the adoption of security automation, several organizations have created applications to assist with creation and validation of security automation content and SCAP data streams.

## Enhanced SCAP Editor (eSCAPe)

G2's eSCAPe application provides a friendly interface for creating and editing SCAP documents. It is available for download at this book's website and includes XCCDF and OVAL file creation and editing capability including the ability to search and tailor individual documents.

eSCAPe includes two interfaces for creating SCAP documents. The first is the *standard interface*. Most features of the editor can be accessed through this interface, including many of the more advanced features such as editing of Open Vulnerability and Assessment Language (OVAL) and Extensible Configuration Checklist Description Format (XCCDF) documents. The *wizard-driven interface,* or mode, by comparison is designed for rapid SCAP content creation and provides a more limited set of features. The wizards, however, are a powerful way to create SCAP content for simple tasks such as checking for malware.

### Navigating the Interface

When eSCAPe first launches, a mode selection window appears, where you can select either the wizard-driven or the standard mode interfaces. If you choose to start in the wizard-driven interface, the wizard selection window opens and eSCAPe enters wizard mode.

The application includes a Regular Expression (Regex) Validator tool that provides a GUI for constructing and testing regular expressions. Regular expressions are supported throughout eSCAPe in accordance with support for OVAL 5.3 and later. Regular expressions allow users to apply powerful pattern matching to system elements such as filenames and registry keys. The Regex Validator tool allows users to check that their expressions are working as expected. The team at Zytrax have created a helpful guide for creating and using regular expressions, available at http://www.zytrax.com/tech/web/regex.htm.

The Validator tool can be used to perform schema validation on open OVAL and XCCDF documents. This validation will alert the developer if the OVAL or XCCDF document does not conform to the proper structure dictated in the XML schema(s).

## The Breadcrumb Toolbar

eSCAPe includes a breadcrumb toolbar that can aid in navigating an OVAL document. While in standard mode with an OVAL document open and a test selected, you can double-click an object or state, and the editor will jump to that object or state and create a breadcrumb for the parent test in the toolbar. Later, you can click the breadcrumb and the interface will return the user to the test. Figure 7-1 shows a view of an open OVAL document displaying the breadcrumb toolbar in operation.

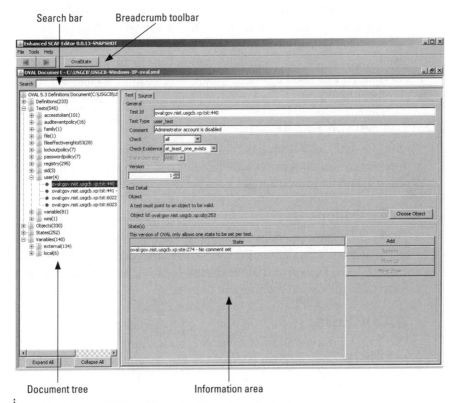

**FIGURE 7-1**  eSCAPe with open OVAL file displaying document tree, breadcrumb navigation toolbar, information area, and search bar

### The Document Tree

In opened OVAL and XCCDF documents, an expandable and collapsible document tree allows for navigation of the SCAP document by structural groupings. For an OVAL file, the highest branching of the tree is the definition level. The tree branches further into tests, objects, states, and variables below.

In an XCCDF document, the first branching is between profiles and groups. Expansion of profile elements reveal selected rules and expansion of groups reveal groupings and then rules. At the bottom of the document tree are buttons for Expand All and Collapse All. These buttons provide a quick way to expand or collapse the entire document tree.

### The Information Area

To the right of the document tree is the information area. Information on the currently selected item in the document tree is displayed in this area. In Figure 7-1, information on the currently selected test is displayed in a Test tab in the information area to the right. The test information can also be edited by adjusting settings such as the test comment in this area.

### The Search Bar

eSCAPe includes a Search bar for searching within open OVAL documents. Searches can be conducted using object comments and object IDs. The Search bar is located at the top of Figure 7-1.

### OVAL Editor

The OVAL Editor provides a range of features for editing OVAL and Common Remediation Enumeration (CPE) OVAL documents. Table 7-1 shows a full list of the available OVAL viewing and editing features in the eSCAPe information area.

### XCCDF Editor

The XCCDF Editor allows for viewing and editing of opened XCCDF files. As different elements of the document are selected in

| Editor | Tree Node | Tabs | Information |
|---|---|---|---|
| OVAL | Definition | General | Displays an overview of the definition including class, ID, title, and version. A summary of the references is also displayed. |
| | | Metadata | Displays metadata including affected platforms/products. Title and description can be edited here. |
| | | Criteria | Displays the criteria logic block. Tests and definition references can be added/removed and operators changed here. |
| | | Source | Displays the XML source of the selected definition. |
| | Test | Test | Contains two panes: General and Test Detail. Under the first pane the test ID, test type, and other attributes are displayed and can be edited. The second pane contains the object and state settings. |
| | | Source | Displays the XML source of the selected test. |
| | Object | Object | Displays and allows for editing of object ID, type, version, comment, behaviors, and parameters. |
| | | Source | Displays the XML source of the selected object. |
| | State | State | Displays and allows for editing of state ID, type, version, comment, behaviors, and parameters. |
| | | Source | Displays the XML source of the selected state. |
| | Variable | Variable | Displays variable type and allows for editing of variable ID, version, data type, comment, possible_value, and possible_restrictions. |
| | | Source | Displays the XML source of the selected variable. |

**TABLE 7-1**   eSCAPe OVAL Editor Tree View Elements and Information Area Options and Settings

the document tree, their corresponding properties and settings appear on the right in the information area, as shown in Figure 7-2.

The XCCDF Editor provides a range of features for editing XCCDF documents. Table 7-2 shows a full list of the available XCCDF viewing and editing features displayed in the eSCAPe information area.

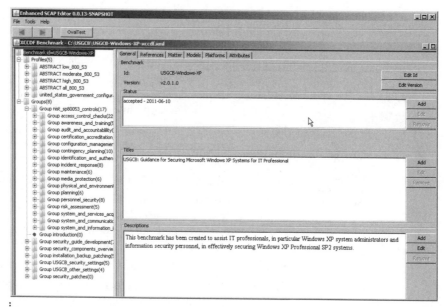

**FIGURE 7-2**  eSCAPe with an open XCCDF file—XCCDF Editor

| Editor | Tree Node | Tabs | Information |
|---|---|---|---|
| XCCDF | Benchmark | General | Editing/viewing of benchmark ID, version, status, titles, and descriptions |
| | | References | Editing of references and notices |
| | | Matter | Editing of front and rear matter metadata |
| | | Models | Editing/viewing of associated benchmark scoring models |
| | | Platforms | Editing/viewing of associated platforms |
| | | Attributes | Editing of associated style elements and the resolved attribute |
| | Profile | General | Editing/viewing of profile ID, version, status, titles, and descriptions |
| | | Attributes | Editing of note-tag, extends, abstract, and prohibit changes attributes |
| | | Children | Editing of all selected and rule elements |
| | | Source | XML source of the selected profile |

**TABLE 7-2**  eSCAPe XCCDF Editor Tree View Elements and Information Area Options and Settings (*continued*)

| Editor | Tree Node | Tabs | Information |
|--------|-----------|------|-------------|
| XCCDF | Group | General | Editing/viewing of group ID, version, status, titles, and descriptions |
| | | References | Editing of references, warnings, and questions |
| | | Attributes | Editing of cluster-id, extends, abstract, hidden, and prohibit changes attributes |
| | | Selectable Item | Editing/viewing of platforms, requires, conflicts, rationales, weight, and selected |
| | | Source | XML source of the selected group |
| | Rule | General | Editing/viewing of rule ID, version, status, titles, and descriptions |
| | | References | Editing of references, warnings, and questions |
| | | Attributes | Editing of cluster-id, extends, abstract, hidden, and prohibit changes attributes |
| | | Selectable Item | Editing/viewing of platforms, requires, conflicts, rationales, weight, and selected |
| | | Role/ Severity | Setting of multiple options, and selection of role and severity attributes |
| | | Checks | Editing/viewing of selected check content refs and check exports |
| | | Source | XML source of the selected rule |
| | Value | General | Editing/viewing of value ID, version, status, titles and descriptions. |
| | | References | Editing of references, warnings, and questions |
| | | Attributes | Editing of cluster-ID, extends, abstract, hidden, and prohibit changes attributes |
| | | Values | Editing/viewing of type, operator and set values |
| | | Source | XML source of selected value |

**TABLE 7-2**   eSCAPe XCCDF Editor Tree View Elements and Information Area Options and Settings

## CPE Dictionary Editor

The CPE Dictionary Editor allows for viewing and editing of opened CPE Dictionary files. Figure 7-3 illustrates the CPE Dictionary Editor with an open CPE dictionary file.

The CPE Dictionary Editor provides a range of features for editing CPE Dictionary documents. For a full list of user-available

CPE Dictionary viewing and editing features displayed in the eSCAPe information area, see Table 7-3.

## The eSCAPe Wizards

The eSCAPe Wizards are designed for rapid creation of SCAP content. The wizards completely abstract the creation of the underlying SCAP documents and therefore present the user with the lowest requirement of understanding regarding SCAP protocols. Each wizard requires only two steps to create content and produces both an OVAL test file and an accompanying XCCDF checklist. The wizards are capable of creating only one test at a time. However, the OVAL Merger utility included with eSCAPe can be used to group many OVAL tests created with the wizard into a single file for distribution. See the section "Using the Merge OVAL Documents Tool" later in this chapter for information on how to use the OVAL Merger tool.

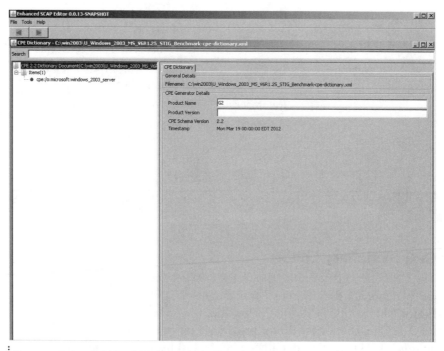

**FIGURE 7-3** eSCAPe CPE Dictionary Editor tree

| Editor | Tree Node | Tabs | Information |
|---|---|---|---|
| CPE Dictionary | CPE Dictionary | CPE Dictionary | Displays CPE file details and allows for editing of generator product name and product version |
| | CPE Item | General | Displays and allows for editing of CPE ID, version, status, titles, and descriptions |
| | | Titles | Editing/viewing of associated titles |
| | | Notes | Editing/viewing of associated notes and notes containers |
| | | Reference | Editing of associated references |
| | | Checks | Editing/viewing of associated check refs |
| | | Source | Displays XML source of selected CPE Dictionary |

**TABLE 7-3**  CPE Dictionary Viewing and Editing Features Displayed in the eSCAPe Information Area

Three wizards are currently available for the rapid creation of SCAP content:

- Windows File Test Wizard
- UNIX File Test Wizard
- Windows Registry Test Wizard

## Opening and Navigating an SCAP Data Stream

To open an existing SCAP Data Stream in eSCAPe, choose File | Open | SCAP Data Stream, and then navigate to and select either a data stream archive (ZIP) file or an XCCDF file that is part of an SCAP data stream. An SCAP Data Stream window will appear with the chosen CPE Dictionary files displayed, as shown in Figure 7-4.

## Example: Finding Malware with SCAP

The eSCAPe wizards are particularly well suited for the generation of malware detection content. Often the presence of malware on a system can be detected by checking for malware artifacts such as files or registry keys. These artifacts can be detected with certain OVAL tests. The following examples demonstrate the steps necessary to create an OVAL test and accompanying XCCDF document to check systems for malware registry or file artifacts.

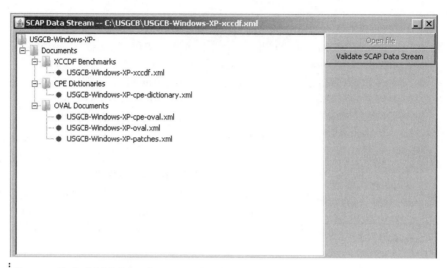

**FIGURE 7-4** SCAP Data Stream window displaying stream files

## Creating Content: Registry Test Example

As an example, to create an SCAP data stream that will search the Windows registry for a known malicious entry, perhaps in response to a vulnerability bulletin from US-CERT, follow these steps:

1. Start eSCAPe

2. In the window that opens, enter Wizard Mode in one of two ways:

   Click the Wizard-Driven button (as shown next) or choose File | Wizard Mode.

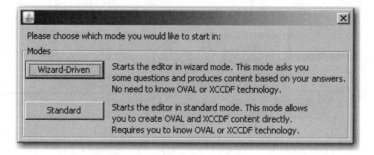

3. Adjust the Target OVAL version and set the OVAL namespace identifier. The choice of OVAL version will be most constrained by the OVAL version supported by the vendor tool in which the content will be run. At the time of this writing, many vendors still fully support only OVAL 5.3.

4. From the list of available wizards, select Registry, and then click Go, as shown next:

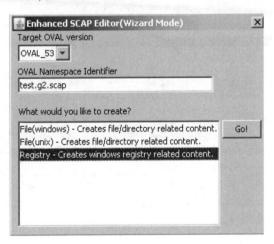

5. In this example, we will be checking for the presence of the following malicious registry key entry: HKLM\ SOFTWARE\Microsoft\Windows\CurrentVersion\Run\ Goodprogram = C:\WINDOWS\Temp\Badprogram.exe.

6. In the window that opens, you'll see fields for entering the title and the registry key information. The use of a descriptive title will easily identify what the OVAL definition is checking for. For this example, type the following registry test title in the Title field: **Registry Check for malicious key - 'Badprogram.exe'**.

7. Because we are checking for both the existence of a registry key and its value, make sure that in the What Is To Be Tested area, the Value Of Hive\Key\Name radio button is selected.

8. Next, from the drop-down Registry Hive menu, select HKEY_LOCAL_MACHINE. Figure 7-5 shows the layout of this window and the list of registry hives available.

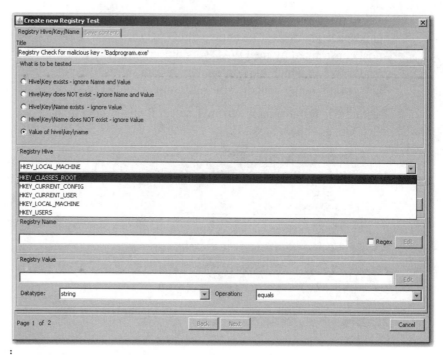

**FIGURE 7-5** Registry Test Wizard window, with Title and Registry Hive

**9.** Next, you'll enter the key, name, and value. For this example, in the Registry Key field, enter **SOFTWARE\ Microsoft\Windows\CurrentVersion\Run**. In the Registry Name field, enter **Goodprogram**. In the Registry Value field, enter **C:\WINDOWS\Temp\Badprogram.exe**. The Datatype field can be set as String, and the operation field can be set as Equals, as shown in Figure 7-6.

**10.** Click Next to move to the last step and save the content. In the next screen, click the Browse button, navigate to where you want to save the file, enter a destination filename, as shown next. Then click Save.

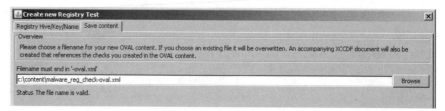

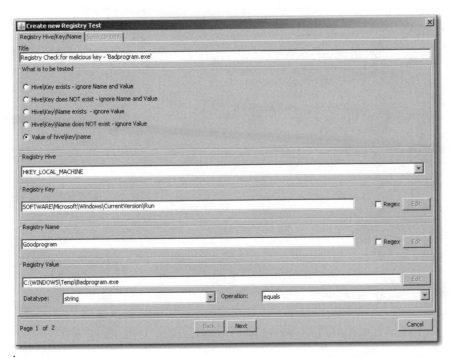

**FIGURE 7-6** Registry Test Wizard window with Registry Key, Name, and Value

The final step is to save the files via the **Save Content** tab shown in Figure 7-7. It is an SCAP convention to name OVAL files with "-oval" at the end and to save XCCDF files with a trailing "-xccdf". At this last step in the wizard, the application requires that the destination filename match those formats. If an OVAL filename is entered without the appropriate suffix, a red error message will appear above the field. The path may be entered manually or selected via the browse function, as shown.

**11.** Finally, locate and view the two files that you created:

- malware_reg_check-oval.xml

- malware_reg_check-xccdf.xml

The OVAL file contains the body of the checks for the malicious registry entry and the XCCDF file references those checks. These files are now ready to be handed off to a NIST-validated SCAP scanner.

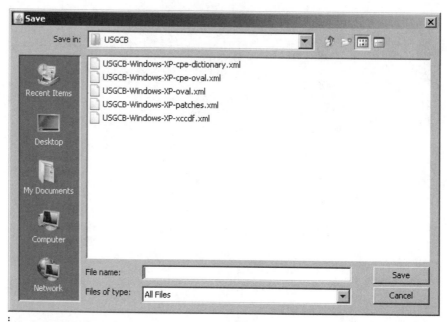

**FIGURE 7-7** Registry Test Wizard window Browse to Save dialog box

## Example: Creating Content to Check for Malicious File

This example will demonstrate how to create SCAP content to check for the presence of a malicious file on a system. In this example, we will be checking for the presence of the following malicious file:

| Path | Filename | Size (KB) | MD5 |
|------|----------|-----------|-----|
| C:\ WINDOWS\ Temp | 34564.exe | 89,829 | 31125f0cef9b543911b0e68589c3acf5 |

**1.** Start eSCAPe and enter the Wizard Mode.

**2.** Select the OVAL file version, as shown in the following illustration, and type the Namespace Identifier, and then choose the File(windows) wizard and click Go!

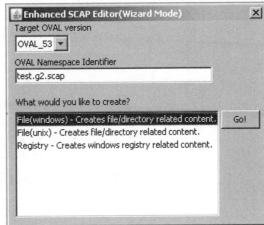

**3.** The next window contains all the settings for creating the Windows file test. Enter a title into the Title field: **Test for malicious file '34564.exe'**

**4.** In the Path field, you can specify a path in two ways. In the first way, enter the specified path, **c:\windows\temp** in the Path field, as shown next:

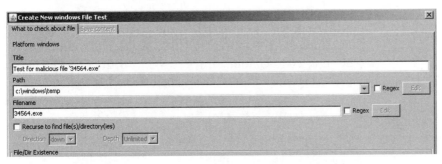

The second way to specify a path is to use one of the predefined path shortcuts available, as shown in the next illustration:

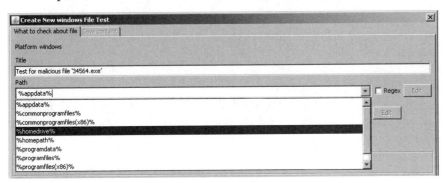

Using one of these shortcuts will result in the creation of an OVAL test capable of determining the actual path on the destination system. In certain circumstances, this is preferred to hard-coding a path that might not be the same on all installations. For example, it is possible to set the systemroot, which is generally C:\WINDOWS, to a non-standard path such as C:\temp\WINDOWS. Such a choice would mean that content that assumes that systemroot is set to C:\WINDOWS might not effectively perform the test. The currently supported path shortcuts and examples of how they might be expanded are displayed in Table 7-4.

**5.** Selecting Recurse To Find File(s)/Directory(ies) at this step will apply behaviors to the file test, directing it to continue through the directory tree until it finds the file or directory. For example, if the file path is not known, the root directory (generally C:\) can be specified and the content will direct the scanner to start at the root level and search down the directory tree. The default recursion Direction is down and Depth is Unlimited, but other options can be selected. Direction can be adjusted to Up or None and Depth can be adjusted to Unlimited, 1, 2, 3, 4, 5, 10, 20, or 100. The following illustration shows sample recursion settings.

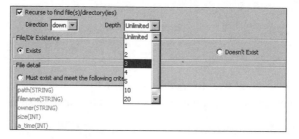

**6.** Next, we will add file details to check for properties of the file. In the File Detail area, make sure the radio button Must Exist And Meet The Following Criteria is selected.

**7.** In the selection box under the button, choose size(INT) and then click the Add button to the right of the field.

| Path Shortcut | Common Value on Target System |
|---|---|
| %appdata% | C:\Documents and Settings\user\Application Data |
| %commonprogramfiles% | C:\Program Files\Common Files |
| %commonprogramfiles(x86)% | C:\Program Files\Common Files (x86) |
| %homedrive% | C:\ |
| %homepath% | C:\Documents and Settings\user |
| %programdata% | C:\Documents and Settings\All Users\Application Data |
| %programfiles% | C:\Program Files |
| %programfiles(x86)% | C:\Program Files (x86) |
| %systemroot% | C:\WINDOWS |

**TABLE 7-4** eSCAPe File Wizard Path Shortcuts and General Values

8. In the next window, in the Operation drop-down, choose Equals, and enter the file size in bytes in the Data field; then click OK.

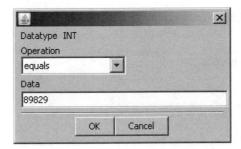

9. At the bottom of the next window, you'll see "size(INT) equals 89829" in the Added area. For each file detail attribute check that is added, a line item appears.

10. Click md5(STRING) in the list of file details, and in the dialog that opens, choose equals for the Operation drop-down and then enter the MD5 hash in the Data field, as shown in the following illustration; then click OK. If a string of the wrong length is entered for the md5 hash, the field

will appear in red and the OK button will be disabled until a
valid md5 hash string is entered.

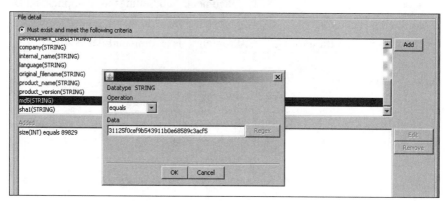

**11.** Click Next to move on to save the file. On the next screen,
shown next, click the Browse button, navigate to where you
want to save the file, enter a destination filename, and then
click Save.

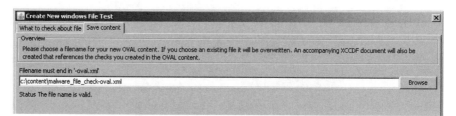

**12.** Finally, locate the two files that you created: malware_file
_check-oval.xml andmalware_file_check-xccdf.xml. The
OVAL file contains the body of the malware check for the
malicious file and the XCCDF file references those checks.
These files are ready to be handed off to a validated SCAP
scanner.

## Using the Regex Validator Tool

eSCAPe includes support for regular expressions throughout OVAL
and for convenience includes a regular expression (Regex) Validator
tool. This tool can be used to compose and test regular expressions

before saving them in an OVAL document. To access the Regex Validator tool, choose Tools | Regex Validator.

To test a regular expression, enter it into the Pattern field and then, in the Text To Match field, enter a sample string that the regular expression should match. Last, click Match, and if the regular expression is working, the sample string will be listed after Matched Text. In Figure 7-8, a regular expression intended to match Service Pack 2 through Service Pack 4 is entered. In regex notation, square brackets indicate a directive to match a single character, in this case within the numeric range of 2-4.

Notice that the string "Service Pack 3" proved to be a match; this demonstrates the proper working of the regular expression.

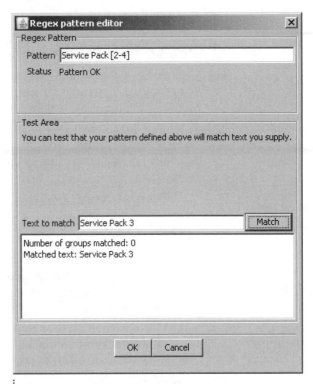

**FIGURE 7-8** Regular Expression Validator

## Using the Merge OVAL Documents Tool

Included with eSCAPe is a utility for merging OVAL files. To access this tool, choose Tools | Merge OVAL Documents.

If several OVAL files were made with the wizards, which allow for the creation of only a single test for each generated definition OVAL file, it might often make sense to merge those files together if they all pertain to the same security issue. The OVAL merger tool features two merge styles: Simple and With Wrapper Definition. The Simple merge style combines all the definitions, tests, objects, states, and variables together into a single file. The With Wrapper Definition option adds a definition at the top of the OVAL file that references all the combined tests. This utility also addresses any possible object ID collisions.

# SOME USEFUL TIPS FOR CREATING CONTENT

Writing SCAP content can be a complex task, and data streams that encompass a complete security policy are often large and convoluted. Here we present some best practices for creating SCAP content that make it easier to create, maintain, and interpret SCAP data streams.

These are simply suggested best practices; as long as your content is built according to the specifications, it should perform as expected, but following these suggestions makes it easier for you and/or others to use your documents.

## Explain Yourself

Commenting your content is one of the biggest favors you can do for your future self and for anyone else who needs to view, interpret, or maintain your content. Although your intentions might seem self-evident at the time you write content, in three months your intentions and the content's purpose might not be as clear.

The purpose of comments is not to make more work for you, although it often seems that way, but to ensure clarity and make maintenance easier.

### Simple Comments

Almost every construct in an SCAP document supports a comment attribute. This attribute should be used to enter a concise comment that explains the purpose of the element. This comment should be a human-readable description that defines the intent of the element, not a simple restatement of other content in the element.

### Complex Comments

In some cases you may want to insert more complex comments than the comment attribute accommodates. In these cases, you can use an XML comment to document the logic or intent of your constructs. You should be aware that these comments can be lost if the content is placed in a repository or used by other individuals.

### Comment Best Practices

Adding comments as you create the content offers several benefits. The content is fresh in your mind, you understand what you are trying to do and how you are trying to do it, and it's less of a chore to do it as part of the content creation rather than waiting until later—when the content is "cold" and you might have forgotten your original intentions. Having to go through an entire document to add comments is an unappealing task.

Following are a few more tips:

- *Make your comments concise.* Although your comments should clearly explain the intent of the content, don't include unnecessary details or off topic information.

- *Make your comments clear.* Although you want to avoid unnecessary verbosity in comments, you need to make sure that your thought process and logic related to the content is clearly communicated.

- *Use a consistent style.* If you use shorthand indicators such as "TODO:" to indicate some need or behavior, don't mix up the styles. For example, don't use a mix of "TODO:", "todo:", "To Do", and so on in your document to indicate the same thing. Also make sure you actually finish these to-do's before releasing your data stream.

- *Keep comments up to date.* Although you should comment as you initially create the content, it is equally important to update your comments any time you change the content in a significant manner.

## Make Sure It Works

Always thoroughly test your content using a variety of tools if possible. After making sure the content is syntactically valid, you should ensure that it functions properly as well. This involves running the content against a variety of systems in a known state and checking the output of the tool against the expected result.

## Version Your Artifacts

Whenever you directly update any SCAP elements, you should increment the associated version number. This helps when you're trying to determine when a change was made, why it was made, what effect it should have, or other reasons for modification.

### Version Bubbling

Whether or not the version of an element that is indirectly updated should be incremented is often contested within the security automation community. For example, if you start with an OVAL definition that references an OVAL test, which in turn references an OVAL object, and that object is changed (causing one to increment the version number of the OVAL object), should the version number of the OVAL test and the OVAL Definition change, too? What about rules that reference an OVAL definition—should their version be incremented when the OVAL definition version is incremented? There are pros and cons on both sides of these issues, so the best we can suggest is to research the arguments and make your own decision; but be consistent.

## Reuse of Artifacts

Many developers agree that reuse of code is a good thing. In many ways, automation content creation is similar to other development efforts and many best practices apply to both. Reusing artifacts leads to less work, smaller file sizes, potentially clearer documents, and easier repair of an issue (such as a single fix that can be made if an error in the content is found or if it needs to be changed).

The major downside of content reuse is the fact that multiple dependencies might exist and changes might have unintended consequences. Software developers have the same issue and use a process called "regression testing" to deal with it. Regression testing looks for new errors that have occurred in something that was working previously.

If you are reusing content, check to see how many different places an artifact is used. The more places it is used, the more potential for introducing unanticipated problems. If you find that an artifact you need to change is used heavily, you may be better off creating a new artifact instead of changing the existing one.

Also consider how often you expect an artifact to change before you decide to reuse it. States are much more likely to change than objects, so although it might make sense to reuse objects, reusing states might not make as much sense.

## Content Correctness

Make sure your content is syntactically correct. It should meet all the requirements and obey all the restrictions imposed by both the component specifications and SCAP itself.

A variety of tools can be used to test the syntax of your content. The specifications all have an XML Schema Definition (XSD) associated with them, and these files are used to validate the basic syntax of the document, ensuring that each is well formed and without syntax errors.

The SCAP Content Validation (SCAPVal) tool, available from NIST at http://scap.nist.gov, performs additional testing to ensure that the content meets the requirements of the SCAP program. Any errors reported by the tool should be corrected, and you should attempt to correct any warnings produced.

## Least Version Principle

A wide variety of SCAP validated products are on the market and in use, some new and some quite old. Because many of these products were validated against differing SCAP versions at different points in time, not all products are able to run all SCAP content. Although SCAP Product Validation requirements mandate backward-compatibility, this means that products validated to process SCAP 1.2 content must be able to process valid SCAP 1.0 content, but older products might not be able to process newer content.

If it is possible to perform the necessary functions using OVAL 5.3, you shouldn't use OVAL 5.10 just because it is the latest version. Using OVAL 5.3 gives your content its best chance of running correctly with the broadest range of tools. That being said, you need not avoid taking advantage of the capabilities of a later specification if those are necessary, but be sure that the tools you are using can support them. Each of the applications on the SCAP Validated Products List must clearly list the versions and capabilities supported, aiding the content creator in ensuring that the intended product(s) will be able to process the planned content.

## Design for People

Ninety-nine percent of the time, the output of an SCAP product is targeted for human consumption. What this means in practice is that users will thank you if you fill in all the text blocks with well-written, valid, and useful content that helps them do their job. Think of times in the past when you've received a report full of meaningless technical jargon or unhelpful text and you've been responsible for taking action based on that report. Recipients of reports based upon your content will appreciate it if you don't emulate that model.

Remember that spelling counts, and use a spelling checker on the parts of your content intended to be read by people.

## Follow the Rules of the Road

SCAP is a complicated set of specifications. As with any complex system, you'll find that it is often possible to produce content that is technically correct, but that violates the intentions of the specification designers. Such content that follows the "letter of the specification" but violates the "spirit of the specification" will often not perform as expected.

The specifications are written in such a way that you are not likely to write this content accidently; you have to work pretty hard to do so.

## Minimize Extension Depth

Extending a definition is a straightforward way to build upon previous work. It can save time and effort, assists in maintenance, and helps ensure correctness. However, once you are at your fourth or fifth level of extension, content readability and logic start to suffer. Eventually you can reach a point where you need a separate diagram to understand the extension relationships in your content.

Try to keep your extensions at a depth of two or three levels. If you start getting deeper, you may want to reevaluate the organization of the definitions you are extending, or consider using separate criterion instead of extension.

## Granularity

Keeping the content well organized and focused will assist in maintenance and reuse later on. There is often a fine line between keeping the content granular and encouraging reuse.

## Customization

If you are writing your content only for your organization, with no plans to change it or share it on a regular basis, you may not need customization. On the other hand, if you are writing content that changes frequently or you plan to distribute it, it is often worth your effort to make it customizable.

Customizability is usually provided through the use of external variables in the XCCDF file. This allows users to create a new profile that changes these values without editing any of the other content files and reduces the risk of errors being introduced in the content.

## Performance

It is always worth thinking about the performance of your content in real-world situations. Any time you are writing content that looks at all of a particular artifact type, whether it be files, user accounts, registry keys, or any other artifact that can have a variable number of occurrences, you run the risk of causing the target system to use more resources than intended. This is an important aspect of the testing process.

Although you can't always predict this impact, and sometimes you have no choice but to look at everything, when you start to write content like this you should sit back and ask yourself, "Is there another way to do this?" If so, you should probably implement the alternative method.

## Regular Expressions

The regular expression syntax used in the SCAP specifications has switched between subsets of the Portable Operating System Interface for UNIX (POSIX) and Perl Compatible Regular Expressions (PCRE) specifications as OVAL has evolved. Prior to OVAL 5.6, the OVAL spec called for POSIX as the default, while SCAP content has previously used the PCRE standards. OVAL 5.6 and later have specified PCRE as the default, with POSIX as an option.

Your best bet when writing content is to use the allowed subset of PCRE. For the most compatible content, you should try to substitute constructs that are valid as both PCRE and POSIX regular expressions.

For example, instead of using **\d** (PCRE syntax) or **[:digit:]** (POSIX syntax), you should use **[0-9]**. The Wikipedia page for "Regular Expression" (http://en.wikipedia.org/wiki/Regular_expression) contains a table that identifies a potential ASCII regex that performs the same matches as the various POSIX and PCRE character class constructs.

# Chapter 8

## Putting Security Automation to Work in the Enterprise

Throughout this book, we have described how security automation works and some of the values it brings to an organization. The potential uses and benefits of automation in the enterprise are significant:

■ When the organization defines its security requirements and baseline configuration policies in a digital, repeatable manner, those baselines and policies become better understood, more easily implemented, and more consistently measurable throughout the enterprise.

■ Standardizing security controls and measures enables effective correlation and integration of various security artifacts (such as system security logs, vulnerability reports, and configuration reviews). This standardization enables security awareness throughout an enterprise without locking the organization into the selection of a single security product.

■ Auditing and tracking compliance with mandates (such as HIPAA and Payment Card Industry [PCI]) are greatly improved.

Fortunately, as commercial products continue to adopt standardized automation languages and protocols, implementation and use of these are simplified and cost-effective. We need all of this at a reasonable cost, built into commercial off-the-shelf products, and based on open industry standards.

The technologies we have described in this book are simply the beginning of a broader set of emerging automation innovations. International standards organizations such as ISO and IETF are supporting these concepts, lending credibility to the hope that the technology will mature and expand. Some examples of forthcoming security automation protocols include the following:

■ **Event Management Automation**    Methods to aggregate and correlate system events, log information, and audit information. This information may be used for incident detection and handling, and for improved situational awareness.

- **Automated Remediation**  Detailed methods for communicating and implementing automated processes to correct system flaws and/or remediate misconfiguration such as the Common Remediation Enumeration (CRE) and a potential remediation language.

- **Enterprise System Information**  A broad set of protocols used to associate policy with assessed security controls and to aggregate/report security results across enterprise boundaries. ESI could include, for example, methods for a branch office to report information consistently to a primary department or from a government bureau to its parent agency.

- **Software Assurance Automation**  Detailed specifications and languages to help people understand the methods used to infiltrate and attack information systems (such as Common Attack Pattern Enumeration and Classification [CAPEC], Common Weakness Enumeration [CWE], and Common Weakness Scoring System [CWSS]). An important component of software assurance includes harnessing information about known vulnerability and compliance issues to perform effective threat modeling.

# HOW ORGANIZATIONS ARE USING SECURITY AUTOMATION

Organizations around the world are implementing these security automation techniques for a broad range of uses. The number and nature of electronic computing devices is growing at an astounding pace—mobile devices, virtual systems, and cloud computing infrastructure are all increasing the breadth of information technology to be monitored, just at a time when economic pressures are constraining the available resources to stay current. The use cases described here discuss how security automation in the enterprise will help managers achieve risk management goals despite budget and labor constraints.

A primary goal of enterprise security organizations is to reduce risk to their information systems. NIST Special Publication 800-30 defines risk as "a function of the likelihood of a given threat-source's exercising a particular potential vulnerability, and the resulting impact of that adverse event on the organization." In the sections that follow, we will explore how automation empowers the security team to measure and monitor that risk.

## Automated Hardware and Software Inventory

Before you can measure risk, you must reliably understand the assets to be protected and their value to the organization. Each system, defined by NIST Special Publication 800-53 as a "discrete set of information resources organized for the collection, processing, maintenance, use, sharing, dissemination, or disposition of information," has physical property value and also has a measurable value to the organization's mission. A system can be defined by its individual components, each of which may be cataloged in an asset management system, and each group of assets may play a role in a larger system—that is, a system-of-systems.

Many commercial products include asset management capabilities such as the following:

- Systems management (such as IBM Tivoli and Microsoft Security Compliance Manager) tools provide a wealth of information and often provide an automated discovery capability, broadcasting special network messages to identify new or changed host devices, tracking their characteristics and reporting back to management repositories.

- Network management products such as Niksun's NetDetector are adept at learning that a new device has entered the environment and often provide the discovered information back to an inventory capability. Network monitoring resources are often an excellent source of host discovery information.

- Most vulnerability scanners are able to identify and characterize the hosts they discover.

There are great benefits to leveraging this broad range of sources for asset inventory, but the disparity among products often leads to conflicting information and missing data. Security automation products and processes enable the organization to collect this disparate data, resolve conflicts, and harmonize the results, leading to a comprehensive asset database of record that is critical to maintaining effective situational awareness. Through the use of protocols such as the Assessment Summary Results (ASR) model, the security organization can quickly understand the types of assets deployed on its networks.

Software inventory is crucial to the organization's ability to monitor and manage its enterprise infrastructure and represents an important component of asset management. Software installation information affects the following aspects of the organization's risk posture:

- The software products in use and the versions installed are the primary locations where vulnerabilities will be introduced. From major operating systems to minor applications, each software product brings unique vulnerability; understanding what's installed and on which hosts is a significant step toward security situational awareness.

- Ensuring that the enterprise is properly licensing the software in use and monitoring adherence to software and use agreements are important elements of security risk management. Many system and desktop management products include the ability to inform system managers of their license compliance status, which may itself become a security compliance artifact to be monitored as part of a larger risk management framework.

- Effective patch management, a critical requirement for managing vulnerability in the enterprise, depends on correctly understanding software inventory.

- Observing the installation of unapproved software is important to reducing exposure. Detecting and mitigating rogue applications quickly will reduce the risk from these threat sources.

Software inventory knowledge and management is possible through manual means, but the growing list of applications and the expanding cloud of assets to be managed make manual inventory a daunting task. The use of automated tools, interoperating through consistent data exchange standards, and reporting results in a repeatable manner (such as through Asset Reporting Format [ARF], Assessment Summary Results [ASR], and Common Platform Enumeration [CPE]) makes a difficult task manageable.

# Security Configuration Management (SCM)

In addition to the ability to discover and compile hardware and software inventory of devices on enterprise networks, security-minded organizations need to assess the configuration of those assets. Security managers need to determine system security settings, assess those settings' compliance with organizational policy and baselines, and, where applicable, compare the observed settings with those agreed upon in security planning documents.

In many cases, these settings may be retrieved and monitored using enterprise-scale commercial tools. Many applications do an excellent job of collecting these settings, some even with the capability of implementing changes (such as applying a patch, correcting a registry setting, or disabling a guest account). Some of these applications work through the use of a resident software component ("an agent"), while others connect to the asset and collect the information as needed.

Although these commercial approaches themselves offer significant security benefit to the organization, significant improvement can be gained by leveraging security automation methods.

## Case Study: U.S. Government

Early in the 21st century, security managers at an agency of the U.S. government recognized the need to collect inventory and configuration information from hundreds of remote locations and discovered that a single commercial solution was not available for newer Windows operating systems. Their information security office decided to contract for a government-based assessment solution, investing in a robust, but proprietary, product that collected registry settings, software inventory, and background services from each host. When commercial off-the-shelf (COTS) solutions eventually appeared, the agency bore the cost and delay of rewriting the compliance policies, and they did so again for the next proprietary enterprise solution.

The former model relied upon written security configuration guidance, manually implemented by network and system administrators and manually reviewed by security auditors, often needing to repeat this process several times throughout an implementation or upgrade.

**An Automated Security Solution** An automated solution for such an agency is to describe the desired security configuration policy through an SCAP-expressed checklist, describing the settings, patches, and other security elements using the SCAP elements described in earlier chapters. Such a standardized checklist ensures that compliance assessment is performed consistently and exactly matches the baseline standard.

Because the security configuration review can be performed through automated means, the security state can be continually monitored for compliance with the agreed-upon controls, resulting in the ability to identify changes in risk posture quickly. This efficient monitoring capability also permits enterprise managers to track security trends, highlighting issues that affect multiple information systems throughout the network. The tasks involved are not trivial, and the implementation of automation technology does not magically eliminate the challenges of managing hundreds of thousands of assets around the globe, but the alternative is very expensive and ineffective.

Use of SCAP-based checklists in the enterprise also enables effective comparison across organizational boundaries. While one group may use a particular commercial compliance assessment product or an enterprise desktop management product, use of the same checklist by an auditor reduces the likelihood of discrepancies and helps to correlate findings. Moreover, the use of a standardized checklist enables multiple branches of an organization to implement their assessment products of choice, while the results may be aggregated, correlated, and monitored at appropriate levels throughout the enterprise.

These benefits are behind the U.S. Government's Configuration Baseline (USGCB) approach (the successor to the Federal Desktop Core Configuration program) that provides common SCAP-expressed checklists for several common platforms. Through the use of this standardized baseline across the entire federal enterprise, the U.S. government ensures that minimum security configuration criteria are implemented on each desktop system. The automated checklists can be implemented on a broad range of commercial and Government off-the-shelf (GOTS) products, with results that may be consistently and reliably correlated within and among agencies. The USGCB initiative offers an example to commercial and government enterprise security practitioners as a model for establishing and monitoring the security configuration posture of IT systems. The checklists themselves are freely available for download from NIST at usgcb.nist.gov and can be tailored and adjusted to meet organizational needs.

### Case Study: Orbitz

In 2009, Orbitz Worldwide's Chief Information Security Officer (CISO), Ed Bellis, described an enterprise project that leveraged SCAP to make sense of organizational vulnerability tracking and remediation.

As an enterprise, Orbitz has a significant infrastructure to support. The company's worldwide brands include dedicated travel-related service sites in more than a dozen countries and span thousands of servers. To track the findings and remediation of common vulnerabilities across hundreds of applications on those servers, Orbitz used SCAP reference data to deconflict and harmonize the vulnerability reports from numerous sensors. Their system downloads the XML vulnerability feed from the National Vulnerability Database (NVD), using Common Vulnerabilities and Exposures (CVE) references to correlate new data with that provided by commercial sources. His team of security practitioners implemented a remediation workflow system that prioritized mitigation of vulnerabilities, recording open flaws and asset management information in corporate JIRA tracking systems, and assigning remediation activities using Remedy's action request system.

Despite a continuous stream of vulnerabilities across a complex infrastructure, Orbitz has managed to stay ahead of the onslaught with limited security resources, thanks in part to the use of security automation technology and common vulnerability enumeration.

# OpenSCAP Security Automation Software in Linux Distributions

OpenSCAP is a framework of Linux software libraries designed to improve accessibility to SCAP through open source, publicly-available products and tools. The libraries were developed by Red Hat with support from G2 and other members of the security automation community. It was originally included in Fedora Linux distribution and subsequently added to Red Hat Enterprise Linux version 5. More details are available at the community website, www.open-scap.org.

Some examples of SCAP-related Linux projects that are enabled by the framework are:

- **scap-workbench**   A graphical tool that provides scanning, editing and validation functionality for SCAP content.

- **oscap-scan**   A command-line security scanner that uses OVAL and XCCDF content.

- **secstate**   A utility to automate the process of maintaining security compliance.  It generates evidence for use in security Certification and Accreditation (C&A) activities and produces automated, tailorable reports about a system's security posture.

- **Plugin for FirstAidKit**   A module that enables the use of XCCDF and OVAL to perform basic security audit steps and to evaluate the results reported.

Links to these and similar projects are available at the OpenSCAP site.

# Use of Security Automation to Track Management and Operational Security

The majority of those implementing security automation have used SCAP to measure and track technical security components for the uses already described, such as for configuration compliance or system vulnerabilities. With the advent of the Open Checklist

Interactive Language (OCIL), however, risk managers are now able to record, track, and correlate management and operational security findings as well. Using an OCIL questionnaire, an organization can create common checklists for use in physical security reviews, security self-assessments, security plans, and other security activities. The use of OCIL permits a consistent method to request data from users through a standard interface, recording the results in a format that can be correlated and aggregated with other security artifacts.

This capability provides significant assistance where security responsibilities are delegated across numerous organizational boundaries.

Compliance with standards often mandates a broad range of manual policy and security requirements. In addition to many technical controls for compliance with the Payment Card Industry's Data Security Standard (DSS), for example, many of the requirements (available at www.pcisecuritystandards.org) relate to human activities. Following are some examples:

- Install personal firewall software on any mobile and/or employee-owned computers.

- Purge unnecessary stored data at least quarterly.

- Follow change control processes and procedures for all changes to system components.

- Limit access to system components and cardholder data only to those individuals whose job requires such access.

Collecting, tracking, and correlating compliance with these types of security controls through the use of OCIL will greatly improve the organization's security situational awareness and contribute to an overall risk management profile.

Similarly, integrating known physical security vulnerabilities with known technical system vulnerability information will greatly increase security managers' understanding of overall risk posture. It is not uncommon for an information security officer to recognize that a server is susceptible to a known software flaw, nor would it be unusual for a physical security officer to record a physical vulnerability, such as a server room door unlocked. Consider, then, the value of a risk management system that can associate the assets in that server room with the physical risks discovered, providing a comprehensive risk score that considers all of the potential vulnerabilities together.

To demonstrate the capability of the OCIL, NIST recently developed an OCIL-based self-assessment tool for healthcare providers to review their compliance with elements of the HIPAA Security Rule. Based upon the answers provided by users in the interactive session through a web-based interface, the application flags potential issues and recommends process changes to help achieve organizational compliance. This toolkit developed by Exeter, with ThreatGuard and G2, is available at the SCAP website: http://scap.nist.gov/hipaa.

## Security Automation to Discover Malicious Software

Another exciting use of security automation is the ability to use inventory and vulnerability scanners to identify potentially malicious software. Although common anti-virus products are able to identify some characteristics of common malware, companies such as CyberESI are researching methods to find suspicious files through other means.

Reviewing software inventory records can yield important information about potential infection of an enterprise host. For example, automated tools' ability to look for executable files or dynamic link libraries within the fonts folder, help folder, or debug folder can point to suspicious activity. Particular tools are commonly used by those conducting malicious activity—for example, specific compression and encryption utilities may indicate that an intruder is actively attacking a given system. Although these attributes and utilities change often, the automated ability to change the search criteria helps keep up with these infiltrators.

## Continuous Monitoring by Integrating Security Systems

SCAP has recently been integrated with a suite of network security standards called Trusted Network Connect (TNC). The TNC standards were developed by the nonprofit Trusted Computing Group. They include two components: device health monitoring protocols and security information sharing protocols.

## Device Health Monitoring

The TNC standards for monitoring device health are a natural fit with the SCAP standards for security content. When both sets of standards are implemented on a device, the device can be checked when it connects to a network (perhaps as a precondition for network admission) and continuously thereafter. Because the TNC standards for health monitoring have been approved as IETF RFCs, they are built into many common operating systems and devices. Even printer manufacturers are working to add support to their devices. When combined with the standard security content of SCAP, the TNC standards will enable a future architecture where all network-connected devices include built-in health monitoring capabilities.

To increase the reliability of TNC health reports when this is needed, the Trusted Platform Module (a standard for security hardware) can be used to validate that devices are not lying about their health, as can happen when a device becomes compromised.

## Security Information Sharing

The TNC standard for sharing information among security systems is the Interface for Metadata Access Points (IF-MAP). This protocol enables security systems to publish information about device identity and health to a central database, where it can be associated with information about user identity and role to determine what level of access a device should obtain. Behavior monitoring sensors and physical security systems can also be tied into this database to provide full-spectrum visibility into expected and actual behavior. Response to abnormal behavior can be automated or manually triggered through the IF-MAP protocol, including quarantine and remediation.

Integration of the TNC and SCAP standards is new, having been initiated by Paul Bartock within the U.S. Department of Defense in 2010. But products implementing this integration have already been built and deployed in production for more than a year. Results are promising so far. After all, network security systems can benefit greatly from information received from endpoint security systems, and vice versa. Attackers share information and use that information to automate their systems, and defenders must do the same. And open standards are the best way to do so, enabling products from multiple vendors to interoperate.

# BUILDING A HEALTHY AND RESILIENT CYBER ECOSYSTEM

In a recent whitepaper from the U.S. Department of Homeland Security, "Enabling Distributed Security in Cyberspace," senior U.S. government officials recognized the following:

> Automation frees humans to do what they do well—think, ask questions, and make judgments about complex situations. Automation allows the speed of response to approach the speed of attack, rather than relying on human responses to attacks that are occurring at machine speed. With the ability to execute at machine speed, defenders could get inside the turning circles or decision cycles of attackers. Further, automation could make it easier to adopt and adapt new or proven security solutions.

It doesn't appear that security automation will replace the human practitioners any time soon, but through improved scalability, speed, and interoperability, security automation gives those security managers a fighting chance to maintain a resilient and healthy infrastructure.

# Chapter 9

## Conclusion

Throughout this book, we have provided the essential information needed for a security practitioner to better understand the general data exchange models that make up today's security automation solutions. There are certainly those who would prefer and could provide a more technical and detailed description, and many express that they are unfamiliar with all of the acronyms and protocols and have difficulty navigating the multiple specifications. We hope that these security practitioners will be helped by this introduction to this aspect of the security automation community.

The work of building security automation is just beginning, even after a decade's labor. To be successful, the pace must improve, and, fortunately, it has. The pioneers of this technology have worked to promote the general welfare of security risk management, inviting all who would listen to share opinions, offer constructive criticism, and contribute to the building project. The community is growing, improving daily with the influx of new partners with new ideas, new technical capabilities, and new missions. That growth brings a tension between newer and better models, and the need to maintain compatibility with legacy infrastructure. This challenge is not unique to security automation; it is the joy and the heartache of nearly every technology since the wheel.

One of the most important challenges that we hear from customers is that we have to find ways to make security automation "real." We have to make it useable by those who aren't professional computer scientists, we have to build practical interfaces, and we must find ways to ensure that these models become pervasive. Interoperability depends upon it. We hope that this book serves a small part in spreading the word to those who can help achieve that reality, including new ideas from automation users and from product manufacturers. Our goal is to encourage growth and support for this exciting technology.

## THE ROAD AHEAD

Among the most exciting facets of security automation work are the continuous improvement and the new areas of exploration. Even as the formal models for inventory, vulnerability measurement, and compliance assessment are forming, new methods for detecting and reporting attack patterns, making observations about malicious activity, and achieving event correlation are coming to the forefront. Knowledge repositories are growing, not in proprietary stovepipes, but in extensible, shareable frameworks. Today, security configuration guidance is nearly completely digital, to the relief of millions of trees that are saved from the paper mill.

This progress is helping to shape the nature of information security itself. Security assessment and system authorization really are becoming part of a healthy ecosystem, moving away from the "paperwork drills" of old to a continuous risk management framework. We recognize that change won't occur overnight, but looking back even a few years shows today's great progress and tomorrow's exciting promise. That's important, because this is serious business, as is borne out by risk assessments from power grids, to water supply, to our financial integrity.

Among the most helpful drivers to accelerate the pace of progress in security automation has been the support of senior leaders in commercial and government sectors. This executive buy-in enables the research, development, and collaboration of those who are building the exchange models. Their support leads to enterprise goals and metrics that drive improvement; these help ensure that the languages, enumerations, scoring models, and reporting methods have meaningful value to stakeholders and thus receive continued funding and attention.

One of the biggest buzzwords in the security community today is "continuous monitoring." Like most of information security, this facet is not new, but the ability to measure ongoing security consistently and accurately in near real time has eluded practitioners for many years.

Figure 9-1 illustrates a recent chart from the U.S. Department of Homeland Security, demonstrating how security automation supports a healthy cybersecurity ecosystem. There is much work yet to be done—we're just beginning to succeed at the "first wave" of automation. The work of the early 21st century has built a good foundation, though, and work is already progressing on second and third wave success. As components such as event management, automated remediation, and incident handling progress, security automation will become more of a holistic enterprise solution.

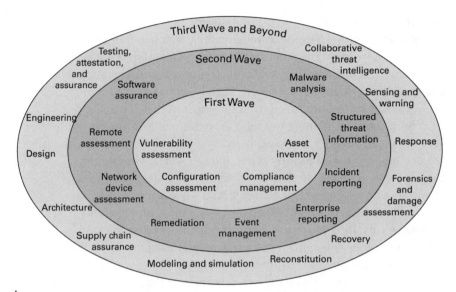

**FIGURE 9-1** DHS' strategic consideration of cybersecurity content automation

The work is rewarding, challenging, and meaningful, so we invite anyone who is willing to make a contribution to join us in the building project. We look forward to hearing from readers on how security automation is changing their viewpoints and actions, and invite all who are willing to join in on some of the international mailing lists used to discuss, debate, and improve the plans and the protocols. We wish you great success in implementing security automation within your own enterprise.

# Appendix

## XCCDF, OVAL, OCIL, and Supporting Enumerations Usage

The example herein is an SCAP 1.2 data stream consisting of OVAL checks for Windows password policy. As you read through the data stream, you'll see that OVAL version 5.8 and XCCDF version 1.2 are used. The main sections in the OVAL and XCCDF are Definitions, Tests, Objects, and States. In these sections, the checks are enabled or disabled, the specific check is defined, and the required value for a pass is defined.

The OCIL portion of the data stream follows with the Questionnaires and Test Actions. The Questionnaires section defines the questions to be asked, and the Test Actions section defines what responses will pass and what responses will fail. The Questions section defines the questions that the user will see during the scan. These examples may seem odd at first—this is because they were developed as part of the validation program rather than a questionnaire for a specific environment. This is useful, though, since it demonstrates a wide range of potential test actions. The Artifacts section is for capturing additional information during the OCIL portion of the scan.

Electronic copies of these and many other data streams are available at the website http://www.g2-inc.com/securityautomation, but we hope this content is useful to the reader to gain a more thorough understanding of how XCCDF, OVAL, OCIL, and supporting enumerations are used.

```xml
<?xml version="1.0" encoding="UTF-8"?>
<data-stream-collection xmlns="http://scap.nist.gov/schema/scap/source/1.2"
    xmlns:cat="urn:oasis:names:tc:entity:xmlns:xml:catalog"
    xmlns:xlink="http://www.w3.org/1999/xlink"
    xmlns:xsi="http://www.w3.org/2001/XMLSchema-instance"
    id="scap_gov.nist_collection_win_password_policy_test-datastream.zip"
    schematron-version="1.0"
    xsi:schemaLocation="http://scap.nist.gov/schema/scap/source/1.2
    http://scap.nist.gov/schema/scap/1.2/scap-source-data-stream_1.2.xsd">
    <data-stream id="scap_gov.nist_datastream_win_pw_datastream.zip"
        scap-version="1.2"
        timestamp="2012-01-31T01:47:39"
        use-case="CONFIGURATION">
        <dictionaries>
        <component-ref id="scap_gov.nist_cref_password_policy_validation_
            content-cpe-dictionary.xml"
            xlink:href="#scap_gov.nist_comp_password_policy_validation_
            content-cpe-dictionary.xml">
            <cat:catalog>
```

```
        <cat:uri name="password_policy_validation_
                content-cpe-oval.xml"
                uri="#scap_gov.nist_cref_password_policy_validation_
                content-cpe-oval.xml"/>
    </cat:catalog>
    </component-ref>
    </dictionaries>

<checklists>
<component-ref id="scap_gov.nist_cref_password_policy_validation_
    content-xccdf.xml"
    xlink:href="#scap_gov.nist_comp_password_policy_validation_
    content-xccdf.xml">
<cat:catalog>
        <cat:uri name="password_policy_validation_
                content-oval.xml"
                uri="#scap_gov.nist_cref_password_policy_validation_
                content-oval.xml"/>
    </cat:catalog>
    </component-ref>
    </checklists>

<checks>
    <component-ref id="scap_gov.nist_cref_password_policy_validation_
        content-oval.xml"
        xlink:href="#scap_gov.nist_comp_password_policy_validation_
                    content-oval.xml"/>
    <component-ref id="scap_gov.nist_cref_password_policy_validation_
                    content-cpe-oval.xml"
        xlink:href="#scap_gov.nist_comp_password_policy_validation_
                    content-cpe-oval.xml"/>
</checks>
</data-stream>

<component id="scap_gov.nist_comp_password_policy_validation_
        content-xccdf.xml" timestamp="2012-01-31T01:47:39">

<xccdf:Benchmark xmlns:xccdf="http://checklists.nist.gov/xccdf/1.2"
        id="xccdf_gov.nist_benchmark_xccdf-for-passwordpolicy-test-
        validation-content"
        style="SCAP_1.2"
        xml:lang="en"
        xsi:schemaLocation="http://checklists.nist.gov/xccdf/1.2
        http://scap.nist.gov/schema/xccdf/1.2/xccdf_1.2.xsd
        http://cpe.mitre.org/dictionary/2.0
        http://scap.nist.gov/schema/cpe/2.3/cpe-dictionary_2.3.xsd">
```

```xml
<xccdf:status date="2011-08-08">draft</xccdf:status>
<xccdf:title>XCCDF Benchmark That References the Validation Content
        for the passwordpolicy_test</xccdf:title>
<xccdf:description>This XCCDF Benchmark references
        the OVAL Definitions in the validation content
         for the passwordpolicy_test.</xccdf:description>

<xccdf:version update="2011-08-08">1.0</xccdf:version>

<xccdf:metadata>
    <dc:contributor xmlns:dc="http://purl.org/dc/elements/1.1/">
     National Institute of Standards and Technology</dc:contributor>
    <dc:publisher xmlns:dc="http://purl.org/dc/elements/1.1/">
     National Institute of Standards and Technology</dc:publisher>
    <dc:creator xmlns:dc="http://purl.org/dc/elements/1.1/">
     National Institute of Standards and Technology</dc:creator>
    <dc:source xmlns:dc="http://purl.org/dc/elements/1.1/">
     http://scap.nist.gov</dc:source>
</xccdf:metadata>

<xccdf:Profile id="xccdf_gov.nist_profile_passwordpolicy-validation"
        prohibitChanges="1">
<xccdf:title>XCCDF Profile That References the Validation Content
        for the passwordpolicy_test</xccdf:title>
<xccdf:description>Password Policy Profile</xccdf:description>
<xccdf:select idref=
"xccdf_gov.nist_rule_-min-passwd-len-with-greater-than-operation-1"
        selected="true"/>
</xccdf:Profile>
<xccdf:Rule id="xccdf_gov.nist_rule_-min-passwd-len-with-
        greater-than-operation-1" selected="true">
<xccdf:title>Test the min_passwd_len entity with the
   greater than operation</xccdf:title>
<xccdf:description>Make sure min_passwd_len properly supports
   the greater than operation.</xccdf:description>
<xccdf:check system="http://oval.mitre.org/XMLSchema/oval-definitions-5">
<xccdf:check-content-ref href="password_policy_validation_
     content-oval.xml" name="oval:nist.validation:def:1"/>
</xccdf:check>
</xccdf:Rule>
</xccdf:Benchmark>
</component>

<component id="scap_gov.nist_comp_password_policy_validation_
content-oval.xml" timestamp="2012-01-31T01:47:39">
<oval_definitions xmlns="http://oval.mitre.org/XMLSchema/oval-definitions-5"
```

```
xmlns:oval="http://oval.mitre.org/XMLSchema/oval-common-5"
xsi:schemaLocation=
  "http://oval.mitre.org/XMLSchema/oval-definitions-5#windows
   http://oval.mitre.org/language/download/schema/version5.8
   /ovaldefinition/complete/windows-definitions-schema.xsd
   http://oval.mitre.org/XMLSchema/oval-definitions-5#independent
   http://oval.mitre.org/language/download/schema/version5.8
   /ovaldefinition/complete/independent-definitions-schema.xsd
   http://oval.mitre.org/XMLSchema/oval-definitions-5
   http://oval.mitre.org/language/download/schema/version5.8
   /ovaldefinition/complete/oval-definitions-schema.xsd
   http://oval.mitre.org/XMLSchema/oval-common-5
   http://oval.mitre.org/language/download/schema/version5.8
   /ovaldefinition/complete/oval-common-schema.xsd
   http://oval.mitre.org/XMLSchema/oval-definitions-5#linux
   http://oval.mitre.org/language/download/schema/version5.8
   /ovaldefinition/complete/linux-definitions-schema.xsd
   http://oval.mitre.org/XMLSchema/oval-definitions-5#unix
   http://oval.mitre.org/language/download/schema/version5.8
   /ovaldefinition/complete/unix-definitions-schema.xsd">

<generator>
<oval:product_name>NIST Validation Content Script</oval:product_name>
<oval:product_version>1.0</oval:product_version>
<oval:schema_version>5.8</oval:schema_version>
<oval:timestamp>2011-05-25T09:30:59-04:00</oval:timestamp>
</generator>

<definitions>
<definition class="compliance" id="oval:nist.validation:def:1" version="1">
<metadata>
<title>Test min_passwd_len entity with the greater than operation</title>
<description>Make sure min_passwd_len entity properly supports
        the greater than operation.</description>

<expected_results>
   <result configuration="1">PASS</result>
   <result configuration="2">FAIL</result>
   <result configuration="3">PASS</result>
   </expected_results>
</metadata>

<criteria>
<criterion comment="Test to see that the min_passwd_len is greater than 0."
           test_ref="oval:nist.validation:tst:1"/>
</criteria>
```

```
</definition>
</definitions>

<tests>
<passwordpolicy_test xmlns="http://oval.mitre.org
              /XMLSchema/oval-definitions-5#windows"
check="all"
comment="Test to see that the min_passwd_len is greater than 0."
id="oval:nist.validation:tst:1" version="1">
<object object_ref="oval:nist.validation:obj:1"/>
<state state_ref="oval:nist.validation:ste:1"/>
</passwordpolicy_test>
</tests>

<objects>
   <passwordpolicy_object xmlns="http://oval.mitre.org/XMLSchema
       /oval-definitions-5#windows"
   id="oval:nist.validation:obj:1" version="1"/>
</objects>

<states>
      <passwordpolicy_state
      xmlns="http://oval.mitre.org/XMLSchema/oval-definitions-5#windows"
       id="oval:nist.validation:ste:1" version="1">
      <min_passwd_len datatype="int"
      operation="greater than">0</min_passwd_len>
</passwordpolicy_state>
</states>

</oval_definitions>
</component>

<component id="scap_gov.nist_comp_password_policy_validation_
    content-cpe-oval.xml" timestamp="2012-01-31T01:47:39">
  <oval_definitions xmlns=
     "http://oval.mitre.org/XMLSchema/oval-definitions-5"
  xmlns:oval-def=
     "http://oval.mitre.org/XMLSchema/oval-definitions-5"
  xmlns:win-def=
     "http://oval.mitre.org/XMLSchema/oval-definitions-5#windows"
  xmlns:ind-def=
     "http://oval.mitre.org/XMLSchema/oval-definitions-5#independent"
  xmlns:oval=
     "http://oval.mitre.org/XMLSchema/oval-common-5"
  xsi:schemaLocation=
  "http://oval.mitre.org/XMLSchema/oval-definitions-5#windows
  http://oval.mitre.org/language/download/schema/version5.3/ovaldefinition
```

```
    /complete/windows-definitions-schema.xsd
  http://oval.mitre.org/XMLSchema/oval-definitions-5#independent
  http://oval.mitre.org/language/download/schema/version5.3/ovaldefinition
    /complete/independent-definitions-schema.xsd
  http://oval.mitre.org/XMLSchema/oval-definitions-5
  http://oval.mitre.org/language/download/schema/version5.3/ovaldefinition
    /complete/oval-definitions-schema.xsd
  http://oval.mitre.org/XMLSchema/oval-common-5
  http://oval.mitre.org/language/download/schema/version5.3/ovaldefinition
    /complete/oval-common-schema.xsd">

<generator>
  <oval:product_name>National Institute of Standards and Technology
  </oval:product_name>

  <oval:schema_version>5.3</oval:schema_version>
  <oval:timestamp>2009-12-09T09:49:40.000-05:00</oval:timestamp>
</generator>

<!-- ================================================================ -->
<!-- ============    DEFINITIONS    ================================= -->
<!-- ================================================================ -->
<definitions>
  <definition class="inventory" id="oval:gov.nist.cpe.oval:def:1"
              version="3">
      <metadata>
        <title>Microsoft Windows 7 is installed</title>
        <affected family="windows">
          <platform>Microsoft Windows 7</platform>
        </affected>
        <reference ref_id="cpe:/o:microsoft:windows_7" source="CPE"/>
        <description>The operating system installed
              on the system is Microsoft Windows 7 (32-bit)
        </description>
      </metadata>
      <criteria>
          <criterion comment="the installed operating system is
                  part of the Microsoft Windows family"
      test_ref="oval:org.mitre.oval:tst:99"/>
          <criterion comment="Windows 7 is installed"

    test_ref="oval:org.mitre.oval:tst:10792"/>

      </criteria>
    </definition>
  </definitions>
```

```
<!-- ================================================================= -->
<!-- ============  TESTS  ============================================ -->
<!-- ================================================================= -->

<tests>
        <family_test xmlns="http://oval.mitre.org/XMLSchema
                /oval-definitions-5#independent"
         check="only one"
         check_existence="at_least_one_exists"
         comment="the installed operating system
                is part of the Microsoft Windows family"
         id="oval:org.mitre.oval:tst:99"
         version="1">

         <object object_ref="oval:org.mitre.oval:obj:99"/>
         <state state_ref="oval:org.mitre.oval:ste:99"/>
      </family_test>
      <registry_test xmlns="http://oval.mitre.org/XMLSchema
            /oval-definitions-5#windows"
         check="at least one"
         check_existence="at_least_one_exists"
         comment="Windows 7 is installed"
         id="oval:org.mitre.oval:tst:10792"
         version="4">
         <object object_ref="oval:org.mitre.oval:obj:5590"/>
         <state state_ref="oval:org.mitre.oval:ste:5027"/>
      </registry_test>
   </tests>

<!-- ================================================================= -->
<!-- ====================  OBJECTS  ================================== -->
<!-- ================================================================= -->
   <objects>
        <family_object xmlns="http://oval.mitre.org/XMLSchema
                /oval-definitions-5#independent"
         comment="This is the default family object.
                Only one family object should exist."
         id="oval:org.mitre.oval:obj:99"
         version="1"/>

        <registry_object xmlns="http://oval.mitre.org/XMLSchema
        /oval-definitions-5#windows"
            comment="This registry key identifies the Windows ProductName"
            id="oval:org.mitre.oval:obj:5590" version="1">
            <hive>HKEY_LOCAL_MACHINE</hive>
            <key>SOFTWARE\Microsoft\Windows NT\CurrentVersion</key>
```

```
            <name>ProductName</name>
        </registry_object>
    </objects>


<!-- ================================================================ -->
<!-- ===================  STATES  ================================= -->
<!-- ================================================================ -->
<states>
        <family_state xmlns="http://oval.mitre.org/XMLSchema
                /oval-definitions-5#independent"
        comment="Microsoft Windows family"
        id="oval:org.mitre.oval:ste:99" version="2">
        <family operation="equals">windows</family>
    </family_state>
    <registry_state xmlns="http://oval.mitre.org/XMLSchema
            /oval-definitions-5#windows"
        comment="The registry key matches with Windows 7"
        id="oval:org.mitre.oval:ste:5027" version="4">
        <value operation="pattern match">
        ^[a-zA-Z0-9\(\)\s]*[Ww][Ii][Nn][Dd][Oo][Ww][Ss] 7[a-zA-Z0-9\(\)\s]*$
        </value>
    </registry_state>
</states>


</oval_definitions>
</component>
<component id="scap_gov.nist_comp_password_policy_validation_
        content-cpe-dictionary.xml" timestamp="2012-01-31T01:47:39">
    <cpe-list xmlns="http://cpe.mitre.org/dictionary/2.0"
            xsi:schemaLocation="http://cpe.mitre.org/dictionary/2.0
                http://cpe.mitre.org/files/cpe-dictionary_2.1.xsd">
    <cpe-item name="cpe:/o:microsoft:windows_7">
    <title xml:lang="en-US">Microsoft Windows 7</title>
    <notes xml:lang="en-US">
    <note>This CPE Name represents version 6.1.7600 of the Windows OS</note>
    </notes>
    <check href="password_policy_validation_content-cpe-oval.xml"
            system="http://oval.mitre.org/XMLSchema/oval-definitions-5">
            oval:gov.nist.cpe.oval:def:1</check>
    </cpe-item>
</cpe-list>
</component>
</data-stream-collection>

<?xml version="1.0" encoding="UTF-8"?>
<Benchmark xmlns="http://checklists.nist.gov/xccdf/1.2" style="SCAP_1.2"
```

```
xmlns:xsi=http://www.w3.org/2001/XMLSchema-instance
xmlns:cpe="http://cpe.mitre.org/dictionary/2.0"
xmlns:cpelang=http://cpe.mitre.org/language/2.0
xmlns:dc="http://purl.org/dc/elements/1.1/"
xmlns:xhtml="http://www.w3.org/1999/xhtml"
xmlns:dsig="http://www.w3.org/2000/09/xmldsig#" id="OCIL Content Validation"
            resolved="0" xml:lang="en-US"
xsi:schemaLocation="http://cpe.mitre.org/dictionary/2.0 cpe-dictionary_2.2.xsd
http://purl.org/dc/elements/1.1/ simpledc20021212.xsd
http://cpe.mitre.org/language/2.0 cpe-language_2.0.xsd
http://checklists.nist.gov/xccdf/1.1 xccdf-1.1.4.xsd
http://www.w3.org/2000/09/xmldsig# xmldsig-core-schema.xsd">
        <status date="2011-07-20">draft</status>
        <title>Validation Program OCIL Content</title>
        <description>This benchmark contains OCIL definitions for
requirements from the Validation Program for SCAP 1.2.</description>

<reference>
<dc:publisher>Content Test Utility</dc:publisher>
</reference>
        <version time="2011-08-20T08:00:00" update="1">20110820</version>
        <Profile id="ValidationProgram">
                <title>Validation Program Questions</title>
                <description>These questions ensure that key
                  OCIL functionality is checked.</description>
                <select idref="V-14500" selected="true"/>
        </Profile>
        <Rule id="V-14500" selected="false" severity="medium" weight="10.0">
                <title>All Questions</title>
                <description>Answer all questions as indicated.</description>
                <check system="http://scap.nist.gov/schema/ocil/2">
                        <check-content-ref href="validation_program_ocil-ocil.xml"
                          name="ocil:validation_program:questionnaire:1"/>
                </check>
        </Rule>
</Benchmark>

<?xml version="1.0" encoding="UTF-8"?>
<ocil xmlns="http://scap.nist.gov/schema/ocil/2.0"
      xmlns:xsi="http://www.w3.org/2001/XMLSchema-instance"
      xmlns:xhtml="http://www.w3.org/1999/xhtml"
      xsi:schemaLocation=
      "http://scap.nist.gov/schema/ocil/2.0
       http://scap.nist.gov/schema/ocil/2.0/ocil-2.0.xsd">
```

```
<generator>
   <schema_version>2.0</schema_version>
   <timestamp>2011-03-02T20:00:00</timestamp>
</generator>

<document>
<title>OCIL Content for Validation Program</title>
</document>

<!--**********************************************************************
                            QUESTIONNAIRES
************************************************************************-->

<questionnaires>
<questionnaire id="ocil:validation_program:questionnaire:1">

<title> OCIL Validation Checklist </title>

<actions>
 <test_action_ref>ocil:validation_program:testaction:1</test_action_ref>
 <test_action_ref>ocil:validation_program:testaction:2</test_action_ref>
 <test_action_ref>ocil:validation_program:testaction:3</test_action_ref>
 <test_action_ref>ocil:validation_program:testaction:4</test_action_ref>
 <test_action_ref>ocil:validation_program:testaction:5</test_action_ref>
 <test_action_ref>ocil:validation_program:testaction:6</test_action_ref>
 <test_action_ref>ocil:validation_program:testaction:7</test_action_ref>
 <test_action_ref>ocil:validation_program:testaction:8</test_action_ref>
 <test_action_ref>ocil:validation_program:testaction:9</test_action_ref>
 <test_action_ref>ocil:validation_program:testaction:10</test_action_ref>
 <test_action_ref>ocil:validation_program:testaction:11</test_action_ref>
 <test_action_ref>ocil:validation_program:testaction:12</test_action_ref>
 <test_action_ref>ocil:validation_program:testaction:13</test_action_ref>
 <test_action_ref>ocil:validation_program:testaction:14</test_action_ref>
 <test_action_ref>ocil:validation_program:testaction:15</test_action_ref>
 <test_action_ref>ocil:validation_program:testaction:16</test_action_ref>
 <test_action_ref>ocil:validation_program:testaction:17</test_action_ref>
 <test_action_ref>ocil:validation_program:testaction:18</test_action_ref>
 <test_action_ref>ocil:validation_program:testaction:19</test_action_ref>
 <test_action_ref>ocil:validation_program:testaction:20</test_action_ref>
 <test_action_ref>ocil:validation_program:testaction:21</test_action_ref>
 <test_action_ref>ocil:validation_program:questionnaire:2</test_action_ref>
 <test_action_ref>ocil:validation_program:questionnaire:3</test_action_ref>
</actions>
</questionnaire>
```

```
<questionnaire id="ocil:validation_program:questionnaire:2"
      child_only="true">
      <title>Should be nested</title>
 <actions>
  <test_action_ref>ocil:validation_program:testaction:22</test_action_ref>
 </actions>
</questionnaire>

<questionnaire id="ocil:validation_program:questionnaire:3"
      child_only="true">
 <actions>
  <test_action_ref>ocil:validation_program:testaction:22</test_action_ref>
 </actions>
</questionnaire>

</questionnaires>

<!-- **********************************************************************
                        TEST ACTIONS
      **********************************************************************-->

<!-- PASSING TEST ACTIONS -->
<test_actions>
      <choice_question_test_action
            id="ocil:validation_program:testaction:1"
            question_ref="ocil:validation_program:question:1">

<when_choice>
   <result>PASS</result>
   <artifact_refs>
<artifact_ref idref="ocil:validation_program:artifact:1"/>
</artifact_refs>
   <choice_ref>ocil:validation_program:choice:1</choice_ref>
</when_choice>
<when_choice>
   <result>FAIL</result>
   <choice_ref>ocil:validation_program:choice:2</choice_ref>
</when_choice>
<when_choice>
   <result>NOT_APPLICABLE</result>
   <choice_ref>ocil:validation_program:choice:3</choice_ref>
</when_choice>
   <when_choice>
   <result>NOT_TESTED</result>
   <choice_ref>ocil:validation_program:choice:4</choice_ref>
</when_choice>
</choice_question_test_action>
```

```
<string_question_test_action
        id="ocil:validation_program:testaction:2"
        question_ref="ocil:validation_program:question:2" >
<when_pattern>
   <result>PASS</result>
   <pattern>pass</pattern>
</when_pattern>
<when_pattern>
   <result>NOT_TESTED</result>
   <pattern>^unanswered$</pattern>
</when_pattern>
</string_question_test_action>

<boolean_question_test_action
        question_ref="ocil:validation_program:question:3"
        id="ocil:validation_program:testaction:3" >
<when_true>
   <result>PASS</result>
</when_true>
<when_false>
   <result>FAIL</result>
</when_false>
</boolean_question_test_action>

<numeric_question_test_action
        question_ref="ocil:validation_program:question:4"
        id="ocil:validation_program:testaction:4">
<when_equals>
   <result>PASS</result>
   <value>42</value>
</when_equals>
</numeric_question_test_action>

<!--- FAILING TEST ACTIONS -->

<choice_question_test_action
   id="ocil:validation_program:testaction:5"
   question_ref="ocil:validation_program:question:5">
<when_choice>
   <result>PASS</result>
<choice_ref>ocil:validation_program:choice:1</choice_ref>
</when_choice>
<when_choice>
   <result>FAIL</result>
   <choice_ref>ocil:validation_program:choice:2</choice_ref>
</when_choice>
```

```
<when_choice>
   <result>NOT_APPLICABLE</result>
   <choice_ref>ocil:validation_program:choice:3</choice_ref>
</when_choice>
<when_choice>
   <result>NOT_TESTED</result>
   <choice_ref>ocil:validation_program:choice:4</choice_ref>
</when_choice>
</choice_question_test_action>

<string_question_test_action
       id="ocil:validation_program:testaction:6"
       question_ref="ocil:validation_program:question:6" >
<when_pattern>
   <result>PASS</result>
   <pattern>pass</pattern>
</when_pattern>
<when_pattern>
   <result>NOT_TESTED</result>
   <pattern>^unanswered$</pattern>
</when_pattern>
<when_pattern>
   <result>FAIL</result>
   <pattern>fail</pattern>
</when_pattern>

</string_question_test_action>
   <boolean_question_test_action
       question_ref="ocil:validation_program:question:7"
       id="ocil:validation_program:testaction:7" >
<when_true>
   <result>PASS</result>
</when_true>
<when_false>
   <result>FAIL</result>
</when_false>
</boolean_question_test_action>

<numeric_question_test_action
       question_ref="ocil:validation_program:question:8"
       id="ocil:validation_program:testaction:8">
<when_equals>
   <result>FAIL</result>
   <value>13</value>
</when_equals>
</numeric_question_test_action>
```

```
<!-- Step  -->
<boolean_question_test_action
        question_ref="ocil:validation_program:question:9"
        id="ocil:validation_program:testaction:9" >
<when_true>
    <result>PASS</result>
</when_true>
<when_false>
    <result>FAIL</result>
</when_false>
</boolean_question_test_action>

<!-- Passing branching -->
<string_question_test_action
        id="ocil:validation_program:testaction:10"
        question_ref="ocil:validation_program:question:10" >
<when_pattern>
<test_action_ref>ocil:validation_program:testaction:11</test_action_ref>
<pattern>pass</pattern>
</when_pattern>
<when_pattern>
    <result>NOT_TESTED</result>
    <pattern>^unanswered$</pattern>
</when_pattern>
<when_pattern>
    <result>FAIL</result>
    <pattern>fail</pattern>
</when_pattern>
</string_question_test_action>

<numeric_question_test_action
        question_ref="ocil:validation_program:question:11"
        id="ocil:validation_program:testaction:11">
<when_equals>
<test_action_ref>ocil:validation_program:testaction:12</test_action_ref>
<value>1</value>
</when_equals>
</numeric_question_test_action>

<boolean_question_test_action
        question_ref="ocil:validation_program:question:12"
        id="ocil:validation_program:testaction:12" >
<when_true>
<test_action_ref>ocil:validation_program:testaction:13</test_action_ref>
</when_true>
<when_false>
```

```
<result>FAIL</result>
</when_false>
</boolean_question_test_action>

<choice_question_test_action
      id="ocil:validation_program:testaction:13"
      question_ref="ocil:validation_program:question:13">
<when_choice>

<result>PASS</result>
   <choice_ref>ocil:validation_program:choice:1</choice_ref>
</when_choice>
<when_choice>
   <result>FAIL</result>
   <choice_ref>ocil:validation_program:choice:2</choice_ref>
</when_choice>
<when_choice>
   <result>NOT_APPLICABLE</result>
   <choice_ref>ocil:validation_program:choice:3</choice_ref>
</when_choice>
<when_choice>
   <result>NOT_TESTED</result>
   <choice_ref>ocil:validation_program:choice:4</choice_ref>
</when_choice>
</choice_question_test_action>

<!-- Failing branching -->
<string_question_test_action
      id="ocil:validation_program:testaction:14"
      question_ref="ocil:validation_program:question:14" >
<when_pattern>
   <result>PASS</result>
   <pattern>pass</pattern>
</when_pattern>
   <when_pattern>
   <result>NOT_TESTED</result>
   <pattern>^unanswered$</pattern>
</when_pattern>
<when_pattern>
   <test_action_ref>ocil:validation_program:testaction:15</test_action_ref>
   <pattern>fail</pattern>
</when_pattern>
</string_question_test_action>

<numeric_question_test_action
      question_ref="ocil:validation_program:question:15"
      id="ocil:validation_program:testaction:15">
```

```xml
<when_unknown>
   <test_action_ref>ocil:validation_program:testaction:16</test_action_ref>
</when_unknown>
<when_equals>
    <result>PASS</result>
    <value>1</value>
</when_equals>
</numeric_question_test_action>

<boolean_question_test_action
       question_ref="ocil:validation_program:question:16"
       id="ocil:validation_program:testaction:16" >
<when_true>
   <result>PASS</result>
</when_true>
<when_false>
   <test_action_ref>ocil:validation_program:testaction:17</test_action_ref>
</when_false>
</boolean_question_test_action>

<choice_question_test_action
       id="ocil:validation_program:testaction:17"
       question_ref="ocil:validation_program:question:17">
<when_choice>
<result>PASS</result>
    <choice_ref>ocil:validation_program:choice:1</choice_ref>
</when_choice>
<when_choice>
    <result>FAIL</result>
    <choice_ref>ocil:validation_program:choice:2</choice_ref>
</when_choice>
<when_choice>
    <result>NOT_APPLICABLE</result>
    <choice_ref>ocil:validation_program:choice:3</choice_ref>
</when_choice>
<when_choice>
    <result>NOT_TESTED</result>
    <choice_ref>ocil:validation_program:choice:4</choice_ref>
</when_choice>
</choice_question_test_action>

<!-- Multiple when patterns -->
<string_question_test_action
       id="ocil:validation_program:testaction:18"
       question_ref="ocil:validation_program:question:18" >
<when_pattern>
    <result>PASS</result>
```

```
    <pattern>[A-Z]</pattern>
</when_pattern>
<when_pattern>
   <result>PASS</result>
   <pattern>[A-N]</pattern>
</when_pattern>
</string_question_test_action>

<!-- Exceptional Values -->
<choice_question_test_action
      id="ocil:validation_program:testaction:19"
      question_ref="ocil:validation_program:question:19">
<when_choice>
   <result>PASS</result>
   <choice_ref>ocil:validation_program:choice:1</choice_ref>
</when_choice>
<when_choice>
   <result>FAIL</result>
   <choice_ref>ocil:validation_program:choice:2</choice_ref>
</when_choice>
<when_choice>
   <result>NOT_APPLICABLE</result>
   <choice_ref>ocil:validation_program:choice:3</choice_ref>
</when_choice>
<when_choice>
   <result>NOT_TESTED</result>
   <choice_ref>ocil:validation_program:choice:4</choice_ref>
</when_choice>
</choice_question_test_action>

<numeric_question_test_action
      question_ref="ocil:validation_program:question:20"
      id="ocil:validation_program:testaction:20">
<when_error>
   <result>FAIL</result>
</when_error>
<when_equals>
   <result>PASS</result>
   <value>1</value>
</when_equals>
</numeric_question_test_action>

<!-- Substitution -->
<choice_question_test_action
      id="ocil:validation_program:testaction:21"
      question_ref="ocil:validation_program:question:21" >
<when_choice>
```

```xml
    <result>PASS</result>
    <choice_ref>ocil:validation_program:choice:1</choice_ref>
</when_choice>
<when_choice>
    <result>FAIL</result>
    <choice_ref>ocil:validation_program:choice:2</choice_ref>
</when_choice>
<when_choice>
    <result>NOT_APPLICABLE</result>
    <choice_ref>ocil:validation_program:choice:3</choice_ref>
</when_choice>
<when_choice>
    <result>NOT_TESTED</result>
    <choice_ref>ocil:validation_program:choice:4</choice_ref>
</when_choice>
</choice_question_test_action>

<!-- Nesting    -->
<boolean_question_test_action
        question_ref="ocil:validation_program:question:22"
        id="ocil:validation_program:testaction:22" >
<when_true>
    <result>PASS</result>
</when_true>
<when_false>
    <result>FAIL</result>
</when_false>
</boolean_question_test_action>

</test_actions>

<!-- **********************************************************************
                            QUESTIONS
     ********************************************************************-->
<questions>

<!-- Passing Questions -->
<choice_question id="ocil:validation_program:question:1"
    default_answer_ref="ocil:validation_program:choice:4">
    <question_text>Answer Yes below.</question_text>
<choice_group_ref>ocil:validation_program:choicegroup:1</choice_group_ref>
</choice_question>

<string_question id="ocil:validation_program:question:2"
    default_answer="unanswered" >
    <question_text>Type the word "pass" (without quotation marks) below.
</question_text>
```

```
</string_question>

<boolean_question id="ocil:validation_program:question:3"
    default_answer="false" model="MODEL_TRUE_FALSE">
    <question_text>Answer True below</question_text>
</boolean_question>

<numeric_question id="ocil:validation_program:question:4">
<question_text>Type 42 below.</question_text>
</numeric_question>

<!-- Failing Questions -->
<choice_question id="ocil:validation_program:question:5"
    default_answer_ref="ocil:validation_program:choice:4">
 <question_text>Answer No below.</question_text>
 <choice_group_ref>ocil:validation_program:choicegroup:1</choice_group_ref>
</choice_question>

<string_question id="ocil:validation_program:question:6"
    default_answer="unanswered" >
    <question_text>Type the word "fail" (without quotation marks) below.
</question_text>
</string_question>

<boolean_question id="ocil:validation_program:question:7"
        default_answer="false" model="MODEL_TRUE_FALSE">
<question_text>Answer False below</question_text>
</boolean_question>

<numeric_question id="ocil:validation_program:question:8" >
<question_text>Type 13 below.</question_text>
</numeric_question>

<!-- Step  -->
<boolean_question id="ocil:validation_program:question:9"
    model="MODEL_YES_NO">
    <question_text>Do you see the steps below?</question_text>
    <instructions>
    <title>You should see me!</title>
    <step>
       <description>This is step 1</description>
    </step>
    <step>
       <description>This is step 2</description>
    </step>
</instructions>
</boolean_question>
```

```
<!-- Passing branching -->
<string_question id="ocil:validation_program:question:10">
   <question_text>Enter "pass" with no quotation marks</question_text>
</string_question>
   <numeric_question id="ocil:validation_program:question:11">
   <question_text>Enter 1</question_text>
</numeric_question>
   <boolean_question id="ocil:validation_program:question:12"
      model="MODEL_YES_NO">
   <question_text>Select Yes</question_text>
</boolean_question>
   <choice_question id="ocil:validation_program:question:13">
   <question_text>Select Yes</question_text>
<choice_group_ref>ocil:validation_program:choicegroup:1</choice_group_ref>
</choice_question>


<!-- Failing branching -->
<string_question id="ocil:validation_program:question:14">
   <question_text>Enter "fail" with no quotation marks</question_text>
</string_question>
   <numeric_question id="ocil:validation_program:question:15">
   <question_text>Enter 2</question_text>
</numeric_question>
<boolean_question id="ocil:validation_program:question:16"
      model="MODEL_YES_NO">
<question_text>Select No</question_text>
</boolean_question>
   <choice_question id="ocil:validation_program:question:17">
   <question_text>Select No</question_text>
<choice_group_ref>ocil:validation_program:choicegroup:1</choice_group_ref>
</choice_question>


<!-- Multiple when patterns -->
<string_question id="ocil:validation_program:question:18">
   <question_text>Enter "A" without the quotation marks.</question_text>
</string_question>


<!-- Exceptional Values -->
<choice_question id="ocil:validation_program:question:19">
   <question_text>Select Not Applicable</question_text>
<choice_group_ref>ocil:validation_program:choicegroup:1</choice_group_ref>
</choice_question>


<numeric_question id="ocil:validation_program:question:20">
   <question_text>Enter "fail" with no quotation marks</question_text>
<!-- this should generate an error -->
</numeric_question>
```

```xml
<!-- Substitution -->
   <choice_question id="ocil:validation_program:question:21">
   <question_text>#<sub var_ref="ocil:validation_program:variable:1"/>
     # Is the text between the pound sign "apple"? If yes, select yes.
</question_text>
<choice_group_ref>ocil:validation_program:choicegroup:1</choice_group_ref>
</choice_question>

<!-- Nesting -->
<boolean_question id="ocil:validation_program:question:22"
   model="MODEL_TRUE_FALSE">
<question_text>Select True</question_text>
</boolean_question>

<!-- choice group(s) -->
<choice_group id="ocil:validation_program:choicegroup:1">
<choice id="ocil:validation_program:choice:1">Yes</choice>
<choice id="ocil:validation_program:choice:2">No</choice>
<choice id="ocil:validation_program:choice:3">Not Applicable</choice>
<choice id="ocil:validation_program:choice:4">Not Answered</choice>
</choice_group>

</questions>

<!-- ***********************************************************************
                        ARTIFACTS
***********************************************************************-->

<artifacts>

<artifact id="ocil:validation_program:artifact:1" >
   <title>Additional Information</title>
   <description>Any additional comments go here.</description>
</artifact>

</artifacts>

<variables>
<constant_variable id="ocil:validation_program:variable:1" datatype="TEXT">
<value>apple</value>
</constant_variable>
</variables>
</ocil>
```

# Index

# O